The Single Market Review

IMPACT ON COMPETITION
AND SCALE EFFECTS

ECONOMIES OF SCALE

The Single Market Review series

EUROPEAN COMMISSION

The Single Market Review

IMPACT ON COMPETITION
AND SCALE EFFECTS

ECONOMIES OF SCALE

The Single Market Review

SUBSERIES V: VOLUME 4

OFFICE FOR OFFICIAL PUBLICATIONS
OF THE EUROPEAN COMMUNITIES

KOGAN PAGE . EARTHSCAN

This report is part of a series of 39 studies commissioned from independent consultants in the context of a major review of the Single Market. The 1996 Single Market Review responds to a 1992 Council of Ministers Resolution calling on the European Commission to present an overall analysis of the effectiveness of measures taken in creating the Single Market. This review, which assesses the progress made in implementing the Single Market Programme, was coordinated by the Directorate-General 'Internal Market and Financial Services' (DG XV) and the Directorate-General 'Economic and Financial Affairs' (DG II) of the European Commission.

This document was prepared for the European Commission

by

Economists Advisory Group Ltd

It does not, however, express the Commission's official views. Whilst every reasonable effort has been made to provide accurate information in regard to the subject matter covered, the Consultants are not responsible for any remaining errors. All recommendations are made by the Consultants for the purpose of discussion. Neither the Commission nor the Consultants accept liability for the consequences of actions taken on the basis of the information contained herein.

The European Commission would like to express thanks to the external experts and representatives of firms and industry bodies for their contribution to the 1996 Single Market Review, and to this report in particular.

Office for Official Publications of the European Communities
2 rue Mercier, L-2985 Luxembourg
ISBN 92-827-8804-0   Catalogue number: C1-71-96-004-EN-C

Kogan Page . Earthscan
120 Pentonville Road, London N1 9JN
ISBN 0 7494 2337 4

Table of contents

List of tables

List of figures

List of abbreviations

CAD	computer-aided design
CAM	computer-aided manufacturing
CEEC	Central and Eastern European country
EAG	Economists Advisory Group Ltd
EDI	electronic data interchange
EEC	European Economic Community
EFTA	European Free Trade Association
EOS	economies of scale
Esprit	European strategic programme for research and development in information technology
EU	European Union
Eureka	European Research Co-ordinating Agency
Eurostat	Statistical Office of the European Communities
FDI	foreign direct investment
FMCG	fast moving consumer goods
GATT	General Agreement on Tariffs and Trade
GBV	gross book value
GVA	gross value added
HST	high speed train (*TGV: train à grande vitesse*)
IT	information technology
kt	1,000 tonnes
M&A	merger and acquisition
MECU	million ECU
MES	minimum efficient scale
MFMD	median of the first moment distribution
mhl	million hectolitre
MNE	multinational enterprise
MPV	multi-purpose vehicle
mtpa	million tonnes per annum
NACE	general industrial classification of economic activities within the European Communities
OPT	outward processing trade
OTC	over the counter
p.a.	per annum
PC	personal computer
PCB	printed circuit board
PET	polyethylene terephthalate
PIMS	PIMS Associates Ltd
PTA	pure terephthalic acid
PVC	polyvinyl chloride
R&D	research and development
RACE	research and development in advanced communications technologies in Europe
ROCE	return on capital employed
ROI	return on investment
SM	single market
SME	small and medium-sized enterprise
TC	textiles and clothing
tpd	tonnes per day
Type 1	industries facing production based competition
Type 2A	industries facing advertising based competition
Type 2AR	industries facing advertising and R&D based competition
Type 2R	industries facing R&D based competition
VISA	Variables for Industrial Structural Analysis
WVTA	Whole Vehicle Type Approval

Acknowledgements

The project was directed by Prof. Bruce Lyons (University of East Anglia) and managed by Jeremy Holmes (EAG), in collaboration with Mary Beth Sutter Childs (EAG), Tony Clayton (PIMS Associates), Prof. Steve Davies (University of East Anglia), Laura Rondi (CERIS, Turin), Alessandro Sembenelli (CERIS, Turin) and Prof. Peter Hart (EAG).

Other project members included Prof. Leo Sleuwaegen (University of Leuven), Prof. Reinhilde Veugleurs (University of Leuven), Giampaolo Vitali (CERIS, Turin) and Odile Janne (University of Reading).

1. Summary

The aim of this study was to evaluate the impact of the single market (SM) programme on economies of scale, as reflected primarily in changes in firm size by type of industry.

The study overall has reflected the following approach:

(a) A comprehensive review of the economic literature.
(b) A detailed analysis of changes in the actual size of firms over the period 1986–91, as compared with the period 1981–86.
(c) An econometric analysis of the effect of the SM programme on these changes and on changes in industrial concentration.
(d) An examination of firm-specific data held on the PIMS database to identify important shifts in performance related to scale between the pre-1985 and post-1985 periods.
(e) Sectoral case study research into the impact of the SM.

This report presents the key findings of the study in five chapters. Chapter 2 reviews the existing literature on economies of scale with relevance to the SM. Chapter 3 presents the statistical background to the empirical analysis using Eurostat data. Chapter 4 presents the analytical assessment of the influence of the SM. Chapter 5 discusses business scale, profitability and costs based on PIMS data. Chapter 6 presents a summary of the case study research in eight manufacturing and two service sectors.

The following sections of this summary deal with each chapter in turn and then provide some overall conclusions. The appendices to the report present detailed information on the case study research (Appendix A) and outline technical assessments by industry sector (Appendix B), in recognition of the influence of technical change in economies of scale. A bibliography is presented at the end of the report.

1.1. Literature review

There is an extensive literature on economies of scale. The basic distinction is between technical economies of scale in production, and dynamic economies of scale in firm level activities such as management, R&D and advertising (discussed in this study as endogenous sunk costs). In addition, there may exist economies of scale that are external to the firm or industry.

The most significant reductions in production costs (and an increase in concentration) as a result of the SM were expected to be in industries experiencing a high level of national protection. Also, as the SM was intended to allow firms access to larger markets, economies of scale could result from increasing specialization over a narrower range of products, with increased production runs. In the service sectors, economies of scale were expected to be largely national rather than pan-European.

The full realization of both scale economies and competition requires large and open markets, particularly if the dangers of oligopoly are to be avoided. Market integration could also stimulate technological progress through better dissemination of knowledge and an increased stock of knowledge resulting from increased competition.

Significant recent work has been undertaken on the distinction between exogenous and endogenous elements of sunk costs, and the relationship between these costs and industrial structure. Davies and Lyons [1996] develop this distinction into a typology of industries based on the type of competition which they face – production based (Type 1), advertising based (Type 2A), R&D based (Type 2R) or both advertising and R&D based (Type 2AR). This typology has been extensively used in the present study.

Advertising and R&D expenditure may be seen as a competitive weapon rather than as a means to reach economies of scale. Nevertheless, the SM might be expected to offer opportunities for spreading R&D costs over a larger output, or for reducing duplication of R&D effort, and for exploiting scale economies through the marketing of pan-European brands.

The question of external economies of scale has often been neglected, but the theory of multinational enterprises indicates that firms may choose to invest in a particular country or region in order to take advantage of local labour market pooling or agglomerative economies related to specialized inputs and services. The question of regional specialization has not been extensively explored in the present study but external economies may, in principle, be a source of high potential gains reinforced by the process of economic integration.

The first conclusion of the literature review is that the removal of non-tariff barriers and regulations may not be a sufficient condition for the exploitation of existing potential scale economies by firms. Technological change and rationalization may be equally important.

Secondly, technical inefficiency could be reduced by improving internal and external competition within industries. This conclusion relates indirectly to the type of competition experienced in any given industry. Thirdly, the SM may reinforce existing geographic clusters of activity, or create new centres for agglomeration economies.

Finally, the SM programme cannot be disassociated from other important influences on the attainment of economies of scale, including the economic cycle, the GATT agreements and the process of industrial globalization.

1.2. Statistical background

Chapter 3 analyses the available Eurostat data relating to firm size and growth. Two different measurements of scale were explored, using the survivor method and the median of the first moment distribution (MFMD). However, data limitations are severe in terms of Member State coverage, and for practical reasons a calculation of average firm size was preferred.

The potential to exploit economies of scale in selected three-digit manufacturing sectors was identified by means of the ratio of Minimum Efficient Scale (MES) to the five-firm concentration ratio at the European level. Using a measure of average market share (average sales divided by EU market size), 47 out of 53 manufacturing sectors were calculated to have unexploited economies of scale (EOS potential).

Sectoral sensitivity to the SM was then identified according to the four groups of industrial sectors analysed by Buigues et al. [1990]. A quadrant analysis of sectors by EOS potential and SM sensitivity was then undertaken.

Changes in firm size by real gross value added were calculated by quadrant, by Member State and by type of competition. For SM-sensitive industries with high EOS potential, the average size of firm decreased by 11% between 1981 and 1986, and by 13% between 1986 and 1991. By Member State, Germany and Denmark showed the strongest recovery in the second period. Type 2R and 2AR industries contain firms of larger typical size than other types, and also possess the greatest potential for economies of scale. Type 1 industries have the smallest average size but the greatest achievement of MES.

In terms of employment, firms considered most sensitive to the SM and with the greatest EOS potential experienced the greatest declines in employment in both time periods. They increased their average labour productivity by 7% between 1981 and 1986 (compared with 10% for all industries), and by 14% between 1986 and 1991 (compared with 8% for all industries). German firms demonstrated the strongest productivity growth.

The ranking of industry types by average employment is the same as for gross value added (although Type 1 industries as a whole account for the largest proportion of total employment). Based on these employment data, Type 2R industries appear to have emerged from recession later than the other industry types.

These firm size data were then placed in the context of intra-EU trade. Trade openness was measured by exports plus imports over production (turnover). Smaller countries are generally more open, but there appears to be a growth in openness in all Member States over both periods, 1981–86 and 1986–91. R&D-intensive industries are by far the most open and Type 2A are the least open.

A version of comparative advantage was measured by exports minus imports over production (turnover). Here there is a clear pattern of smaller countries being more specialized, with a dramatic increase in specialization in Ireland, and a steady increase in Germany. Standardizing for industry types, a small reduction in specialization in 1981–86 was reversed in 1986–91.

1.3. The influence of the single market

Chapter 4 discusses the theory of firm size, scale economies and trading costs, and poses two questions: what factors determine the average size of business units, and how might a reduction in trade barriers affect those relationships?

It is inaccurate to characterize the SM simply as an expansion of market size, since most industries in the mid-1980s already operated to an extent at the international level. The SM should therefore be viewed in terms of a marginal/quantitative change rather than a discrete/qualitative change in market size.

The removal of border controls was expected to reduce the fixed cost of exporting, and so allow the growth of smaller firms which had previously been restricted to national markets. However, where we do not have data on firms with less than 20 employees and we do not have industry-specific price deflators, analysis of this effect must be qualified.

Expansion of demand due to the SM was also expected to reduce the operation of firms at inefficiently small scale. A further mechanism applies if firms are not initially on the minimum attainable cost curve, given their output level.

Based on these principles, an empirical model was specified, aiming to capture the different aspects of intra-EU trade barriers in the different types of industries. The key variables in this model reflect an industry's level of public procurement, the influence of national regulations, the level of intra-EU trade openness and the level of comparative advantage. A measure of initial disadvantage is also incorporated, reflecting the expectation that the SM would have a greater effect on business size where average size had been low in relation to MES. Finally, we would expect to see a greater effect in industries which were previously most affected by trade barriers, and this is also incorporated in the model.

In Type 2 industries, a larger market is more likely to result in larger firms than would be the case in Type 1 industries, as a direct result of the escalation of fixed costs in R&D and advertising. The role of production economies of scale in determining firm size is much less important in Type 2 industries.

Differences between Type 1 and Type 2 industries in terms of the relationship between barriers to trade and firm size depend on the type of barrier. The effect of national regulations is also not straightforward, although they may allow larger scale production in Type 2 industries by deterring domestic entry. In Type 2 industries there is also a high incidence of firms that are multinational within the EU (particularly in Type 2R), but a different relationship exists between firm size and trade in different types of industry.

Analysis of developments in industry concentration shows that there has been a significant increase at the EU level between 1987 and 1993, particularly in Type 2R industries. There has also been a greater increase in concentration in industries where EOS potential is high (many of which are Type 2R). Industries with a relatively low EOS potential have experienced a larger increase in concentration if they have a high level of SM sensitivity; but SM sensitivity exerts no extra impact where EOS potential is high.

More detailed analysis shows that EU concentration increases where: average business size grows more rapidly than industry size in Member States; business size inequalities within individual Member States increase; specialization by Member State increases; and intra-EU multinationality increases.

In Type 1 industries, average national business size grew by approximately 6% between 1987 and 1993, national concentration stayed roughly constant and EU level concentration increased slightly. This implies a small increase in intra-EU multinationality and/or an increase in specialization within the EU.

In Type 2A there were quite dramatic increases in the typical business size within Member States, but EU level concentration increased at about the same rate as national concentration, suggesting little change in multinationality and/or specialization.

In Type 2R, average business size tended to decline slightly, along with a decline in national concentration. However, there was a rapid increase in EU level concentration, reflecting increasing specialization and substantial increases in intra-EU multinationality.

In Type 2AR industries, average business size grew substantially but industry size increased more moderately, along with a small increase in national concentration. Concentration at the EU level also increased slightly, but not as much as in Type 2R.

Overall, the analysis confirms that in the manufacturing sector there was potential for further achievement of economies of scale at the start of the SM programme. However, industries have been affected differentially by national boundaries and by the type of competition which they face.

The clearest effects are in the R&D-intensive industries, where firm size is positively related to specialization in Member States with a comparative advantage. However, as a group these industries were also experiencing negative industry growth, so this relative effect did not translate into greater absolute size on average.

There is also evidence that firms have been responding to the SM through M&A activity, with a substantial effect on EU concentration. This activity is likely to have been prompted by R&D and marketing economies, although the resulting corporate rationalization may also feed through into production economies.

1.4.   Business scale, profitability and costs

Chapter 5 uses data on 128 pan-European business units from the PIMS database, which shows that there have been significant changes in the performance of such businesses since the mid-1980s. The data were split into a pre-1985 set and a post-1985 set.

In terms of return on capital employed, pan-European businesses performed significantly worse than national or regional (i.e. sub-national) businesses in the pre-1985 period. In the subsequent period, the gap closed due to a worsening performance by the national and regional businesses.

Pre-1985, the better performing pan-European businesses were: less likely to be exploiting scale economies (on the whole they were not European market leaders); more likely to be focused on a narrow range of products, services and customer types; very likely to have high marketing costs; and less likely to have a high level of innovation. This is largely consistent with the characteristics of Type 2A industries.

There is also some evidence that the ability to exploit external economies of scale was a significant success factor pre-1985 as the better performing businesses tended to be more dependent on a few suppliers.

Post-1985, the more successful businesses tended to be: in the top three in terms of European market share; more dependent on mass market products with little customization; operating in markets where advertising is a significant cost; more innovative; and even more focused on a few major suppliers.

This pattern is consistent with Type 2A industries exploiting scale economies faster than most, but also implies some catch-up by Type 2R and Type 2AR industries. Overall, the PIMS data indicate that, in the post-1985 period, stronger margins were more clearly associated with larger scale relative to competitors. There is also some support for the theory of vertical disintegration based on value added/sales ratios.

The PIMS analysis also considered the relationship between changes in costs and changes in output. For manufacturing costs a 1% increase in output pre-1985 is associated with a 0.73% increase in costs. This is consistent with the exploitation of economies of scale but could be attributed to other causes (including excess capacity, although this was also examined). The propensity for costs to increase in marketing, R&D and administration was higher than for manufacturing costs alone.

It was hypothesized that industries with a steep slope to their cost curve would have most to gain from the SM, and so should have experienced the largest increase in business size, as analysed in Chapter 3. However, no clear pattern was found, so a quantification of the cost savings achieved in industries which experienced business size growth was not possible.

PIMS data were also used to examine the performance of businesses which have experienced major technological change relative to all other manufacturing businesses. There are significant differences in return on sales and employee productivity. This implies that the benefits of technological change arise from sales growth (reflected in scale) rather than from improved single efficiencies.

1.5.   Summary of the case study research

Sector case studies were undertaken in three Type 2R industries (rail stock, pharmaceuticals and computers), two Type 2A industries (chocolate confectionery and beer), one Type 2AR industry (motor vehicles), two Type 1 industries (glass and clothing) and two service industries (insurance and retailing). Chapter 6 summarizes the findings and Appendix A provides the full case studies.

These case studies are set in the context of industrial change (including patterns of concentration and the impact of new technology) and the process of globalization. In each sector, the nature of the opportunities for exploitation of scale economies has evolved in a way that has been largely independent of the SM programme. Generally speaking, technical and dynamic economies of scale have been more important than external economies of scale.

Strategies of product differentiation, cost reduction and increased focus are all evident in the case studies, with a high degree of overlap between the first two of these strategies. In the Type 2R industries there has been a move towards greater focus in terms of product specialization, particularly in the computer sector.

The Type 2A industries show divergent trends in marketing, with chocolate experiencing economies through more pan-European activity and more specialization in terms of products, and beer experiencing increased costs through more country-by-country marketing and an expansion in the scope of activities. Both the service sectors studied exhibit the characteristics of industries which still largely retain national markets.

The specific impact of the SM is also analysed by type of industry. In the Type 2R industries, rail stock has benefited from the opening up of public procurement in terms of reduced product complexity and some longer production runs. Industry consolidation prompted by the SM has also facilitated more knowledge transfer in R&D and component sourcing, which has helped to maintain the international competitiveness of the European industry. The impact on the pharmaceutical sector has so far been limited, but some benefits in terms of movement of personnel and pan-European marketing may be emerging.

In computers, restructuring of the industry and public procurement liberalization have led to dynamic economies of scale through greater focus and product/service specialization in R&D. External economies have also become more important in relation to supplier inputs.

In the Type 2A and Type 2AR industries studied, the most significant impact of the SM has been in the elimination of national restrictions on raw material inputs to the chocolate confectionery industry, although the scope for technical economies of scale may be limited by the Chocolate Directive (73/241/EEC, as amended).

In the beer industry, the free movement of both products and capital has assisted the realization of technical scale economies, and knowledge transfer in both marketing and R&D is leading to a greater diversity of products. In motor vehicles, the impact of the SM, with the exception of Whole Vehicle Type Approval (Directive 70/156/EEC, as amended), is thought to be limited when compared with the wider issues of globalization in the industry.

In the Type 1 industries, market growth for flat glass has been stimulated by EU regulations on energy efficient buildings (see Appendix C), although the buildings market has been nationally defined until relatively recently. The internationalization of this sector may have been partly assisted by the improved market access and regulatory harmonization embodied in the SM programme. In the clothing industry, the SM has also opened up new market opportunities, which have had a growth effect on the supplier industry. Combined with increased levels of outsourcing, this has led to increased realization of external economies of scale.

In the service industries studied, common European approaches in marketing and personnel development are emerging in insurance, but these are only due in part to the SM programme. Nevertheless, dynamic economies of scale have been achieved, particularly in the non-life sector, and the free movement of capital has allowed operators to move towards a single business structure within the EU.

In retailing, knowledge transfer is increasing, and membership of the European Council was mentioned as being influential in this. The free movement of products has assisted cross-border sourcing, and the widening frame of reference for innovation has been assisted by expectations of the SM programme.

1.6. Overall conclusions

Industries considered sensitive to the SM and with high EOS potential exhibited declines in firm size in both 1981–86 and 1986–91. However, labour productivity in these industries accelerated substantially in the second period (14% growth compared to 8% for all industries).

Industries which face R&D based competition (Type 2R) or both advertising and R&D based competition (Type 2AR) contain firms of larger typical size than other industries and also possess the greatest potential for economies of scale. R&D-intensive industries are also the most open in terms of intra-EU trade.

In 1987–93 there was a significant increase in concentration at the EU level in Type 2R industries, and in industries where EOS potential is high (many of which are Type 2R). Industries with a relatively low EOS potential experienced a higher increase in concentration if they had a high level of SM sensitivity.

In the R&D intensive industries firm size is positively related to specialization in Member States with a comparative advantage. However, these industries also experienced negative growth, so this effect did not translate into a growth in absolute firm size. At the Member State level Type 1, Type 2A and Type 2AR industries all exhibited increases in firm size.

Analysis of PIMS data indicates that Type 2A industries have realized economies of scale most quickly, but also that there is now some catch-up being shown in Type 2R and Type 2AR industries. In the period since 1985 business profitability is more closely associated with scale than was the case prior to 1985.

The impact of the SM in relation to economies of scale therefore differs according to the type of competition faced in an industry. This finding was reinforced by the case study research, which also confirmed the importance of public procurement liberalization and industry restructuring in the exploitation of scale economies in Type 2R industries.

2. Economies of scale and the single market: a review of the literature

The theoretical importance of economies of scale is enormous, and much has been written on their impact. In fact, one of the most research-active branches of economics in the last 20 years has been industrial organization, which can be defined as the study of markets in the presence of economies of scale. Rather less research effort has been put into the quantification of such economies. A significant reason for this is the fact that measurement is such a difficult task, riddled with methodological problems. The first task of this chapter is to introduce these problems, and how people have tried to get round them. The second task is to introduce some of the ways in which the single market programme might affect the achievement of scale economies. There is not enough space to go into detail on specific industries, so we concentrate on general issues; leaving it to Chapter 4 to go into more detail on the mechanisms through which the single market will affect different industries.

We begin, in Section 2.1, by separating out some basic concepts. Three main sources of scale economy (production, endogenous overhead costs, and external economies) are identified, and we also suggest that economies of scale cannot be assessed independently of other types of technical efficiency. This gives us four main areas to look at in more detail in Sections 2.2 to 2.5. In each case, we identify the sources of economies of scale, review the evidence on their importance, and introduce the expected impact of the single market. Section 2.6 highlights some important influences on the achievement of economies of scale, other than the single market. These will be important in our later attempts to isolate a single market effect.

2.1. Basic concepts of economies of scale

This section offers a brief discussion of the meaning of economies of scale, and the theoretical basis for increased exploitation of these economies as a result of regional integration.

Scale economies may be defined initially (and traditionally) as those benefits that result when the increased size of a single operating unit (plant), producing a single product, reduces the unit cost of production. The minimum efficient scale (MES) is in theory the size of plant at which all economies of scale are exhausted and beyond which the long-term average cost curve either turns upward, or remains flat (reflecting constant returns to scale in production). The cost gradient is defined as the slope of the cost curve. The long-run average cost curve identifies minimum average costs for each production level, assuming given factor prices and quality, and state of technology.

In order to understand economies of scale, it is important to identify their different dimensions. Scale economies may be internal or external to the plant, internal or external to the firm, internal or external to the industry, static and/or dynamic. There are economies of scale in production and possibly in functions such as distribution, management, marketing and research.

Technical economies of scale for production are the theoretically best-known type and relate to estimates of the MES and cost gradients. The sources of those economies have been amply described by Pratten [1988]. We discuss their measurement in Section 2.2. These cost savings can accrue from a better division of labour within the production unit, the spreading of fixed costs, and longer production runs. Besides these static scale economies, there is the phenomenon of learning effects associated with increasing experience gained through the production of a product or a service. The learning curve postulates that the average cost for a product is a decreasing function of the total production of that product in the past, i.e. there is an average cost reduction over time due to production experience.

Technical economies of scale should not be confused with technical efficiency, which requires the minimization of costs for any given output (as distinct from average costs varying with output). However, when it comes to measurement issues, the two concepts are inevitably inter-twined, so we discuss technical efficiency in Section 2.3, albeit at rather less length.

There are economies of scale arising from firm level activities which are distinct from those arising from large plants, large outputs for individual products and long production runs. Such firm level economies concern activities in management, advertising, research and development, and risk taking (e.g. possibilities for obtaining finance and innovation) and are sometimes known as dynamic economies of scale, though we shall discuss them as endogenous sunk costs (see Section 2.4). There may also be economies of rapid firm (and market) growth. These arise from better scope for taking advantage of economies of scale, technical progress, and a relatively healthy working climate. Some economies may also result from the operation of multiple geographically-dispersed plants as an integrated system (multi-plant economies). However, Scherer and Ross [1990] suggested that these may not be significant. Multi-product economies can result from the production of a diversified range of products (economies of scope).

External economies of scale usually refer to those that are external to the firm; the average costs of the firm depend on the size of the entire industry. A large industry in a country might generate a labour force with skills and habits useful for industrial life, support an extensive infrastructure, allow many specialized crafts to develop, etc. An important reason for scale economies at the industry level is a greater division of labour. Scale economies are national if they depend on the size of the national industry. They are international if they depend on the world-wide (or possibly EU) size of the industry. External economies are discussed in Section 2.5.

Economies external to the industry may also arise. They can also be national (external to the industries but internal to their home country) or international. Such economies result from cross-industry externalities. More particularly, they can arise from industrial inter-dependence such as that between buyers and suppliers of raw materials or intermediate products.

Potential economies of scale, as measured by rated capacity, are physical characteristics of the production facilities. Actual economies of scale, as determined by the actual amount of material processed within a specific time period, are organizational [Chandler, 1990]. Those economies would then depend on the organizational human capabilities essential to exploit the potential of technological processes such as knowledge, skill, experience and teamwork and/or the willingness of the firm (or industry) to reach them.

Potential economies of scale vary widely between different countries, industries and different time periods. It has been argued [Chandler, 1990] that those differences in economies of scale (and scope) result from differences in technologies of production and distribution, and differences in the sizes and location of markets. This is particularly relevant at a time of rapid technological change and changing market characteristics. Findings from research on economies of scale are debatable, requiring careful and sophisticated evaluation.

Economies of scale have been recognized as important determinants of the structure of an industry. Scale economies relate to the industrial organization literature in three main aspects. First, they are an important determinant of productive efficiency. Second, we wish to explain market concentration and to inquire whether industries are more concentrated than necessary to secure production efficiency. Third, we are concerned to know whether economies of scale represent a barrier to the entry for new firms (although it could be the presence of sunk costs rather than economies of scale that acts as a barrier to entry).

In the area of industrial structure, Sutton [1991] distinguishes between the effects of exogenous and endogenous sunk costs. Production has exogenous sunk costs, but some expenditures on advertising and on research and development are endogenous overheads (sunk costs) and can be used strategically by competing firms. Furthermore, Dasgupta and Stiglitz [1988] have suggested that learning-by-doing also involves a form of (exogenous) sunk cost that is the cost to produce.

The conventional theory of economic integration is largely associated with neo-classical and factor-endowment trade models, in which the measurement of the impact of economic integration is provided by the concepts of trade creation and trade diversion. This analysis is based on the assumptions that markets are characterized by perfect competition and production by constant returns to scale. It can be argued that the traditional theory is 'static' and that 'dynamic' effects also need to be considered because economic integration can yield significant growth-related gains.

These dynamic gains relate to enhanced economies of scale and scope linked to effective single market size as rates of capital formation, human resource development, technological change and entrepreneurial activity accelerate. A new literature has emerged in the study of economic integration, embracing dynamic effects and concentrating on imperfect competition, economies of scale and product diversity. In addition, when dynamic gains are considered, their locational distribution becomes an important issue.

2.2. Technical economies of scale

2.2.1. Methods of measurement

Empirical estimates of scale economies are fairly well covered in the standard literature so that the review here will be brief. There are three main techniques of estimation: statistical cost analysis, engineering estimates, and the survivor test.

The statistical approach relates costs to output volume of plants or firms of different sizes. A fairly large number of variables have to be taken into account to give significance to the results. Firms and plants classified in the same industry often have differences in product mix, differences in the age of the capital stock (and hence in the embodied technology), differences in input prices, cumulative output volume, and so forth. In practice, complete, reliable data are hard to come by. Moreover, this approach may reflect short-run rather than long-run average costs, especially as long-run costs often incorporate rents, and so reveal little about economies of scale.

The engineering approach looks directly for opinions from engineers and managers about the shape and position of the cost curves, and so tries to estimate the minimum efficient scale (MES) directly based on the use of the 'best current practice' techniques. This approach is in principle the most promising. However, engineering estimates require a substantial, costly and time-consuming research process, so that they often give comparable estimates for only a small range of (manufacturing but not service) industries and deter researchers from employing them. Also, engineering data are necessarily hypothetical in the sense that they do not allow for managerial diseconomies, inelastic factor supplies, potentially greater strike activity in larger plants, transport costs, and heterogeneous products, etc. Nevertheless, they provide a useful benchmark, and we use the Davies and Lyons [1996] standardization of Pratten's [1988] compilation in Chapter 4.

The survivor technique attempts to identify the size class which is seen to be increasing its share of industry output over a period of time, and suggests that the average size of this class represents MES. The idea is that, taking all market considerations into account, the most successful size must be most efficient. There are limitations to this technique. It does not say anything about the level of costs and does not always clarify the shape of the cost curve. Survival patterns are not always stable over time and the criteria for distinguishing surviving from non-surviving size classes embody a certain amount of arbitrariness. Survivor estimates may be tainted by pecuniary conditions, when plants (and most certainly firms) may increase their market share not because they have lower costs but because of increased market power. The results of the 'survivor test' may also reflect differences between firms using different technologies and showing different innovative performances over a particular period of time. Lastly, the selected survival size class contains different plants over time as plants move in and out of their size class. We attempt survivor estimates of MES in Section 3.2.

Measures of typical size

Faced with these problems, many analysts use existing size data, derived from census size distributions (say sales or employment) as a proxy variable for the minimum efficient scale. It is important to recognize that these are measures of 'typical' firm size, and not of MES. They have no theoretical foundation as direct measures of technical (or any other) economies of scale. However, because firm size and economies of scale are intimately related, they will be strongly correlated. For this reason, typical firm size is often used as a proxy for MES in empirical work. For some purposes, that may be reasonable, but on its own, a measure of typical size says nothing about the attainment of scale economies. Where these measures become truly revealing is when they are related to an independent measure of scale economies, such as engineering estimates. In Chapter 4, we provide a detailed analysis of the relationship between typical firm size and economies of scale, and estimate an econometric relationship between the two.

Various proxy measures for MES figure in the empirical literature. The simplest measure is to take the arithmetic average (this is used extensively in Chapters 3 and 4). A more refined proxy is the average size of plants comprising the upper half of an industry's size distribution. Another example of typical size is the Florence median plant size, i.e. the size of plant of the midpoint of the size distribution in the sense that 50 per cent of industry size is accounted for by plants in excess of the midpoint. Formally, this is the median of the first moment distribution (MFMD). We calculate this in Section 3.2.

Units of measurement

Whatever measure of MES or typical size is chosen, we must also choose the units of measurement. Common units of measurement are total assets, net assets, sales, employment and value added. Empirical results are affected by the choice of size measure since the available measures are not perfectly correlated. In this case, studies which use different size variables are likely to reach broadly similar but different conclusions. This is a serious problem if, for example, the same firm is assigned to different size groups according to which size measure is used. In practice, gross value added, sales and employment are the variables most likely to be available for use in the measure of size.

Theoretically the most appropriate measure of a firm's activities is offered by value-added. This is what we adopt in Chapters 3 and 4. However, this measure excludes contributions from all inputs other than labour and capital, and is affected by the degree of vertical integration of the firm. If the size measure is the turnover of the firm, it refers to the money values of its different products. Difficulties may arise in finding an appropriate deflation index when using data over time, or exchange rates when comparing data from different countries. Similar problems surround the valuation of fixed assets. In addition, firms may use different accounting procedures due to different depreciation methods, or differences in the lifetime of capital assets that is assumed for depreciation purposes. Firms also have different capital structure, e.g. representing a collection of capital of different vintages. The use of all these size measures may further be complicated by product mix variations between firms or plants.

Employment is the most common, often unique, measure used in size distributions of firms, contained in published national census of production data. Employment, i.e. the numbers of workers, is only an approximation of labour input for the firm which is better measured by man-hours. In the current period, this may be especially important as there is a large number of part-time workers. Bearing all the above points in mind, special care must be exercised in interpreting the results from size measurement.

Real and pecuniary economies of scale

The measurement of economies of scale is primarily concerned with the 'real' economies of scale, i.e. those arising from the reduction of inputs consumed per unit of output at higher scales of output. Those technical economies of scale, as defined by Shepherd [1990], arise from the actual physical organization of production activities. They result in an increase in economic efficiency and a reduction of costs. Yet other economies and advantages of large scale may be obtained by individual firms or industries, such as pecuniary gains, but these do not reflect any improvement in real efficiency. Pecuniary gains may refer to bargaining power to obtain supplies at lower prices, privileged access to the capital market or effective lobbying. As mentioned by Shepherd [1990], both technical and pecuniary gains occur together, and no easy method has yet been designed in research to exclude all pecuniary elements from measures of scale economies. Only engineering estimates can explicitly exclude them.

2.2.2. Recent empirical studies

Technical economies of scale are the theoretically best known type of production economies. Apart from production economies of scale, economies achievable in other common functions at the level of the firm, such as promotion, research and development, management and financing, were often regarded as less significant and/or more difficult to quantify [Owen, 1983; Pratten, 1988]. Some of these will be taken up in more detail later.

A feature of the existing analysis on economies of scale is that the information available forces a focus on manufacturing. For service industries it is not currently possible to provide a comprehensive assessment of scale economies similar to that in manufacturing industries. However, the manufacturing sector in Europe has, on the whole, been able to maintain its important role in the European Community despite the wild speculation on the 'de-industrialization' of Europe.

Currently, the main references concerning estimates of economies of scale have been published by the Commission of the European Community. An extensive survey was made by Pratten [1988] of engineering estimates of the minimum efficient scale (MES) and cost gradients for a number of European industries. He concluded (p. 162) that 'there are substantial scale effects for products and production runs to be obtained in a wide range of manufacturing industries'. Industries where economies of scale were found to be the largest included transport equipment, machinery and instrument manufacture, chemicals and paper and printing. Other industries such as textile and clothing, food, drink and tobacco were considered as generally having a limited scope for technical economies of scale.

Engineering estimates are believed to be reasonably reliable estimates of production scale economies. However, those estimates have been criticized elsewhere [e.g. Davis et al, 1989] and it has been argued that the importance of economies of scale has been grossly exaggerated in much of the manufacturing sector as well as in other areas. Many studies have reported relatively small optimal plant size (MES), roughly constant costs at the firm level and relatively flat cost gradients [Shepherd, 1990]. In addition, Shepherd suggested that estimates of cost gradients, especially at the firm level, probably contain a degree of bias as a result of pecuniary economies. It may also be that upward bias of estimates of internal economies of scale in Europe come from not taking into account the effects of other dynamic and external economies in those estimates.

Many studies have used the United States as a reference point for evaluating economic performance in Europe. In a comparative study of managerial enterprise in the United States, the United Kingdom and Germany from the 1880s through to the 1930s, Chandler [1990] attributes the success of (large-scale American) enterprises to large long-term investments in manufacturing, marketing and management. Chandler suggests that economic conditions over the period made large-scale firms necessary in order to reap the benefit of economies of scale and scope.

However, there cannot be universal generalization, and the success of American managers in the first years of the 20th century has to be placed in the context of the use of techniques of mass production and mass distribution. For many industries, especially those making differentiated products, new flexible manufacturing systems may have reduced the minimum optimal scale [Holmes, 1989]. But for other industries, especially mass production ones, there may be unexploited, even increasing, economies of scale in production. Technological innovations, often sponsored by changes in demand, generate a continually evolving process of change.

As far as services are concerned, estimates of economies of scale are scarce and difficult to construct empirically. Several attempts to measure technical economies of scale in services have produced different results [Emerson et al, 1988a]. It would seem that those economies of scale are generally small and less than for manufacturing [Pratten, 1988]. Economies of scope, however, may play a more important role in services [Emerson et al, 1988a].

2.2.3. Expected impact of the single market

One of the key motivating factors for the 1992 single market programme was the belief that it would boost efficiency and the rate of economic growth in Member States. The basis for this belief was that with the abolition of remaining border controls on intra-EC trade, as well as the harmonization or mutual recognition of standards and other regulations, the efficiency of resource use and investments would increase through greater intra-EC competition and better exploitation of economies of scale. The scale factor has been considered to be a fundamental economic reason for integrating the markets of the Community. Indeed, the European Commission [1988] estimated that over one-third of the economic benefit of the 1992 programme would have at its source the further exploitation of economies of scale. In recent years, there has been an increasing body of empirical work concerning increasing returns in Europe and the impact of the single market programme.

According to Owen [1983], a very large part of the gains from the initial formation of the European Economic Community (EEC) came from the exploitation of economies of scale. Engineering estimates of Pratten [1988] suggest that there are substantial unexploited economies of scale in the EU (see Chapter 3). The potential gains from greater exploitation of scale economies in Europe seems to be corroborated by the finding of generally larger production runs and bigger plant sizes in the United States than in Europe [Flam, 1992].

Many studies, however, have found quite small gains available from unexploited economies of scale [e.g. Davis et al, 1989; Shepherd, 1990]. In the business community's perception of the completion of the single market 's effects on costs, a large minority (36%) does not expect any effect, while a few are unenthusiastic (2%) and expect their costs to increase [Nerb, 1988]. However, it is noted that the effect reported was defined as the direct effect of the removal of barriers, and that the indirect effect of greater exploitation of economies of scale and scope is not being taken fully into account in this estimate.

Where there are large production economies of scale in one industry, and consequently predominantly exogenous sunk costs, the level of the concentration of this industry is likely to increase with more European market integration [Davies and Lyons, 1996]. Davies and Lyons found that the greatest potential for economies of scale are in Type 1 and Type 2R industries, in which they expect to observe an increase in European industrial concentration with further market integration. In particular, some highly protected Type 2R industries, e.g. among the public procurement industries, are likely to incur significant reductions in production costs and an increase in concentration as a consequence of the single European market.

In the context of the realization of the single market, the most significant reductions in production costs are expected in industries which have experienced high levels of national protection. Even the sceptics agree that there are important unexploited economies of scale in the most highly regulated sectors such as the public procurement sector, including power-generating, rail transport and telecommunication equipment. In these public procurement markets, access restrictions are more or less prohibitive throughout the Community and further market integration may mean greater competition, even with fewer firms overall in the Community.

The single market programme, giving access to spatially larger markets, may also induce large gains from increasing specialization over a narrower range of product lines, and hence increasing the length of production run. Effectively, if a specialized plant is constrained to suboptimal scale because of the limited size of its market, the manager may possibly react by diversifying the plant's output mix [Caves, 1989]. Thus, producers may respond to an increased market size by selecting larger plant sizes, but they may also include fewer product lines in a plant of any given size. Both can be interpreted as reaping economies of scale, but the latter would not be picked up on most measures.

The services identified as the most sensitive to the completion of the single market belong mainly to the insurance, distribution and banking sectors. Major growth has been experienced in insurance and other financial services. There have also recently been complex interlinkages between firms, especially within financial institutions. Those corporate strategies of co-operative arrangements may have been motivated by the spreading of the risks and costs of product development or research [Farrands and Totterdill, 1993] and stimulated by the single market perspective. Motives for new corporate strategies are nevertheless often confused and, in this case, may be different from a stimulus to change from the single market programme. For example, in their study of Britain and Germany, Mayes and Hart [1994] claim that the 1992 programme did not address the most important factors which led to the segmentation of the market in the insurance sector.

In addition, many service sectors are designed by their very nature to serve local markets, often tailored to domestic taste. Economies of scale in those sectors are suggested to be national rather than international ones, and consequently the scope for economies of scale through the completion of the European market is sometimes believed to be limited. Nevertheless, some authors [e.g. Mayes et al, 1991] claim that some of the major gains from the single market may come from the stimulus to investment and the extension of competition to areas such as services and industries, dominated by public procurement.

It is difficult to know whether, and to what extent, internal economies of scale have already been exhausted in the European Community. As suggested by Pratten [1988], pure scale economies and rationalization economies are often likely to be associated. Holmes [1989] argues that significant scale economies may still be available from rationalization. He suggests, therefore, that economies of scale have been systematically under-exploited because of a lack of competitive pressure. This problem is directly linked to issues addressed in competition policy regarding the operation of mergers. For example, if potential economies of scale are large in some sectors, there may be scope for mergers in order to reap them. Yet this may not be true of other sectors which attempt mergers. Furthermore, it has been suggested that there is a tendency in manufacturing industries for the actual concentration to be higher than required by scale economies [Holmes, 1989; Scherer and Ross, 1990].

This observation consequently raises questions about the merits of the merger boom in Europe, as mergers doubled between 1982–83 and 1985–86 and again by 1988–89 [Mayes et al, 1991]. The influence of the single market programme on mergers and acquisition may be to make them more desirable and/or to help to make them easier. At the heart of the European competition policy is the prediction that the motive of these mergers may have been the strengthening of market position rather than reasons related to economies of scale. In many industries the trade-off between exploitation of economies of scale and competition may not be relevant. As a consequence, an intensified competition and decrease in public subsidies may lead to diseconomies of scale (and unrealized economies of scope) in a number of sectors as a result of ill-advised past mergers or acquisitions.

According to Mayes et al [1991], changes in ownership in themselves do not involve more efficiency, economies of scale or more innovation. As illustrated by Holmes [1989], there may be significant economies of scale available from rationalization. Within the Community, exploiting some economies of scale may depend on the willingness and rapidity of individual firms and their consequent new corporate strategies.

Within this perspective, given the existing extent of unexploited scale economies, it seems that a strong and (more) credible competition policy should be implemented by authorities; i.e. a change in business expectations would only come from a strong string of regulatory changes and other measures to increase competition.

The European economy is dominated by oligopolies such as electronics, telecommunications, chemicals, automotive production, and those in a growing range of service industries. Large firms in those sectors have been estimated as necessary in order to compete at European and global levels. The full realization of both economies of scale and competition require large and open markets. With the completion of the single market, these gains would require global competition if the dangers of oligopoly are to be avoided.

A study by Venables and Smith [1988] has been used to illustrate the possible gains from integration of the European market, taking into account economies of scale and the effects of product differentiation. Their model investigates two interpretations of the European integration. The first involves a quantitative change on the assumption that the markets stay segmented. The second describes a qualitative change in firms' behaviour on the assumption of an integrated market (in which prices net of transport costs are equalized). The gains from the second scenario are substantially higher than those in the first, since there is the added effect of rationalization and thereby a further lowering of average costs and prices.

A study by Mayes and Hart [1994] on the stimulus to change from the single market in Britain and Germany indicates that where a substantial stimulus exists, few examples have been found of existing activity actually being shifted in order to exploit an improved cost structure in the single market. This research focuses on the effect of the SM on four industries: retailing, pharmaceuticals, insurance and machine tools. It was found for the period considered that there was a lack of strong incentives to alter behaviour offered by the SM programme. The results show effectively that strong pressures from other barriers in these industries, not tackled by the SM programme, did overcome the impact of the SM programme. Much of the stimulus to change offered by the SM programme is still to come, as many of the market measures have yet to take effect.

2.3. Technical efficiency

2.3.1. X-inefficiency

The concept of efficiency in economics expresses the success with which resources are utilized, and indicates the extent to which firms are best utilizing their available inputs to produce the maximum potential output. In practice, such fully efficient behaviour is never realized for the economy as a whole.

A measure of technical inefficiencies, as first defined by Farrell [1957], is the distance from the production frontier. For example, two identical firms with the same technology and same combination of inputs may produce two different levels of output. This source of inefficiency could be explained by the management's (in)ability to manage and organize the firm, which is accounted for in X-inefficiency [Leibenstein, 1966]. X-inefficiency – internal inefficiency – can be broadly defined by the outcome of some non-optimal conduct [Torii, 1996]. It refers to a failure to keep the cost down to the minimum possible level; X-efficiency is reached by being on the average cost curve.

X-efficiency and economies of scale are two separate concepts. As the average cost curve is the lower bound to the set of possible average costs, departures above the curve involve X-inefficiency, a degree of bad management and unnecessary costs. On the other hand, scale inefficiency is represented by departures away from the optimum scale of production on the curve where costs are minimized.

This distinction is especially important when examining the economic effects of the SM. It is possible that the increased competitive pressure on firms, resulting from the SM, forces inefficient firms to improve their performance and move towards the production frontier. If they do not, they will be driven out of business. The net result is that the average economic performance of firms, measured, for example, by labour productivity, will increase not because firms become larger and achieve economies of scale, but because they adopt best-practice techniques and reduce their costs. In this scenario, the dispersion and skewness of the distribution of firms by labour productivity will decrease as firms move towards the production frontier. It is also a phenomenon that does not fall within the definition of economies of scale, and so lies outside the scope of this study. However, it is a theme to which we shall return in interpreting our data.

2.3.2. Recent empirical studies

Studies on determinants of productivity or efficiency have been numerous, and clearly stress a considerable variety of performance. For example, comparisons have been made at the industry level of productivity differences between countries [Hooper and Larin, 1989]. Some of this variation could be explained by the difference in size of individual plants within each industry and by their choice of inputs. However, there are other sources of variation to be considered.

In production, the firm can suffer from different types of inefficiencies: scale inefficiency due to suboptimal scale to minimize costs, X-inefficiencies, and inefficiency in 'catching-up' the technology frontier or in adopting a new, more efficient technology. Evidence seems to indicate that technical inefficiency is a significant factor in explaining the under-performance of firms [Mayes, Harris and Lansbury, 1994].

It has been suggested that in practice, in the typical industry, many firms operate inside the production frontier so that only a few best-practice firms operate on the frontier, along with a 'tail' of inefficient ones [Mayes, 1996; Mayes, Harris and Lansbury, 1994]. Therefore, firms could improve their productivity without even altering the quantity, type or combination of factors of production.

A study by Lansbury and Mayes [1996b] has investigated, for the United Kingdom, the United States, Japan, Australia, Canada and South Korea, how far the change in performance in the 1980s is due to an improvement in what can be achieved by the technology available (given the inputs employed); and how far it is due to a reduction in the level of technical inefficiency, compared with that frontier, of what could be achieved. In other words, they have tried to determine how much of the change in performance was due to either shifts in the production function, or 'clustering' of individual firms to the production frontier. Their results show that the tail of less efficient plants has changed little in size during the 1980s, so that on average there has been a small reduction in technical inefficiency in the manufacturing industry. However, when inefficiency has fallen, the main determinants involved have been more effective internal and external competition. It was furthermore suggested that major gains may be reached by a country through catching up with the technology of its more successful competitors.

2.3.3. Expected impact of the single market

Scale economies and X-efficiency can be seen as two different sources of cost reductions. Diverse hypotheses have been tested, and have found some support in the literature as regarding constraints on efficiency [Caves, 1989]. Those hypotheses include tariff protection, social attitudes and priorities, industrial subsidies, public sector protectionism, collusive agreements, etc. If X-inefficiency is widespread, there is a very large potential scope for efficiency gains arising from the single market brought about by increased competition. Higher competitive pressure in the European Community may not only force inefficient firms and plants to close, but also induce more effort from entrepreneurs and less slack within firms.

Furthermore, it may be that part of the spread in performance is due to the use of more or less efficient technologies. This gives some strength to the argument that emphasis should be given in industrial and related policies to acquiring and encouraging the adoption of best practice technology (e.g. support for R&D, encouragement of the venture capital industry). There may be room for reducing gaps between best practice technology in competing countries, and this may represent major gains in the whole of each industry in Europe.

In addition, it has sometimes been argued that market integration itself could induce technological progress (e.g. Pelkmans, 1984). Market enlargement may enable a better diffusion of a given stock of knowledge, and increased competition may lead to an improvement of the stock of knowledge.

2.4. Endogenous sunk costs

2.4.1. Economies of scale, market size and industrial concentration

Recently in the theory of industrial concentration, researchers have focused on understanding how different types of economies of scale affect industrial structure. Looking more carefully at the determinants of concentration has provided new insights on the role for concentration of

(1) the prevalent competitive process between firms in the industry, and (2) the different types of scale economies. The relationship between industrial concentration and market size is then emphasized as theoretically revealing and empirically robust.

Sutton [1991] investigated a new approach to the theory of concentration by distinguishing between exogenous and endogenous elements of sunk costs, which interact with each other in determining the equilibrium pattern of industrial structure. As a consequence, relations between concentration and market size are estimated for two different groups of industries, and the corresponding processes of market consolidation and evolution are analysed empirically. The first group represents industries in which exogenous sunk costs are predominant and the form of competition is mainly through price. Exogenous sunk costs are associated with those of requiring a plant of minimum efficient scale (set-up costs) and possibly some advertising and R&D outlays can be treated as exogenous.

In the second group, sunk costs are endogenous to the firm, and consequently consist of business decision variables such as advertising and R&D outlays. Endogenous sunk costs can be used as competitive weapons by the firms, and consequently may involve a competitive escalation of those outlays. Sutton's analysis outlines the specificity of markets in which advertising plays a major role but his theory 'can be applied in principle to any form of sunk outlays that increase consumers' willingness-to-pay for a given firm's product(s)' [Sutton, 1991, p. 313].

The role of production economies of scale can be introduced as involving exogenous sunk costs to produce at the minimum efficient scale. These are determined by the nature of the underlying technology. Dynamic economies of scale, such as those in R&D and marketing activities, can be treated as involving a choice to the firm of incurring sunk costs to enhance its demand. The study has therefore provided a useful insight to the implications of advertising and R&D outlays for market structure. Firstly, when sunk costs are exogenous, the lowest viable concentration decreases to zero when market size increases. Size differences could consequently be traced to particular decisions or innovations that apparently provided long-lived competitive advantages. Secondly, when advertising sunk costs are endogenous and advertising competition is important, concentration not only stays away from zero whenever advertising competition is sufficiently tough; but it also does not decline significantly with relative market size.

Referring to the work of Sutton [1991], Davies and Lyons [1996] analyse the structure of manufacturing in the European Union, with particular reference to the European integration. A classification of manufacturing sectors is more fully developed according to the type of competition which prevails in the markets, and the way that product differentiation is created. The two main sources of product differentiation for firms are advertising and R&D spending which are considered as endogenous sunk costs creating economies of scale. Their analysis distinguishes Type 1 industries, which engage in little advertising or R&D, from Type 2 industries. Type 2 industries are further subdivided into three different categories: Type 2A industries engaged only in advertising (e.g. food, drink and tobacco), Type 2R only in R&D (e.g. machinery, instruments and transport equipment) and Type 2AR in both (e.g. cars, domestic electrical appliances, pharmaceuticals). With this typology, the authors further investigate the mechanisms which relate the different types of economies of scale to the different elements of structure for the four industry types.

The influence of production economies of scale on concentration is stressed in Type 1 industries, whereas such scale economies have a much reduced role in Type 2 industries and little influence in Type 2AR. In addition, Davies and Lyons suggest that endogenous sunk costs such as R&D and advertising may have increased as the result of competitive escalation rather than economies of scale. This typology of industries is used extensively in Chapters 3 and 4 of this report.

2.4.2. Scale economies in the process of innovation and marketing

Next consider the efficiency with which R&D inputs are converted into useful outputs. According to Schumpeter, large firms with monopoly power may have more resources for R&D and innovation than their smaller competitors, conferring on them an advantage in innovation. The assumption of economies of scale for R&D inputs in producing innovative outputs has led to hypotheses of inherent advantage for large firms in innovative activity. In addition, monopoly power allows better appropriability of the returns to innovation, providing better incentives and consequently higher rate of innovation.

The optimal size of the R&D effort could refer to the 'critical mass' a R&D unit should achieve in order to make full use of all its resources. These resources may be expensive, high capacity pieces of equipment or a large team of various specialists. The main source of economies of scale in R&D activity was identified by Pratten [1988] as the spreading of R&D costs. However, if minimum efficient scale in R&D is relevant, it relates only indirectly to the optimal size of the firm.

It is widely known that large firms undertake the bulk of industrial R&D. Scherer [1991] concludes nevertheless that after several attempts to find these economies of scale in R&D, the relationship between firm size and technological innovation remains uncertain. The empirical evidence suggests [Acs and Audretsch, 1991b] that economies of scale do not play any significant role in producing innovative output, and that small firms can be at least as innovative as their larger counterparts in some industries. Though large firms are more R&D-intensive, some empirical results indicate diminishing returns to scale as the rule. Indeed, it has been argued that the relative contribution of small and large firms to innovation may depend on industry conditions.

As pointed out by Shepherd [1990], technical progress may be closely related to economies (or diseconomies) of scale and there may be different 'optimal size' at the invention or innovation level. There may be such important and pervasive innovations, which require a long development period, that only a large firm is able to gather the needed funds, equipment, talent and sustained effort. Firms of large size may undertake incremental R&D activities that would not otherwise be possible. The need for a large R&D unit may be necessary in some sectors. This has been suggested, for instance, in the semiconductor industry, in which R&D collaborative arrangements have increased recently to allow for global competition.

Some of the literature has also focused on attributes other than size that are assumed to make a firm more innovative, such as expertise. Pavitt [1992] stressed that firms from different industries are facing technological threats and opportunities which are of very different natures. The rate and direction of technical change are often seen to be important factors in an explanation of the structure of many industries. Moreover, the technological performance of firms may depend on an effective technological strategy, especially with increasing international competitive pressure. There are many constraints on the choice of technological strategies for firms, such as those of the firm's size and principal products. These characteristics reflect the accumulated competencies and skills of the firm, upon which strategic decisions are built [Pavitt, 1992]. Pavitt and Patel [1991], for instance, stressed that large firms are more likely to have a relatively broad range of technologies and product markets than small firms, which are typically more specialized.

It may finally be said 'there is no optimum size of firm but merely an optimal pattern for any industry, such a distribution of firms by size, character and outlook as to guarantee the most effective gathering together and commercially perfecting of the flow of new ideas' [Jewkes et al, 1958, p. 168].

As far as marketing is concerned, there may be economies of scale in some sectors (especially in certain consumer goods industries). Some economies are pecuniary (e.g. media discounts) and some are real (e.g. threshold levels of advertising to get through to consumers). However, marketing expenditure would normally stay national, if only because of language and culturally-based taste differences. According to Davies and Lyons [1996], some advertising-intensive industries may be competing only at the national level, so that the competitive escalation of advertising expenditures is unlikely to occur above this level. On the other hand, R&D expenditures may increase through EU-wide or even global competitive escalation.

The learning phenomenon must also be considered. The sources of learning are diverse and their importance varies between sectors; they include suppliers, customers, competitors and more general development in pervasive technologies [Pavitt, 1992; Pavitt and Patel, 1991]. Learning could be firm-specific and cumulative. Similarly, technological competencies could also be the result of a firm-specific cumulative process [Pavitt, 1992].

Learning from experience in production, or learning-by-doing, is suggested as being important in many industries [Dasgupta and Stiglitz, 1988]. This is a form of dynamic economy of scale in production. It has been argued that many European industries which show such learning effects still have their volume of output artificially constrained by various barriers and national policies [Emerson et al, 1988]. As a consequence, the single market programme would contribute to the greater exploitation of this type of scale economy.

Since production is necessary as a form of (exogenous) sunk cost to allow learning effects, there will be an irreversibility in production possibilities (due to increasing returns to production). This phenomenon of 'path-dependent' and cumulative processes has also been investigated for technologies by Arthur [1989]. His study shows that modern and complex technologies often involve increasing returns to adoption. In a spatial dynamic dimension, this would mean the emergence of geographical areas locked in by historical events or chance to different technologies, and encourage the technology gaps between countries to remain and even widen. Similarly, firms may be locked in to certain types of production and technologies.

The study by Dasgupta and Stiglitz [1988] shows that powerful learning possibilities encourage the growth of industrial concentration and the emergence of dominant firms. Thus, when the scope for learning is large, a structure which is oligopolistic rather than competitive might emerge.

2.4.3. Expected impact of the single market

The completion of the single market may bring new opportunities for exploiting economies of scale in advertising with, for example, the introduction of European brands. However, the relevant geographical range of advertising expenditure is often identified at the national level, typically dependent on national media, culture and language.

A major expectation of the European economy regarding dynamic economies of scale is the achievement of significant dynamic efficiency gains which enhance Europe's technological performance. Assuming that the single market will lead to more competitive markets, what will be the impact on investment in R&D and the rate of innovation? Empirical research on the relationship between firm size and innovation, and economies of scale in R&D, is inconclusive. Opportunities of R&D economies of scale offered with further European integration might be twofold [Pratten, 1988]. First, firms would be allowed to spread development costs over a larger output and/or benefit from growing faster development. Second, R&D resources could be used more efficiently because of less duplication of both research and development.

It has been suggested that the required size of R&D activity and technological strategy may vary from industry to industry. In the semiconductor industry for example, strategic decisions are increasingly being made towards technological diversification, acquisition and collaboration [Hobday, 1989]. On the one hand, firms with a broad range of activities will be more likely to exploit the developments of the increasing complexity and interrelatedness of new technologies. On the other hand, strategic decisions on acquisition and collaboration (such as joint ventures or strategic alliances) might be seen as a method of dealing with the current technological complexity. Firms may find it difficult to cover the entire cost and the risk of increasing high financial investment alone, and would begin to look for alternative solutions.

The 1980s saw the emergence of a new generation of European-based multinational enterprises in the semiconductor industry, which undertook strategic partnerships as well as aggressive investment and marketing strategies in order to compete within a global framework. Those new competitive strategies may well have been stimulated by the single market programme. Furthermore, the developments often received direct government support and led to a range of European Commission collaborative programmes such as Esprit, Eureka and RACE.

When looking at the impact and the role of the single European market, Davies and Lyons [1996] show that a large number of mergers which occurred since 1987 involve advertising or R&D intensive industries. According to their analysis, the reasons for those mergers were primarily the further exploitation of economies of scale rather than the strengthening of market position. With such mergers, they suggest that some rationalization is needed in order to achieve lower production costs. However, the authors expect to find the highest impact of the single market programme in Type 1 industries that compete predominantly through price, and in low-trade R&D industries that do not compete at the European level (e.g. some public procurement intensive industries).

2.5. External economies of scale

2.5.1. Sources

The question of external economies and their measurement has often been neglected. There has been much controversy about the actual extent of external economies and the effect of the completion of the single market. The further exploitation of economies from greater division of labour, concentration and agglomeration may represent important additional gains and opportunities from the single market programme.

External economies are often considered as location factors for enterprises, and referred to as technological externalities, or technological spillovers. Other factors leading to localization are labour market pooling or the availability of non-tradeable specialized inputs and services [Krugman, 1991 a&b].

In addition, there has been a historical shift towards the formation of more closely integrated international networks in the organization of multinational enterprise [Dunning, 1993]. As to the role of external economies, a multinational enterprise may, for example, decide to invest in a particular country in order to take advantage of the agglomerative economies and/or benefit from further international division of labour. The geographical dispersion of activities in global multinational enterprises may be further reinforced when located in an economically integrated region.

It has been argued that international scale economies due to greater division of labour may be important in the European Community [Ethier, 1988] because European integration was followed by intra-industry trade rather than inter-industry specialization. European integration would then provide firms with incentives to organize an international division of labour in which productive (and innovatory) activity in each country becomes more highly specialized. On the other hand, national economies of scale could also be considered, arising from geographical concentration of an industry in a particular country. The trade pattern would then be more inter-industry. By allowing increased specialization by the partner countries, further economic integration can result in gains via such economies. Country size influences the importance of national economies of scale, as a small country is less likely to have industries composed of firms of efficient scale.

It is often claimed that the bigger the potential economies of scale, the greater the gains from specialization and trade integration, particularly for a small country. However, the combination of dynamic effects and external economies may lead to dynamic advantage or disadvantage for some countries (or regions). As a consequence, it seems important to understand how this dynamic process takes place with the development of the single market programme because international trade may not contain self-equilibrating mechanisms to ensure a convergence of economies.

2.5.2. Evidence on external economies

Clusters of economic activity already exist in Europe, around which there are external economies of scale related to a thick market in inputs, a local informal knowledge base, and a dynamic competitive spirit (for example, financial services in London). Moreover, a recent study for the European Commission by the Netherlands Economic Institute [1993] stressed the importance of the desire for companies to be close to other companies carrying out similar activities as a significant location factor. Those clusters should be allowed to develop as any industrial policy measures to prevent such external economies would not be consistent with the single market programme [Davis, 1993].

The study of geographical clustering has given some support to the view that dynamic economic development is closely linked to the agglomeration and attraction of economic activity. The model of 'new industrial districts' corresponds to a new dynamic conception of regional economic development [Farrands and Totterdill, 1993]. An industrial district is characterized by agglomerations of inter-dependent and co-operative small and medium-sized enterprises, and by a general environment of co-operation and confidence (such as partnership with local authorities, industry associations and trade unions). Successful experiences of this structure, relying on the dynamic interplay between external economies of scale, have opened new perspectives in regional development policy in some European regions.

As far as the location of innovative activity is concerned, a significant geographic agglomeration may then be expected due to the cumulative, non-transferable or location-specific character of knowledge [Feldman, 1993]. Innovation is expected to agglomerate geographically in areas that provide agglomeration economies – or concentration of specialized resources – that enhance and facilitate the innovation process. Feldman's conclusion supports the proposition of a general significant tendency for innovations to cluster geographically, this tendency being still more pronounced when considering individual industries. More particularly, her model revealed the importance of having a broad technological infrastructure for states. The major factors identified as increasing innovative activity are those of spillovers across industries (but still within state boundaries), spillovers of university research, and the presence of related industries and specialized business services. According to this spatial approach to innovative activity, states that contain concentrations of innovative inputs will develop a comparative advantage for innovative industries. However, the author warned that this advantage may be lost in the translation of scientific knowledge into new commercial innovations.

Caballero and Lyons [1990] have further investigated, and found, important national external economies from cross industry externalities in four selected European countries (West Germany, France, the United Kingdom and Belgium). They conclude that, with the single market programme, external economies have a significant role which has generally been underestimated and merits further research. National external economies may be particularly relevant to the services industries which are often country-specific. However, it may be that some industries already benefit from international economies (such as big car makers), having already completed a single market [Cohen, 1990]. Oulton [1996] has applied the method employed by Caballero and Lyons to UK manufacturing industries in order to test for external scale economies due to the expansion of manufacturing as a whole. His results show that, whereas returns to scale stay constant at the industry level, there are non-negligible external effects at the level of aggregate manufacturing on individual industries.

It is against this background that we have conducted our case studies (Appendix A, summarized in Chapter 6). It is not possible to quantify external economies in simple statistical measures, but insights can be gained from the views of experts in the industry.

2.5.3. Convergence or divergence in the single market

Neven [1990] argues that the main beneficiaries from the single market programme are likely to be the southern European countries 'both in terms of exploiting comparative advantages and in terms of exhausting scale economies' (p. 46). Opposing this view, many arguments have been advanced to suggest that the benefits of economic integration will accrue to some of the central regions to the detriment of the peripheral regions. They often refer to the new literature on the existence and the role of market imperfections, external economies of scale and learning curves for individual firms.

In one contemporary approach to interregional trade, Krugman [1991a] proposed a model of regional specialization. The nature of considered externalities is general rather than specific to a particular industry. There are pecuniary externalities associated with either demand or supply linkages (as opposed to purely technological spillovers). The general set of assumptions implies imperfect competition with economies of scale and transportation costs for manufactured goods, and the mobility of workers. There are two regions in the economy, and two sectors: a mobile or 'footloose' manufacturing sector; and a non-manufacturing sector, e.g. agriculture, using a location-specific input and facing a competitive market. Enterprises concentrate because of strongly increasing returns to scale, and mobile labour moves into the region. In order to minimize transportation costs, firms will be more likely (other things being equal) to locate in regions with a relatively large local demand. As firms concentrate, demand will expand which will attract more firms and lead to a circular process of agglomeration (similar to a dynamic cumulative process) and regional divergence. The determination of regions in which this process starts will essentially depend on initial conditions such as the spatial distribution of the non-rural population.

However, the results of the model stress the large degree of indeterminacy of the locational choice of firms and therefore of the pattern of regional specialization. There are several possible final locations of enterprises, depending on the key parameters of transportation costs, the size of the economies of scale and the share of consumption expenditure on manufactured goods. A small change in these parameters induces the self-feeding process of agglomeration to occur either in the preferred centre – accentuating divergence, or in regions in which the initial demand potential was relatively small – favouring convergence. This indeterminacy supports regional policy measures, since the economies of scale in the existing agglomerations may prevent a substantial relocation in the periphery following the elimination of barriers of trade in the process of the economic integration. In another model Krugman [1991b, p. 89] suggests that, for the region that becomes the periphery, 'close integration is good but a limited move towards integration may hurt' [see also Krugman and Venables, 1990].

As a consequence, there should be no strong reasons to expect the elimination of regional problems and the centre-periphery pattern through the free interplay of market forces. On the contrary, such problems could be aggravated. For example, regions at the centre of the European Community are able to exploit their natural positional advantage of being closest to the main population centres. In addition, this positional advantage may be reinforced by the fact that the central regions contain nearly all the major urban concentrations as well as the financial and administrative capital cities. Those big cities have better transport and telecommunications facilities as well as access to large and well-qualified labour forces: on the whole, these advantages involve external economies of scale and favour the further concentration of firms and industries in the central regions. The increasing global and footloose nature of international production and other activities, due to both the single market programme and the globalization phenomenon, may be likely to reinforce and accelerate patterns of 'circular and cumulative causation' within countries and/or regions. The potential impact of external economies is therefore great.

2.6. Non-single market influences on the attainment of economies of scale

To assess the economic effects of the implementation of the single market programme, one needs to isolate the effects of European integration from all the other effects associated with the passing of time, such as the natural development of trade flows, the growth of income, global trade liberalization, etc. To do so, the existing situation should be compared with one in which the institutions and policies of the SM are totally absent. However, in practice some speculation cannot be avoided. Therefore, important forces other than the single market programme must be identified that influence changes in European industrial structures. In the literature, three main influential forces are suggested: cyclical variations in the economy, the technological change and the phenomenon of the globalization of industry.

2.6.1. Economic cycles

It has been suggested that measures of changes in scale efficiencies or other efficiencies are correlated with changes in general economic conditions. Cyclical movements would therefore be captured in measures of firms' sizes. The general economic climate may be itself an explanation for greater exploitation of economies of scale. In recession years, for example, managers may pay much closer attention to costs than in expansion periods.

As far as X-inefficiencies are concerned, there could be more room in the market for inefficient producers during growth periods of the economy [Mayes, Harris and Lansbury, 1994]. Recessions could induce a general reduction in inefficiencies and even the exit of the least efficient firms or plants. Since tails of inefficient businesses remain in industries, the influence of economic cycles on production costs may be important. As a consequence, an observed downward trend in firms' sizes could be attributable to a recession period rather than to any single market effects.

In addition, the production frontier may also be shifted as a result of economic cycles. For instance, the frontier may be shifted because of increased incorporation of new technologies in industries experiencing economic growth [Mayes, Harris and Lansbury, 1994; Lansbury and Mayes, 1996b].

In these circumstances, to identify the extent and determinants of greater exploitation of economies of scale is not an easy task. In Europe, economic cycles in the 1980s would broadly show a phase of decline in the early 1980s and of growth later in the decade. In our econometric work in Chapter 4, we take explicit account of industry-specific growth.

2.6.2. Technological change

Changes in the economies of scale over time are also subject to debate. On the one hand, Pratten's [1971] estimates show that there are reasons to believe economies of scale increase, rather than decrease, in most industries over time. Technical progress may consist, for example, of inventing ways in which small scale processes can be profitably scaled up. On the other hand, it has been argued that no broad trend toward greater scale economies can be identified, be it in manufacturing industry or in other sectors. In many industries, changes in technology and production management have had a decentralizing impact, promoting small scale production and reduction of optimal size. Such tendencies can be found resulting from the impact throughout manufacturing of technological development in, for example, electricity generation, the direct reduction process of steel manufacture, and the reduction in size of computers and communications systems. Our sectoral reviews in Appendix B attempt to assess these technological trends.

Increased computerization may allow small production units to gain access to the latest technology, and reduce the cost advantages of large scale and long production runs. Typically, industry studies indicate that the range of cost variations between firms of similar size is much greater that the cost variations associated with scale [Smith, 1992]. In the car industry for example, the apparently important cost advantages of Japanese firms (with their efficient lean product development process) over European firms do not seem to be based primarily on advantages of scale.

2.6.3. Globalization

There has been a growing realization that much more work is required on the globalization phenomenon, with the emergence of globally-oriented multinational enterprises and the establishment of global networks of trade, production and R&D facilities. In an increasingly globalized market, competitive pressures have increased in Europe. In particular, competition has intensified between the European Community, the United States and Japan. It has been argued that the restructuring of the Community industry that took place in the 1980s is the result both of competitive pressures from non-European multinationals and of anticipation of the single market [Sharp, 1992]. Furthermore, the globalization process is likely to reinforce single market effects.

However, the European Community is not the only vehicle of trade liberalization since the GATT agreement 'bound' the Member States not to raise tariffs on industrial products and agree to a series of tariff cuts. The European Community is part of the GATT, although the signatories of GATT are the Member States. It has nevertheless been argued that the European Community represents a more constraining commitment from the Member States than that of the GATT [Holmes, 1992].

2.7. Conclusion

The extent and nature of increasing returns in European industries is a topic of lively debate. Although it is believed that the realization of potential economies of scale represents a clear gain, empirical evidence on their extent is not conclusive. To quantify and measure the different types of scale economies remains difficult and uncertain.

It has been argued that technical economies of scale in production have often been overestimated. Reasons for this may be the impossibility of separating them from other pecuniary, external and dynamic economies. Greater production economies of scale may also be brought about by a reduction in product variety and consequently longer production runs. In addition, the effect of technological change on those economies of scale has not been well defined. Whether there are unexploited internal economies depends on the sector considered. The highest potential economies of scale are usually expected in the most protected industries, especially in public procurement industries.

Moreover, the removal of non-tariff barriers and regulations may not be a sufficient condition for the exploitation of existing potential scale economies by firms. Rationalization may be an equally important condition for this exploitation. This belief leads to the idea that an important impact of the single market on economies of scale may arise through a strong and credible competition policy, which would change business expectations and behaviour. It is further argued that many of the recently increased number of mergers were not necessarily driven by the need to exploit new economies of scale, but rather by a desire to expand market shares. It has been suggested that this may have been particularly true in R&D and advertising intensive sectors, where the size of the market is fundamental in determining the incentive to invest in these endogenous sunk costs.

Technical inefficiency could be reduced in the European Community by improving internal and external competition within industries. The removal of barriers within the European Community, as part of the single market programme, could be expected to lead to an increase in average technical efficiency, given the increase in competition faced by domestic producers.

It has been argued that R&D and advertising expenditures may be seen as a competitive weapon rather than as a means to reach economies of scale. However, opinions remain divided in the literature as to whether there are economies of scale in the conversion of inputs to outputs in these activities.

In some industries there may be economies of scale in R&D through the spreading of costs and risks. Large R&D resources may be needed, such as large teams of specialists or expensive specialized equipment, which a small R&D unit could not afford. This would be especially relevant if one assumes an increasing complexity and interrelatedness of new technologies. The need for a large R&D unit may then be necessary in some sectors, as suggested more particularly in the semiconductor industry, in which collaborative strategies in R&D have emerged. Therefore a possible impact of the single market programme may be to stimulate such strategies in selected industries. In fact, direct actions have been taken at the European level through some EU initiatives in the semiconductor industry.

In advertising, it is not clear whether an increase in a firm's expenditure is motivated by the exploitation of scale economies or by the acquisition of more monopolistic power. One impact of further European integration may be to allow the development of new European brands. Further exploitation of learning economies of scale may be a benefit of the completion of the single market, due to the expected increases in the production level. These dynamic scale economies in production may lead, as they accumulate, to advantages or disadvantages as firms become locked in to some production processes (or technologies).

External economies may also be a source of high potential gains reinforced with the processes of economic integration. Benefits often relate to a greater division of labour and agglomeration economies. However, in a dynamic perspective, the further exploitation of external economies may lead to 'circular and cumulative' processes to the advantage or disadvantage of some countries (or regions).

The positive impacts of the completion of the single market with regard to agglomeration economies are twofold. Firstly, there may be further exploitation of existing economies, with the reinforcement of existing clusters of economic activity. Secondly, there may be the creation of new centres for agglomeration economies in which economic activity would start to accumulate.

Finally, one can argue that the effects of the single market programme cannot be satisfactorily disassociated from those arising from other important driving forces, such as the GATT agreements or the globalization of industries. However, the European Community may involve more constraining (and influential) commitments from Member States than GATT. Global change itself may be a driving force for the changes within Europe, and we should expect to observe changes as a result of cyclical economic factors as well as the single market programme.

In the next chapter, we begin our analysis by describing what has actually been happening to the size of firms across the EU, and provide a background of economic growth and intra-EU trade. In Chapter 4, we start to disentangle some of the influences of the single market.

3. Statistical background on firm size and growth

In this chapter, we begin our analysis of the Eurostat size distribution data, and try to discern the major trends. In Section 3.1, we discuss some of the limitations of the data and justify our later use of average enterprise size, measured by gross value added, as a reasonable measure of attained scale. This measure is analysed in some depth in Chapter 4, and the remainder of this chapter aims to provide a descriptive background to that work.

Two important factors must underpin an understanding of firm size (we use the terms firm, enterprise and business unit interchangeably in this chapter – the precise empirical definition of what we mean is given in Section 3.1.1). First, in the context of this study, size is only relevant relative to potential economies of scale; and second, the achievement of any given size depends on the type of competition that firms engage in. A deeper analysis of the precise ways in which these fit together is left to Chapter 4, but here we present two typologies based on the potential for further gains from economies of scale (3.2.1), and the type of competitive mechanism typically used in the industry (3.2.2). These typologies are then used to arrange the descriptive statistics on the average size of business unit (3.3). It is of considerable policy interest to know how the achievement of economies of scale varies across different countries, so we also present the summary data by Member State. Finally, in assessing the role of the single market programme, we shall be making use of two measures of integration based on intra-EU trade. Summary statistics by industry type and Member State are presented in Section 3.4.

3.1. Measurement of scale using Eurostat data

3.1.1. Eurostat definitions

Data used in the analysis of firm size come from Eurostat, which collates data at the enterprise (or *Unternehmen*) level. 'Enterprise' is defined as the smallest legally autonomous business unit, which is quite different from the standard definition of the term 'enterprise' in English-speaking countries, where it refers to a group of companies comprising the parent company and all of its subsidiaries. In this study we shall call this the business unit or enterprise, or often simply 'firm' for short, but the reader should always bear Eurostat's definition in mind. Note that Member States can differ somewhat in their interpretations of a business unit, so cross-Member State comparisons may be partly definitional. However, this should not affect the cross-industry comparisons within Member States. The databases used include all firms employing at least 20 people (except for Spain which includes all firms) in three-digit NACE manufacturing industries. (Luxembourg is excluded due to insufficient data.)

Part of the analysis utilized a database which distributes data by employment (known as the Series D database). Due to the limited number of countries available, this analysis was superseded by one which utilized a more comprehensive database, but which lacked distribution into size categories (the VISA database).

Prior to using the data to measure change in firm size, two decisions had to be made: (i) what unit of measurement to use (employment vs gross value added vs turnover); and (ii) what measure of scale?

3.1.2. Unit of measurement

The ideal unit to measure for the presence of scale economies would be quality adjusted volume of production, but this measure is not available. Employment is the most widespread and concrete measure; however, it is often affected by both long-term, labour-saving, technological change and by short-term cyclical fluctuations in the European economy. Productivity growth means that employment continually falls even if production volume rises. Sales/turnover, properly adjusted for inflation, gets close to output volume, but is sensitive to the position in the production chain – e.g. brokers and traders can have huge turnover, but still operate on a small scale because they add little value to the product. Gross value added captures the contribution of the industry to real production. This is therefore our preferred measure. It is adjusted to general inflation, using annual GDP deflators, although we would have preferred an industry specific index (which was not available). The trend towards specialization on core activities (vertical dis-integration) would tend to bias this measure downwards (e.g. the same number of cars is produced, but value added of gearboxes is now contracted out).

3.1.3. Measurement of scale

We attempted two measures of economies of scale using size distribution data: the survivor method (which attempts direct measure of scale economies by identifying the firm size most successful in the market); and a measure of typical size called the median of the first moment distribution, whereby half the output is produced in larger firms and half in smaller (a popular measure of central tendency of firm size; if 50% of the output is always produced by firms of less than MES, it is a direct measure of MES, otherwise it still gives a good measure of typical scale). Unfortunately, however, we found that the quality of data was insufficient to provide reliable results; there were few observations, a short time series and size classes which were too broad.

Our pilot of 31 industries gave the following results:

Table 3.1.   Results of MFMD and survivor employment calculations: 1986

	MFMD		Survivor	
	Employment	No. of Obs	Employment	No. of Obs
UK	2,316	19	77	19
France	3,643	28	688	28
Italy	1,163	22	913	26

The only countries which had sufficient data for these calculations were the UK, France and Italy. As Table 3.1 shows, the two calculations yielded very different results; the weighted averages of industries for each of the UK, France and Italy were much smaller than the corresponding MFMD estimates. The reason for this is that in many cases the survivor size class was the smallest class, the lower employment bound to this size class being 20. This had the effect of pulling the average survivor class down.

In order to identify empirically which estimate, MFMD or survivor, was more reasonable, we assumed that sales were positively correlated with employment and ran two regressions; one regressing the log of the SPES/Pratten MES estimate (measured in sales) on the log of the MFMD estimate, with a dummy variable taking the value 0 for Pratten's estimates and 1 for SPES estimates; and one regressing the log of the SPES/Pratten estimate on the log of the survivor estimate and the SPES/Pratten dummy. Outlying observations were excluded. The R^2 from the regression using the MFMD method was 0.58 while that for the survivor method was 0.38. The MFMD was therefore deemed to be more accurate.

The next step was then to calculate the MFMD for two additional years, 1981 and 1991, to identify whether any changes took place in firm size before and after 1986. The results are given in Table 3.2. They show that there were dramatic changes in the median size of firms in the three countries where data were available. The MFMD declined in each of the three countries between 1981 and 1986 (by 39% in the UK, 59% in France and 62% in Italy) and in two of the three between 1986 and 1991 (by 18% in the UK and 49% in France). Only in Italy did the MFMD increase in the latter period, by 73%.

Table 3.2.   Results of MFMD calculations for 1981, 1986 and 1991 (weighted averages of 31 manufacturing sectors)

	1981	1986	1991	% change 1981–86	% change 1986–91
UK	3,791	2,316	1,900	-38.9	-18.0
France	8,905	3,643	1,834	-58.1	-49.7
Italy	3,079	1,163	2,013	-62.2	73.1

Since the number of industries under investigation using the MFMD method was limited to 31 and in only three countries, an alternative method of calculating typical firm size was then employed: this involved calculating the average firm size, which has the virtue of simplicity and wide availability, but is also sensitive to the inclusion/exclusion of smaller firms.

3.2.   Typologies of sectors

3.2.1.   EOS potential

Early in the project, we had to identify potentially interesting sectors to investigate in those parts of the project for which there were insufficient resources to be comprehensive (i.e. case studies, and concentration). For selected three-digit manufacturing sectors, a classification of their sensitivity to the SM programme against their potential to exploit economies of scale was undertaken. The potential to exploit economies of scale was identified by means of the ratios of MES (as indicated by Pratten, 1988) to the five-firm concentration ratio at the European level (as indicated by the SPES database for 1987, and referred to as CR5).

We then divided CR5 by 5 in order to calculate the ratio of MES to the average production of the largest five firms. When this calculation was carried out, only two sectors (tractors and agricultural machinery, and aerospace) had EOS potential greater than 1, indicating that only these two industries had unexploited economies of scale. EAG therefore used average market share rather than the average of the largest five firms in order to calculate EOS potential. Average market share was calculated as average sales divided by EU market size. By this calculation 47 out of 53 manufacturing sectors had unexploited economies of scale.

Sectoral sensitivity to the SM programme was identified according to the four groups of industrial sectors that were expected to be most affected (Group 1 being the most sensitive) as given by Buigues et al [1990]. This classification resulted in the ranking of sectors according to EOS potential as shown in Table 3.3 and the matrix shown in Figure 3.1.

Quadrant A includes those manufacturing sectors which were considered to have both a high sensitivity of the SM programme, and the potential to exploit economies of scale. The quadrant separations for each variable are based on the average of the 53 sectors shown. The horizontal line in Figure 3.1 indicates that 8.65 is the average EOS potential. The vertical line indicates that 1.2 is the (theoretical) average SM sensitivity; in practice quadrants A and C contain all those sectors in Groups 1, 2 and 3 as analysed by Buigues et al.

3.2.2. Type of competitive mechanism

For our more comprehensive econometric work, we preferred to directly model EOS potential and disaggregate the sources of barriers to the single market. However, following work reported in Davies and Lyons [1996], we expected to observe different patterns depending on the type of competition prevalent in the industry. A Type 2 industry is one in which typically or innately (i.e. most countries and in most time periods) firms engage in advertising and/or R&D competition. Roughly speaking, this means industries which have an advertising to sales ratio and/or R&D to sales ratio in excess of 1%. A Type 1 industry is one in which firms engage in neither type of competition. Within Type 2 we identify three subsets: a Type 2A industry is one in which firms typically engage in advertising, but not R&D competition; a 2R is one engaging in R&D but not advertising; and a Type 2AR industry is one in which firms typically engage in both advertising and R&D competition.

Type 2A industries (13 industries, accounting for 12% of EU manufacturing production) mostly come from the food, drink and tobacco sectors; Type 2R industries (22 industries, accounting for 26% of production) include some chemicals, but mainly come from machinery, instruments and transport equipment; Type 2AR industries (nine industries, accounting for 14% of production) include some chemicals such as pharmaceuticals, and soaps and detergents, and consumer durables such as cars and domestic electrical appliances; and Type 1 industries (56 industries, accounting for 48% of production) are mainly associated with processing materials, including iron and steel, cement, foundries, grain-milling and the textile and wood processing industries.

Table 3.3. EOS potential and SM sensitivity of EU manufacturing sectors listed in decending order of EOS potential

Industry	NACE	MES (MECU)	S (1) (MECU)	MES/S = Ideal mkt share	Avg sales 1986 MECU	Avg mkt share = Avg sales/S	EOS potential = (MES/S)/ Avg sales/S	SM sensitivity (2)	Quadrant
Tractors & agricultural machinery	321	1,000	15,216	6.57	13.6	0.09	73.31	1	B
Aerospace	364	4,000	32,804	12.19	82.3	0.25	48.63	1	B
Electric lighting	347	250	6,653	3.76	9.3	0.14	26.93	1	B
Non-ferrous metals	224	1,000	32,059	3.12	46.0	0.14	21.75	0	B
Electrical machinery	342	250	36,240	0.69	12.7	0.04	19.68	2	A
Shipbuilding	361	250	15,368	1.63	14.7	0.10	16.96	2	A
Iron & steel	221	2,000	52,628	3.80	135.8	0.26	14.73	0	B
Rubber	481	250	23,583	1.06	18.5	0.08	13.50	1	B
Man-made fibres	260	500	8,278	6.04	46.9	0.57	10.67	0	B
Telecom & measuring equipment	344	250	60,624	0.41	23.9	0.04	10.44	4	A
Tobacco	429	2,000	31,748	6.30	202.2	0.64	9.89	0	B
Insulating wires & cables	341	250	18,168	1.38	25.5	0.14	9.80	2	A
Rail stock	362	250	5,309	4.71	26.3	0.49	9.52	3	A
Radio & TV	345	250	36,461	0.69	26.9	0.07	9.28	1	B
Cycle & motor cycle	363	100	3,765	2.66	11.1	0.30	8.98	0	B
Beer	427	250	19,851	1.26	28.9	0.15	8.65	3	A
Industrial & agricultural chemicals	256	250	34,496	0.72	29.9	0.09	8.37	1	D
Fish products	415	100	7,253	1.38	12.7	0.17	7.88	0	D
Domestic electrical appliances	346	250	15,951	1.57	32.1	0.20	7.80	1	D
Machine tools	322	50	17,540	0.29	6.6	0.04	7.61	1	D
Steel tubes	222	250	10,324	2.42	36.7	0.36	6.81	0	D
Paper & pulp	471	250	25,244	0.99	38.1	0.15	6.57	0	D
Pharmaceuticals	257	250	41,599	0.60	38.2	0.09	6.54	3	C
Wine & cider	426	100	10,174	0.98	16.7	0.16	6.00	3	C
Glass	247	100	18,988	0.53	17.1	0.09	5.86	1	D
Medical instruments	372	25	6,565	0.38	4.5	0.07	5.57	4	C
Food & chemical machinery	324	50	21,820	0.23	9.4	0.04	5.29	1	D
Motor vehicles	351	8,000	151,214	5.29	1,516.3	1.00	5.28	1	D
Soft drinks	428	100	11,411	0.88	19.0	0.17	5.26	3	C
Paper & wood & etc. machinery	327	50	13,338	0.37	10.7	0.08	4.65	1	D
Oils & fats	411	250	17,147	1.46	53.8	0.31	4.65	0	D
Pasta	417	100	4,442	2.25	22.0	0.50	4.54	2	C
Mining & construction machinery	325	50	32,841	0.15	12.0	0.04	4.15	1	D
Basic chemicals	251	500	102,942	0.49	121.6	0.12	4.11	1	D
Transmission equipment	326	50	13,998	0.36	12.8	0.09	3.92	1	D
Clocks & watches	374	25	1,661	1.51	6.4	0.39	3.89	0	D
Textile machinery	323	50	8,288	0.60	13.3	0.16	3.76	1	D
Flax & hemp	434	25	1,427	1.75	7.1	0.50	3.54	0	D
Chocolate & sugar confectionery	421	100	17,108	0.58	31.7	0.19	3.15	2	C
Boilers & containers	315	25	21,290	0.12	8.0	0.04	3.14	3	C
Computers & office machinery	330	250	30,613	0.82	85.3	0.28	2.93	4	C
Ceramics	248	25	9,720	0.26	9.5	0.10	2.62	1	D
Wool	431	25	14,917	0.17	9.6	0.06	2.60	1	D
Cotton	432	25	19,183	0.13	14.0	0.07	1.79	1	D
Asbestos	244	25	1,627	1.54	18.4	1.13	1.36	0	D
Clothing	453	5	53,097	0.01	4.0	0.01	1.24	1	D
Household textiles	455	5	6,802	0.07	4.1	0.06	1.22	1	D
Starch	418	100	3,455	2.89	101.4	2.93	0.99	0	D
Footwear	451	5	6,367	0.08	5.1	0.08	0.98	1	D
Photo labs	493	5	2,349	0.21	5.6	0.24	0.89	1	D
Carpets	438	5	16,982	0.03	15.2	0.09	0.33	1	D
Miscellaneous manufacturing	495	1	4,075	0.02	4.5	0.11	0.22	1	D
Jewellery	491	1	9,285	0.01	5.4	0.06	0.18	1	D
Averages							**8.65**	**1.2**	

(1) Size of the EU market (production) in ECU.

(2) SM Sensitivity: 4= highest, 0=lowest.

Figure 3.1. Effects of SM measures: EOS potential vs SM sensitivity of EU manufacturing sectors

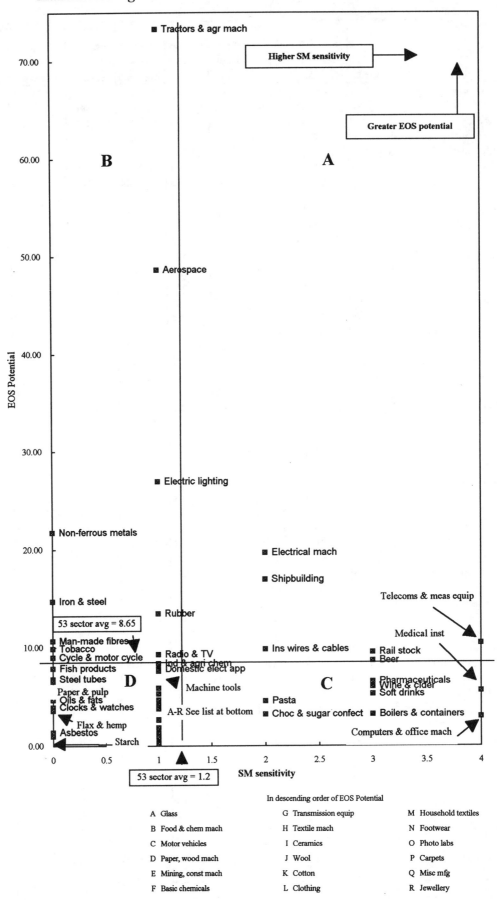

In descending order of EOS Potential

A Glass	G Transmission equip	M Household textiles
B Food & chem mach	H Textile mach	N Footwear
C Motor vehicles	I Ceramics	O Photo labs
D Paper, wood mach	J Wool	P Carpets
E Mining, const mach	K Cotton	Q Misc mfg
F Basic chemicals	L Clothing	R Jewellery

3.3. Average size of businesses

This section provides descriptive statistics on average size, first by value added, which is used in the next chapter. We also provide data on average employment, since this gives insight into labour productivity changes.

3.3.1. Real gross value added

Changes in firm size as measured by real gross value added were calculated in three ways: first by a separation of firms into their respective quadrants (A, B, C etc.); secondly by Member State; and thirdly by type of industry (1, 2A, etc.).

For the quadrant analysis, the calculation of changes in firm size using Eurostat's VISA database included those Member States which had nine pieces of information available: number of enterprises, employment and gross value added for each of the three years, 1981, 1986 and 1991. Countries meeting this criterion were Denmark, France, Germany, Italy, the Netherlands, Spain and the UK. In the event, 112 manufacturing industries were used and there were 577 observations per year.

To test whether there were statistically significant changes in real gross value added before and after 1986, the following regression was carried out: ln Y/N 86 was regressed on ln Y/N 81 and ln Y/N 91 regressed on ln Y/N 86 where Y/N is average gross value added per enterprise. Dummies were added to the regressions to test if there was any significance in the separation into the quadrants A, B, C and D (vs the category with all other sectors used in the analysis).

Table 3.4 shows the results of the average calculations:

Table 3.4.   Changes in real gross value added per enterprise (MECU, 1981 prices)

			1981	1986	1991	% change 1981-86	% change 1986-91
GVA/Enterprise	Quadrant	A	6.59	5.86	5.11	-11.2	-12.7
		B	5.92	6.29	6.20	6.3	-1.4
		C	2.29	2.63	2.85	14.8	8.3
		D	2.44	2.54	2.60	3.9	2.4
		Other	0.89	0.92	1.02	2.8	11.1
		Total	1.65	1.73	1.81	4.7	4.5

There was a slight increase in average real gross value added in the two periods (4.7% in the first and 4.5% in the second), but these were found to be not statistically different from 0. The increase in average size after 1986 was not greater than before 1986, which does not support the view that the year 1986 marks a structural break reflecting the anticipated influence of the SM. Moreover, for the SM-sensitive industries in quadrant A, the average size of enterprise using this measure decreased by 11.2% between 1981 and 1986 and by 12.7% between 1986 and 1991, which does not suggest that the SM led to any economies of scale at the level of the enterprise.

It should be noted that there was a large difference in the number of industries per quadrant: quadrant A included six manufacturing sectors, B included 11, C had eight, D had 28 and 'other' had 59 for a total of 112 sectors.

The following tables (3.5 and 3.6) show the results by Member State, including both total real GVA and real GVA per enterprise. These analyses include all countries for which data are available and only industries for which both 1986 and 1991 data are available, as well as 1981 data. The number of industries included for each country is given in the right hand column.

Table 3.5.   **Total real GVA by Member State and total EU (MECU, 1981 prices)**

Country	1981	1986	1991	% change 1981-86	% change 1986-91	No. of industries[3]
Germany	153,480	192,228	230,415	25.2	19.9	91
France	102,473	86,441	88,837	-15.6	2.8	100
UK	86,158	77,270	71,161	-10.3	-7.9	90
Italy	61,896	51,803	49,132	-16.3	-5.2	102
Spain	39,658	26,196	30,490	-33.9	16.4	97
Netherlands	8,638	16,638	19,203		15.4	52
Belgium	9,965	11,668	12,155	17.1	4.2	52
Denmark	4,377	6,031	7,237	37.8	20.0	58
Ireland	n/a	n/a	4,025	-	-	35
Portugal	n/a	n/a	1,353	-	-	75
Greece	2,774	965	523	-65.2	-45.8	68
Total[1]	469,419	469,239	514,531	-0.04	9.7	-
EUR-12[2]	473,203	438,263	453,567	-7.4	3.5	89

[1]   Total is sum of 11 Member States given above in table.
[2]   EUR-12 is total given in Eurostat VISA database.
[3]   Data are included, where available, for NACE codes 221-495 with the exception of the following for reasons of their dissimilarity from other manufacturing industries: 231, 232, 319, 348, 352, 365, 435.

This table shows that generally there was recession in the first period and recovery in the second. Strongest growth occurred in Germany and Denmark, which is something that will be reiterated later in the chapter. The Greek figures are not considered to be very reliable (and this is confirmed by later employment data).

Table 3.6.   Real GVA per enterprise by Member State (MECU, 1981 prices) and initial disadvantage in 1986

Country	1981	1986	1991	% change 1981–86	% change 1986–91	Initial disadvantage	No. of inds[1]
Germany	4.94	6.35	6.91	28.5	8.8	0.53	91
France	3.72	3.24	3.17	-12.9	-2.2	0.30	100
UK	3.51	3.19	2.80	-9.2	-12.2	0.30	90
Italy	2.35	1.75	1.50	-25.4	-14.3	0.26	102
Spain	0.26	0.19	0.22	-25.5	15.4	n/a	97
Netherlands	3.32	4.01	3.97	21.0	-1.1	0.46	52
Belgium	3.08	3.35	n/a	8.6	-	0.59	64
Denmark	2.22	2.53	3.18	13.8	25.5	0.63	58
Portugal	n/a	n/a	0.16	-	-	n/a	75
Greece	0.79	n/a	0.16	-	-	n/a	68

[1]   Data are included, where available, for NACE codes 221-495 with the exception of the following for reasons of their dissimilarity from other manufacturing industries: 231, 232, 319, 348, 352, 365, 435.

Focusing on 1986, Germany has by far the largest size enterprises, followed by the Netherlands, Belgium, France, and the UK; Denmark has slightly smaller enterprises and Italy significantly smaller. (The figures for Spain are so small due to the fact that enterprises with less than 20 employees are included.) Portugal and Greece seem much smaller, but the reliability of these data is questionable. These averages, however, may say little about attainment of economies of scale, because different countries have different industrial structures.

Initial disadvantage expresses unweighted average size (measured in turnover) relative to our engineering estimates of MES. Thus, a low figure suggests a large gap between attained size and potential EOS, while a number approaching one would suggest that fewer unutilized economies of scale remain. An initial disadvantage equal to 1 would not mean exactly all economies of scale have been attained since firstly, within an industry, size distribution means that even if initial disadvantage were equal to 1, some firms would be smaller than MES and some larger; and secondly, initial disadvantage is an average across all industries, so if it equals 1, it is likely that some industries will have an average in excess and some below. So the interpretation is really just a general indication. Most strikingly, this completely reverses the position of Denmark. This is because Denmark specializes in industries which have relatively low MES. Now, Denmark, Belgium, Germany and the Netherlands have least scale disadvantage, followed by France, the UK and Italy some way behind. Finally, note how there is no clear pattern in average size growth between the two periods when averaged across whole Member States.

Table 3.7.   Total real GVA by type of industry

Type	1981	1986	1991	% change 1981–86	% change 1986–91
1	209,177	177,566	187,366	-15.1	5.5
2A	37,391	32,034	33,653	-14.3	5.1
2R	162,601	166,774	165,596	2.6	-0.7
2AR	64,034	61,889	66,952	-3.4	8.2

Looking at total real gross value added by type of industry (Table 3.7), Type 1 industries still contribute most to gross value added, but are closely followed by 2R. Type 2AR have a few large industries and 2A have a larger number of relatively small industries. Types 2R and 2AR have been most resistant to recession, while Types 1 and 2A have moved in line.

Table 3.8.   Average real GVA by type of industry

Type	1981	1986	1991	% change 1981–86	% change 1986–91	Initial disadvantage
1	0.99	0.97	1.03	-2.5	6.6	0.72
2A	1.62	1.64	1.84	1.6	12.4	0.37
2R	4.85	5.25	5.04	8.2	-4.0	0.17
2AR	6.45	6.65	7.45	3.1	12.0	0.16

The typical size of firms is very much larger in Type 2R and especially Type 2AR, but these industries also have the greatest potential for economies of scale as revealed by the initial disadvantage ratios. Type 1 industries have the smallest average size, but the greatest achievement of MES (note: this sector includes some woodworking and metal treatment industries with very low MES). Note that this arrangement of the data is not independent of the Member State distribution; e.g. Germany is relatively strong in Type 2R industries, so one reason why German firms are larger is because of the industries in which they are engaged. Also, the smaller Member States tend to be disproportionately represented in 2A. This is another reason why the econometric approach of the next chapter is necessary. A more interesting pattern of growth of average size emerges when looking at industry type, which shows recent growth in average size in advertising intensive industries and very little growth in Type 2R industries.

3.3.2. Employment

The following table shows average employment for all industries in each of the three years as well as the average employment for each quadrant. There were slight reductions in average employment in the two periods (4.9% in the first and 2.8% in the second), but these were found to be not statistically significant changes. The figure shows that firms in quadrant A (firms most sensitive to the single market and possessing the highest potential to exploit economies of scale) experienced the greatest declines in average employment (16.7% in the first period, 23.5% in the second).

Table 3.9.   Changes in average employment per enterprise

			1981	1986	1991	% change 1981–86	% change 1986–91
Employment per enterprise	Quadrant	A	324	270	206	-16.7	-23.5
		B	255	232	216	-9.1	-6.9
		C	86	91	92	5.0	1.6
		D	127	117	110	-7.7	-5.8
		Other	47	46	48	-2.7	3.2
		Total	81	77	75	-4.9	-2.8

The employment figures are more complete and less vulnerable to price indexation and disequilibrium problems (although for reasons discussed above, real GVA is still considered to be the preferred method of analysing changes in firm size) than GVA figures. Changes in employment over the two periods largely reflect productivity changes.

If we accept the view that the SM has not yet led to important economies of scale at the enterprise level (Eurostat definition) in the sense of altering the typical production frontier, or lowering the typical average cost curve, it seems very likely that the SM has stimulated more firms to move towards their production frontiers as a result of increased competitive pressure, as explained in the literature survey. The evidence for this important development emerges from Tables 3.4 and 3.9, which show that the decreases in employment exceeded the decreases in output per enterprise.

Hence, there were increases in labour productivity, which is a standard measure of economic performance. For example, the SM-sensitive industries in quadrant A increased their average labour productivity by over 14% during the period 1986–91, compared with an increase of 6.6% during 1981–86. This may be compared with the increase in average labour productivity for all industries of 10% during 1981–86 and of 7.5% during 1986–91. Clearly, the SM-sensitive industries in quadrant A have improved their relative economic performance.

Table 3.10.   Total employment by Member State and total EU

Country	1981	1986	1991	% change 1981–86	% change 1986–91	No. of inds[3]
Germany	6,996,694	6,694,657	7,152,675	-4.3	6.8	91
France	4,554,437	3,964,274	3,776,948	-13.0	-4.7	99
UK	4,577,579	3,936,891	3,701,779	-14.0	-6.0	90
Italy	3,444,605	3,008,276	3,034,522	12.7	0.9	102
Spain	2,391,430	1,950,277	2,062,849	-18.4	5.8	97
Netherlands	359,766	501,060	549,109	39.3	9.6	56
Belgium	478,161	495,896	489,055	3.7	-1.4	66
Denmark	215,010	291,244	267,770	35.5	-8.1	60
Ireland	104,830	94,594	102,858	-9.8	8.7	35
Portugal	578,231	516,406	554,356	-10.7	7.3	68
Greece	313,752	284,848	259,233	-9.2	-9.0	76
Total[1]	24,014,495	21,738,373	21,951,154	-9.5	1.0	-
EUR-12[2]	23,779,928	21,155,099	21,432,564	-11.0	1.3	89

[1]   Total is sum of 11 Member States given above in table.
[2]   EUR-12 is total given in Eurostat VISA database.
[3]   Data are included, where available, for NACE codes 221-495 with the exception of the following for reasons of dissimilarity from other manufacturing industries: 231, 232, 319, 348, 352, 365, 435.

For example, the German figures show very strong productivity growth. In terms of relative Member States, the employment figures largely match the real gross value added figures. However, Portugal and Greece look much closer in size as measured by employment to the others; the difference reflects the massive productivity gap between these two countries and the rest of the EU. It is not really possible to attribute this gap to scale versus technical efficiency. (Note that Spain is unique in including firms of size less than 20 employees.)

Table 3.11.   Employment per enterprise by Member State

Country	1981	1986	1991	% change 1981–86	% change 1986–91	No. of inds[1]
Germany	225	221	215	-1.9	-3.0	91
France	166	149	135	-10.2	-9.3	99
UK	186	162	146	-12.9	-10.3	90
Italy	131	102	93	-22.2	-8.9	102
Spain	16	14	15	-8.1	4.9	97
Netherlands	136	117	110	-14.0	-6.0	56
Belgium	128	126	n/a	-1.5	-	66
Denmark	107	121	116	12.6	-3.8	60
Ireland	110	103	n/a	-7.0	-	35
Portugal	52	54	93	5.0	71.6	68
Greece	84	n/a	79	-	-	76

[1]   Data are included, where available, for NACE codes 221-495 with the exception of the following for reasons of their dissimilarity from other manufacturing industries: 231, 232, 319, 348, 352, 365, 435.

Table 3.12.   Total employment by type of industry

Type	1981	1986	1991	% change 1981–86	% change 1986–91
1	12,335,006	10,579,312	10,751,978	-14.2	1.6
2A	1,528,664	1,315,101	1,342,419	-14.0	2.1
2R	6,967,466	6,589,724	6,665,009	-5.4	1.1
2AR	2,948,792	2,670,962	2,673,158	-9.4	0.1

Type 1 industries now look very much larger than Type 2R as measured by employment. This shows the substantial productivity gap between traditional and technically progressive industries.

Table 3.13.   Average employment by type of industry

Type	1981	1986	1991	% change 1981–86	% change 1986–91
1	56	52	52	-7.1	0.0
2A	64	62	65	-2.7	3.5
2R	204	191	178	-6.5	-6.4
2AR	279	258	260	-7.7	1.1

The ranking of industry types by size is the same as by gross value added. Looking at the difference between gross value added growth in Table 3.8 and employment growth, we get productivity growth. This increased in the second period for Types 1 and 2A, consistent with either a recovery from recession or an SM effect. A different pattern emerges in R&D industries. Type 2R were still in recession in the later period, and this is indicated in low productivity growth (especially compared with the earlier period). Overall, though, these industries had stronger productivity growth. These industries have more global competition, which may be the most important influence on efficiency in R&D industries.

In order to get a better understanding of these descriptive statistics, we need to attempt to isolate the different factors that affect the attainment of scale.

3.4. Intra-EU trade

An important step in achieving this aim is to place the firm size data in the context of the pattern of intra-EU trade. The source of intra-EU trade data is Eurostat's VISA database once again. Certain sectors are excluded from the analysis due to poor availability (such as jewellery and miscellaneous manufacturing).

3.4.1. Openness

Openness is measured by exports plus imports over production (turnover). As expected, smaller countries are more open, i.e. they have a higher trade intensity, although the relationship is not precise (the UK looks slightly low, probably due to greater trade with non-EU partners, and the Netherlands is very high). There appears to be continuing growth in openness in all Member States and in both periods.

Table 3.14.   Openness by Member State

Country	1981	1986	1991	% change 1981–86	% change 1986–91	No. of inds[1]
Germany	0.28	0.31	0.34	13.8	9.1	84
France	0.30	0.35	0.45	15.7	27.5	91
UK	0.21	0.28	0.33	34.6	18.7	82
Italy	0.32	0.35	0.37	9.9	5.4	91
Netherlands	0.63	0.73	0.82	15.6	11.3	19
Denmark	0.50	0.50	0.56	0.3	11.7	48
Ireland	0.55	0.62	0.67	12.1	7.8	33
EUR-7	0.29	0.34	0.39	16.4	14.2	-
EUR-12	0.34	0.40	0.45	18.6	13.3	83

[1]   Data are included, where available, for NACE codes 221-495 with the exception of the following for reasons of their dissimilarity from other manufacturing industries: 231, 232, 319, 348, 352, 365, 435.

Table 3.15.   Openness by type of industry

Type	1981	1986	1991	% change 1981–86	% change 1986–91
1	0.30	0.35	0.39	19.3	9.4
2A	0.20	0.23	0.26	17.6	12.2
2R	0.42	0.48	0.55	14.1	16.0
2AR	0.37	0.45	0.52	22.1	14.1

R&D intensive industries are by far the most open, and Type 2A are the least open. There does not appear to be any particular pattern of differential growth across sectors.

3.4.2. Comparative advantage and specialization

Comparative advantage is measured by exports minus imports over production (turnover). It is not really comparative advantage *per se*, which would express this relative to the overall trade balance, but captures the main idea of intra-EU competitive success in each industry in each Member State. If we look at the weighted averages, this simply reflects the manufacturing balance of trade relative to production, which in 1986 was +16% in the Netherlands and +12% in Ireland; and in other Member States ranged from +5% in Germany to -5% in France. Apart from Ireland's rise, there are no clear trends. By industry, of course, intra-EU trade is in balance (due to measurement errors, in fact it is a very small negative number).

A more revealing presentation of the data is in the standard deviation across industries (Table 3.16) where comparative advantage = standard deviation of [(total exports – total imports)/turnover]. A high standard deviation would reflect greater specialization amongst countries, and a low standard deviation would mean similar trade balances across industries and little specialization.

Table 3.16.   Comparative advantage by Member State

Country	1981	1986	1991	% change 1981–86	% change 1986–91	No. of inds[1]
Germany	0.13	0.14	0.17	12.3	15.8	84
France	0.14	0.15	0.18	7.9	24.2	91
UK	0.11	0.14	0.12	35.3	-15.0	82
Italy	0.26	0.30	0.21	16.4	-30.0	91
Netherlands	0.28	0.24	0.23	-13.8	-4.5	19
Denmark	0.65	0.64	0.64	-0.8	-0.7	48
Ireland	0.38	0.52	1.02	38.0	96.8	33
EUR-7	0.30	0.33	0.39	11.7	19.3	-
EUR-12	0.03	0.02	0.03	-38.8	47.0	83

[1]   Data are included, where available, for NACE codes 221-495 with the exception of the following for reasons of their dissimilarity from other manufacturing industries: 231, 232, 319, 348, 352, 365, 435.

There is a clear pattern of smaller countries being more specialized (although the UK seems somewhat out of line). There is no clear pattern over time except a steady increase in specialization in Germany and France, and a dramatic increase in Ireland.

However, a much clearer pattern emerges when we look at industry types. Standardizing for these industry types shows a small, but consistent pattern: a small reduction in specialization in the first period was reversed in the second.

Table 3.17.   Comparative advantage by type of industry

Type	1981	1986	1991	% change 1981–86	% change 1986–91
1	0.04	0.02	0.02	-47.0	11.4
2A	0.01	0.01	0.01	-21.0	149.2
2R	0.02	0.02	0.04	-13.9	111.6
2AR	0.01	0.01	0.02	-5.1	37.4

The descriptive statistics are informative to a certain extent. To clarify their interpretation, however, we must now turn to a properly specified econometric model in Chapter 4.

4. Assessment of the influence of the single market

In this chapter, we attempt an assessment of the influence of the single market on the attainment of economies of scale. Following on from the previous chapter, we begin by investigating the average size of business unit based on Eurostat data. However, we also take the analysis further, to consider how EU industrial concentration has changed. This is for two reasons. First, we have been able to collect slightly more up-to-date information on concentration; and second, the relationship between changes in the business unit size and in EU concentration reveals some important information on business strategies following the Single European Act.

The analysis of average size requires a two-stage methodology. In the first stage, we develop a model of what determined average firm size in 1986, that is, in a period prior to the single market programme. This provides a background that quantifies the relative importance of influences on size, such as minimum efficient scale, market size, public procurement and openness to trade. Then, in the second stage, we assess how changes in these factors, some due to the single market and others not, have worked to change firm size in the period 1986–91. The latter period is really much too short to properly evaluate the impact, but we have been constrained by the availability of data. Our theoretical model of firm size is developed in Section 4.1. The emphasis is on how various distortions to open competition act to restrict size; how the theory of firm size changes qualitatively once the competitive mechanism includes endogenous fixed costs (as in Type 2 industries); and how the single market is expected to affect the size of firms. Section 4.2 presents and discusses the econometric evidence.

There is a direct identity relationship between average firm size, market size, national and EU concentration, intra-EU multinationality, and intra-EU specialization by Member State. This means that if we can measure what has been happening to some of these variables (e.g. size and concentration), we can imply what has been happening to others (e.g. multinationality and international specialization). We formalize this idea as a statistical decomposition, and apply it in our commentary on recent trends in concentration. Our analysis of concentration includes 1993 as the most recent year for which data are available. When we say 'available' we should stress that these are not published data, but figures we have had to construct from first principles for this project. The methodology is given in detail in Davies and Lyons [1996], as is the 1987 base year data. In Section 4.3, we present our decomposition analysis and analysis of recent trends in concentration. Once again, we pay particular attention to how the relationship differs according to the type of competitive mechanism typical of the industry. Section 4.4 concludes the assessment.

4.1. Firm size, scale economies and trading costs: theory

The mechanisms by which the creation of a fully integrated single market influences the achievement of economies of scale depend crucially on the technologies and competitive strategies adopted by firms. If product designs and technologies are stable, and in particular if they are not themselves affected by market size, then the core mechanism will be in production economies of scale. This is discussed in Section 4.1.1. Such economies are mainly achievable at the level of business units, particularly if production takes place at a single location. However, if firms compete by investing in R&D in order to develop better quality products, then the most relevant economies of scale will arise in the R&D process. An important feature of such economies is that as long as a little more R&D effort results in a little better quality, then it is only the size of the market that limits R&D spending. Advertising competition has similar characteristics. The consequences of this process are discussed in Section 4.1.2. Unlike with production economies, R&D and advertising incentives operate at the aggregate firm level, and so are likely to be shown in industrial concentration as well as in disaggregated business units.

4.1.1. Production economies

It is tempting, but misleadingly inaccurate, to characterize the single market simply as an expansion of market size, as firms shift their horizons from national to EU markets. This is inaccurate because most industries in the mid-1980s already operated to an extent at the international level. The single market effect of reducing or eliminating remaining non-tariff barriers must, therefore, be seen for most firms in the context of a marginal/quantitative change rather than a discrete/qualitative change in market size. This does not necessarily imply that the consequences must be small, but it does mean that estimation of the impact needs careful consideration. In Section 4.2.1, we estimate an econometric model of average business unit size by industry and Member State. In order to specify that model, we must first ask two questions: what factors determine the average size of business? and how might a reduction in trade barriers affect that relationship?

We begin by considering the first question in the context of a hypothetical case, in which there is no room for imperfections of the kind that the single market is intended to redress. In a perfectly competitive world, with no homogeneous products and inefficiency, so all firms face the same U-shaped average cost curves, firm size is determined entirely by the output associated with the minimum point of the cost curve. Technological economies of scale are all that matters, and market size makes no difference.

Next, add some realism by allowing firms to differentiate their products. With horizontal product differentiation, and monopolistic competition, firms would produce at less than the minimum point on the cost curve, but there is little we can say about how market size will affect the attainment of scale economies. This is because the balance of higher output per firm and new entry depends on consumer attitude to more product variety versus lower prices. Nevertheless, Krugman [1979] has argued that at least some of the effect of an increase in market size is likely to manifest itself in higher output per firm.

There is little empirical support for the long-run diseconomies of scale, so next suppose that cost curves are L-shaped. Then, any firm size greater than or equal to the minimum efficient size (MES) may be observed. The average size of such firms is still likely to be positively associated with MES, but larger markets allow for greater growth above that size. In such markets, we may expect average firm size to be positively associated with both MES and market size: $x_{jk} = f(MES_j, \text{market size}_j)$. In terms of practical measurement and following our discussion in Chapter 3, x is the mean size (value added) of business units in industry j and Member State k. The source for MES is Davies and Lyons [1996], where earlier work by Pratten on the collation of engineering estimates is applied and extended consistently across the NACE industrial classification for all manufacturing sectors. Market size is total production within the EU by NACE industry (source: Eurostat). Thus, we start from a hypothetical, integrated market, where national boundaries within the EU do not affect the size of business units.

With this background case in mind, we can consider how market imperfections, especially those associated with trade between different Member States, affect average firm size and the achievement of production economies of scale. In the extreme case of prohibitive non-tariff barriers between Member States, the appropriate measure of market size would be national, not the EU level. Away from this polar case, the relative importance of the size of the EU and national markets depends on the heights of such barriers. Put slightly differently, trade barriers reduce the effective size at the EU market; and their removal increases it towards the EU level. Because of multicollinearity problems, when EU and national size are both included alongside national dummy variables, we build on the latter interpretation when building our econometric model.

A necessary condition for a single market effect is that competition is initially not sufficiently strong to eliminate inefficiency. Thus, there are firms that can survive even though they are of less than MES (or otherwise not minimizing costs). In this context, the Emerson report suggests three mechanisms through which the single market was expected to reduce inefficiency in production. We consider each in turn, and draw out the implications for average firm size.

First, the removal of border controls reduces the fixed cost of exporting, and so allows the growth of smaller firms which had previously been restricted to sell within national borders (see Figure 4.1). Even if some such growth is at the expense of larger firms, there will be a small net addition to total industry supply, and so average firm output and the achievement of production economies of scale should rise, albeit by a very small amount.

There is one theoretical reservation to this proposition, and two important measurement issues. The theoretical reservation is that the greater profitability of small firms may attract new entry, and the net effect could then be to reduce average size. It is then possible that the achievement of scale economies would not be enhanced by reducing fixed export costs. Turning to measurement, if we only observe firms of, say, greater than 20 employees, and the single market allows very small firms to grow through this threshold, then it may appear as if we are observing an entry effect, even though truly there is growth and greater achievement of scale economies. Finally, if we do not have industry-specific price deflators, and can only adjust for general inflation, then value measures may be misleading measures of size. For example, if the industry elasticity of demand is unity, average size (by value) will depend only on firm numbers, and output growth caused by lower prices will be missed. Only if industry demand is elastic will real output be positively correlated with the value of output. Although these problems need not invalidate an analysis of measured average firm size, it is important that they are borne in mind in what follows.

A second mechanism by which the single market was expected to reduce the operation of firms at inefficiently small scale was by expansion of demand (see Figure 4.2). This could be brought about in several ways: even with the same number of firms in the EU, the reduction in marginal trading costs could enhance competition and increase industry output; greater competition could also eliminate some suppliers leaving survivors with greater market shares; and both effects could be reinforced if, as firms move down their cost curves, they become more competitive in extra-EU markets. The measurement problems described in the previous paragraph remain valid.

A third mechanism applies if firms are initially not efficient in production, even given their output level, i.e. if they are not on the minimum attainable cost curve (see Figure 4.3). Then a competitive 'cold shower' effect will force the least efficient firms to either reduce costs or exit from the market. In terms of Figure 4.3, firms finding themselves with costs above the new price line cannot survive for long without improving their efficiency. In the presence of economies of scale, the room for a firm to respond by reducing costs (without changing output) will be more restricted if that firm is small. Inasmuch as this means that relatively more small firms must leave the market, we should observe an increase in the average size of business units. (In the figure, three of the four smallest firms need to adjust, and the smallest cannot do so without gaining market share; only half the larger firms are forced to reduce costs or exit.)

Having established the main mechanisms through which the single market (and its absence) affects firm size, we can move towards specifying an empirical model that allows for the effects to differ across industries. Some barriers to trade, such as border controls, will have affected all industries, while other barriers, such as public procurement bias, will have affected different industries to very different degrees. In our empirical work, we employ four industry-specific measures designed to capture different industry-specific aspects of intra-EU trade barriers. These will be used to establish the extent to which trade barriers differentially distorted the relationship between firm size, technology and EU market size in the mid-1980s (i.e. pre-single market). This will then enable us to quantify the industry-specific effects of the single market programme as these barriers are removed.

The first is a dummy variable, PUB, which equals 1 if the industry was considered to be heavily influenced by public procurement [European Commission, 1990]; and the second is a dummy variable, REG, which equals 1 if the industry was heavily influenced by national regulations [same source]. These are intended to capture the distortions created by public procurement bias and by a profusion of national regulations and technical standards – arguably the two most important types of barrier tackled by the SM programme. We defer our detailed discussion of how these affect the achievement of production economies of scale, but note two important points. First, different Member States have traditionally adopted different attitudes to public procurement and regulation, so we can expect a range of effects depending on the degree of national *dirigisme*. Second, the same governments often adopt different attitudes to different industries; for example, trying to create a national champion in one industry, while attempting even-handed support for all national firms in another. In the next section, we develop a partition of industry types that helps to explain and predict such differences.

The remaining two industry-specific variables, designed to pick up on pre-single market distortions, are based on measures of intra-EU import penetration and the intra-EU export propensity, both measured at the Member State level [source: Eurostat]. There are two separate effects that are picked up by such measures. The first we call the *openness* effect: high intra-EU trade, either imports or exports, suggests that the national market is already integrated into the EU production structure. Put the other way round, the absence of trade may result in firms in a Member State being unable to achieve sufficient size to fully exploit economies of scale. We call the second effect *comparative advantage*: high intra-EU exports accompanied by low intra-EU imports suggests that a Member State has a comparative advantage in that industry, and that an integrated market is exploiting the advantages of international specialization. Some care is needed in interpreting this effect, as it might be the case that the existing achievement of scale economies actually creates a comparative advantage, rather than vice versa. We measure openness by the sum of import penetration and the export propensity, and the comparative advantage effect by the difference between export propensity and import penetration.

Overall, we suggest the following model for explaining the average size of business units prior to the advent of the single market :

$$x_{jk} = f(MES_j, \text{market size}_j, PUB_{jk}, REG_{jk}, \text{openness}_{jk}, \text{comparative advantage}_{jk}) \quad (1)$$

Having established the initial impact of intra-EU trade barriers on the size of business units, we would expect two types of effect on firm size as firms respond to reduced or eliminated barriers to trade. First, a general response to greater competition should affect all industries (e.g. the removal of border controls). Nevertheless, we would expect even pervasive effects to have a greater effect on unit size where average size has been low in relation to economies of scale. This initial disadvantage is measured as the average size of business unit relative to MES. Note that if all firms were the same size, we would only expect an effect where the initial size was less than MES. However, given that there is a distribution of unit sizes, the particular equality of average size and MES has no practical significance; and as long as there are any units below MES, some effect should be observable.

Second, we expect to see stronger effects in those industries which were previously most affected by the barriers to trade. In terms of public procurement bias and regulated industries, since we have no measure of differential implementation of single market measures, we can only pick up a general effect of PUB and REG due to higher initial government-induced distortions. For our trade-based measures, however, we do have more direct measures of changes over time. Thus, our model of changes in average unit size between pre- and post-single market measures is:

$$\Delta x_{jk} = g(\text{initial disadvantage}_{jk}, \Delta \text{market size}_j, PUB_j, REG_j, \Delta \text{openness}_{jk}, \Delta \text{comp. advantage}_{jk})$$
$$(2)$$

The Δ refers to a change between two time periods, which are specified in Section 4.2. As stated before, a fuller discussion of the industry-specific effects must await the next section.

Figure 4.1.   Effects of SM measures: removal of border controls

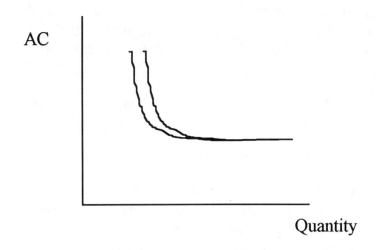

Figure 4.2.   Effects of SM measures: expansion of demand

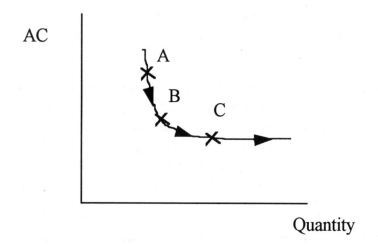

Figure 4.3.   Effects of SM measures: competition reduces X-inefficiency

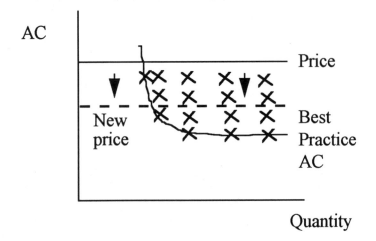

4.1.2. Endogenous fixed costs

Firm size is the result not only of the interaction of demand conditions and production costs, but also of the type of competition engaged in by the industry. The effects of increased price competition as a result of the single market have been discussed in the previous section. Here we focus on how competition in R&D and marketing can affect these outcomes. The crucial difference introduced by competition in R&D and advertising is that these are essentially endogenous overhead costs; and furthermore, the firm which spends most can usually attract a disproportionate market share. For example, the firm which spends most on R&D can generally produce a higher quality product, often without any significant increase in marginal production costs. Advertising campaigns can have a similar effect on the perceived quality of the product. As stated earlier, we call industries competing in: advertising, Type 2A; R&D, Type 2R; both, Type 2AR; and neither, Type 1. As Sutton [1991] shows, the Type 1/Type 2 distinction can have a dramatic effect on the market shares of leading firms. This raises two distinct issues in the context of the present study. First, how does this impact on the achievement of production economies of scale in the single market? Second, what impact has the single market had on the achievement of economies of scale in R&D and advertising? In this section, we concentrate on the first question.

Although endogenous fixed-cost competition typically operates at the broader firm level, rather than at the level of an individual production unit, any competitive mechanism that increases the size of a firm enhances its ability to achieve production scale economies. An important aspect of Type 2 competition is that the larger the market, the greater the incentive to invest in R&D and advertising. Thus, in contrast to the hypothetical, classic, competitive, Type 1 market discussed in the previous section, where firm size depended only on economies of scale and exogenous demand conditions, in a classic Type 2 industry, a larger market will result in larger firms as a direct result of the competitive escalation of fixed costs. The role of production economies of scale in determining firm size is much reduced. Thus, we expect a stronger effect of market size on firm size, and given L-shaped cost curves, this will probably translate into bigger business units. In terms of equation (1), we expect industry size to have a greater effect in Type 2 industries, and MES is likely to have a reduced influence.

How will Type 2 industries differ from Type 1 in the relationship between barriers to trade and firm size? This depends on the type of barrier. For example, the aims of government intervention will be quite different. Public procurement bias is likely to be aimed at creating national champions in Type 2 industries, since distributing largesse across a large number of firms will be much less effective in encouraging innovation and exports. However, in Type 1 industries, procurement bias can be used to support a wide range of domestic producers without such a loss of R&D incentives due to fragmenting sales.

The effects of national regulations are less clear. They deter foreign entry, which means there may be more room in the domestic market in which to expand; but they also deter exports. Inasmuch as Type 2 industries are more concentrated, this may allow leading firms to influence national regulations to their own benefit, allowing larger scale production by deterring domestic entry.

Moving away from government intervention, and to the firm's direct point of view, trade and trade barriers affect firm size differently in different types of industry. There are strong incentives to spread R&D overheads over as wide a market as possible. Thus, these industries tend to have been operating at the EU or even global level for some years, although some Type 2R industries were still not fully integrated by trade as of 1987 [see Davies and Lyons, 1996].

There is also a high incidence of firms that are multinational within the EU, which means that individual firms are able to produce in locations with the strongest comparative advantage. To an extent, these Type 2 effects also apply to Type 2A and 2AR industries, although there are some important modifications. Although marketing expertise can be usefully applied internationally, the economies of international scope are much reduced by differences in language, media and culture across Member States. Evidence of the value of international marketing is found in the fact that Type 2A industries (like Type 2R) are among the most multinational in the operation of firms within the EU, though these industries (unlike Type 2R) tend also to engage in relatively much less international trade [see Davies and Lyons, 1996]. Thus, we expect to observe a quite different relation between firm size and trade in the different types of industry.

Overall, the pervasive influence of different types of competition suggests that any analysis of economies of scale should be carried out separately for different industry types. This is the way we proceed in the following section.

4.2. Econometric evidence on average business unit size

This section provides an econometric analysis of Eurostat data on the average size of business unit disaggregated by industry and Member State. These data have already been described in Chapter 3 of this report. Data on industry size and intra-EU trade were also provided by Eurostat, and the remaining data come from the UEA/SPES database of 100 manufacturing industries. All data are at the three-digit NACE level. Although Eurostat attempts to collect data separately for all 12 Member States and for all industries, so that hypothetically there could be 1,200 observations of average size in each year, in practice there are many gaps. This is partly because many countries do not collect the appropriate data, and partly due to confidentiality when small numbers are involved (e.g. Spain does not provide sales data, and there are very few industries covered by Luxembourg). Also, no historical data are available for the most recent members who joined in 1996.

The data availability problem particularly affects those Member States which joined in the 1980s (Greece, 1981; Spain and Portugal, 1986). In fact, there is respectable industry coverage for just six Member States, including the big four (Germany, France, Italy, the UK, the Netherlands, and Denmark). These are the countries on which we focus, and taking account of confidentiality and other data availability problems, this leaves us with just 426 observations of average business unit size and the associated variables described in Section 4.1.1.

The functional form used for estimation was guided by the strong positive skew in the distribution of variables measured as levels, so logarithmic transformations were made to mean size, EU size and MES. Growth in mean size, growth in EU size and the initial disadvantage were each measured as the difference in the logs, and the changes in trade ratios are simple differences. Since MES is measured in terms of sales (not value added), the initial disadvantage is measured as the difference between MES and mean size measured by sales. Given the institutional differences between Member States, separate public procurement and regulated industry dummies were estimated for each country.

Finally, we included simple dummy variables for each country to pick up more general country effects, perhaps reflecting the way national business unit sizes are related to the size of the home market. Since the regressions are estimated with a constant, one country dummy has to be excluded (to avoid perfect multicollinearity). Germany is the excluded country, so the coefficients on the remaining country dummies should be interpreted as measuring the typical difference in mean size of business unit, as compared with Germany, and having taken into account the other variables in the regression. All variables were then entered linearly into equations (1) and (2). Tables 4.1 to 4.4 present the results of estimating these equations separately for each industry type. The public procurement industries are all to be found in Type 1 and Type 2R sectors, while regulated industries are often associated with consumer protection and are concentrated in the Type 2A and Type 2AR sectors.

Equation (1) is estimated using 1986 data, as the starting point highlighting sources of production inefficiency before the single European Act was implemented; we refer to this as the levels regression. Equation (2), which we call the changes regression, is estimated for changes between 1986 and 1991. The latter date is the last for which Eurostat data were available. Thus, the period is dictated entirely by data availability. This is very unsatisfactory, not least because the implementation of the single market programme was not due to be completed before 31 December 1992, and some measures were still not implemented then (or even as late as 1996!). Thus, the changes equation can give little more than a glimpse at the effects of the single market programme, picking up only the immediate effects of the first measures to be implemented, and the effects of firms with foresight anticipating later measures.

Table 4.1 presents the results for Type 1 industries. First, consider the levels regression. Far and away the most significant variable is MES, which gives an elasticity of firm size with respect to MES of one third (given a degree of product differentiation, we should probably expect to observe an elasticity less than unity). It is striking to observe that there is no effect of the size of the EU market on mean unit size. Thus, in the long run in Type 1 industries, firm size is determined by economies of scale, not market size. Our measures of trade openness and comparative advantage have no effect on mean size, but public procurement does. In all countries, this bias tends to create too many small firms (compared with the general relationship between average size and economies of scale), but the effect is quantitatively strongest in France and the Netherlands, followed by Denmark. Finally, all countries have a significantly smaller average size compared with Germany, but there is no systematic relationship between the size of this effect and the size of the home market. Italy has by far the smallest size firms, and although Denmark has the next smallest, Dutch firms are of similar size to those in France and the UK (once all other factors in the regression model have been taken into account).

Turning to the changes between 1986–91, although there is a suggestion that EU growth feeds through initially into larger firms (in the long run, entry and exit should re-establish the relationship found in the levels regression), there is no evidence of any early single market effect. Industries with a larger initial disadvantage are not increasing in unit size any more than any others, there is still no trade effect (even though intra-EU trade penetration was rising on average), and nor is mean size being made up any faster in public procurement industries. The only systematic effect is that most countries, but particularly Italy and the UK, are falling even further behind Germany in terms of relative size of unit. As will be seen, the case of Italy's low and decreasing relative size of business units is quite pervasive.

As expected, Table 4.2 shows that in Type 2A industries, there is a quantitatively smaller relationship between mean size and MES, and now a positive relationship with EU size emerges. In fact, the effect of market size is three times as large as that of MES. This reflects the fact that advertising spending is higher in larger markets and this enables firms to increase output per business unit. This appears to be an effective way of increasing size in these industries (and contrasts with price-cutting, or whatever other way firms can try to expand demand for their products in Type 1 industries). There is only very slight evidence that comparative advantage allows positive trade balance locations to achieve greater scale, but as we have already stated, integration in Type 2A industries tends to come through multinational firms producing internationally, rather than through international trade. The effect of regulation is much weaker than was public procurement in Type 1 industries. However, it is interesting to note that the predominant effect is now to raise mean size. Presumably, this reflects either the deliberate creation of national champions, or (more likely in these industries) the effective lobbying by market leaders to skew regulation to their own protection. The exception of the (insignificant) negative effect in Germany may be partly due to the way the beer industry was regulated there, with the opposite effect of protecting numerous small brewers. Finally, only Italy and France have significantly smaller average sizes than Germany; and this reflects the strong relative size of Type 2A industries in the UK, Netherlands and Denmark [see Davies and Lyons, 1996].

Turning to the changes regression for Type 2A, EU growth again shows through as enhancing mean size (the short-run effect revealed by the growth coefficient is stronger than in the long run). Changes in trade openness are weakly, but negatively, associated with firm size. Perhaps the most interesting coefficients are on the national intercepts. Firms in the two smallest countries in the sample, Denmark and the Netherlands, are experiencing positive relative growth in this sector, even relative to Germany (the coefficient on REG*DEN should be ignored as there is only one Danish regulated industry in this sample).

Type 2R industries display many similarities with Type 2A. Mean size depends on both MES and EU size, although (rather surprisingly) the quantitative effect lies between Type 1 and Type 2a industries. The trade balance is also a significant determinant of mean size. This suggests that firms are drawn to the most efficient locations, and this helps them achieve more production economies of scale compared with firms in more disadvantaged locations. Public procurement tends to raise unit size in these industries, but this is a significant effect only in Italy and Denmark. The most striking finding is the strong size advantage that German firms have in these high technology industries, with large negative coefficients on all the national intercepts.

The Type 2R industries have much the most interesting changes regression. Only in these industries are there clear signs of a single market effect resisting a decline in (or even raising) average unit size systematically more in industries and locations where size was initially smallest relative to MES (and even here, it is possible that there was some other cause, such as an increase in global competition[1]). The rest of the story is consistent with the previous two industry groups. EU growth is initially channelled into unit size (although in the long run, as shown by the 1986 regression, we expect entry to reduce this effect). Also, the national

[1]   See also Table 3.8.

intercepts show increasing divergence from Germany; with the divergence trend smallest in the smaller countries (Netherlands and Denmark) and France, and greatest in Italy and the UK.

The final, and smallest, group of industries is Type 2AR. In these industries, there is a much fuzzier relationship between business size and technical economies of scale, and a powerful relationship with EU size. In fact, the latter elasticity is not significantly different from unity. In these industries, therefore, firm size is determined by R&D and advertising economies, and production economies of scale have no significant effect. Only in this group does greater openness, manifested in higher trade penetration, feed into higher business unit size. There is also an interesting pattern to the effects of regulation. In the larger countries, particularly Germany, regulation reduces mean size, while in the smaller countries (the Netherlands and Denmark), it raises size. This may be partially compensating for a very strong size disadvantage that the firms in the latter countries seem to have in relation to Germany (compare the size of the country intercept coefficients). The changes regression for Type 2AR tells no interesting story other than the negative finding that we were unable to detect a single market effect.

Overall, in our econometric analysis, we find some strong national differences in the achievement of economies of scale. The relationship between achieved size and production economies of scale depends heavily on the prevalent type of competition in the industry. We also find that government intervention in the form of public procurement bias and national regulations have a systematic effect on average size, as predicted, tending to reduce it in Type 1 industries but raise it in Type 2. However, the trade data reveal only a weak suggestion of trade barriers contributing to the underachievement of scale economies. As expected, 1991 was too early to see very much change as a result of the planned single market. Only in Type 2R industries was there evidence to suggest that firms were increasing the size of business units most strongly where there was a significant size disadvantage, in anticipation of future competition. Finally, one clear picture did emerge from the analysis of changes: the size gap between German firms and those located in other Member States was positive, and increasing systematically across industries.

Table 4.1.   Type 1 industries

	1986 mean size		1986–91 change in mean size
Constant	7.51 (26.63)**	Constant	0.14 (4.49)**
MES	0.33 (14.05)**	Initial disadvantage	-0.01 (-0.62)
EU size	-0.02 (-0.60)	EU growth	0.23 (1.63)
Trade penetration	0.00 (0.06)	Change in trade pen.	-0.02 (-0.61)
Trade balance	0.07 (1.46)	Change in trade bal.	0.10 (0.79)
PUB * GE	-0.21 (-0.76)	PUB * GE	0.01 (0.10)
PUB * FR	-0.83 (-5.14)**	PUB * FR	-0.08 (-1.15)
PUB * IT	-0.20 (-1.06)	PUB * IT	0.00 (0.11)
PUB * UK	-0.16 (-1.54)	PUB * UK	0.01 (0.14)
PUB * NE	-0.52 (-4.25)**	PUB * NE	-0.00 (-0.03)
PUB * DEN	-0.28 (-2.06)*	PUB * DEN	0.02 (0.14)
FR	-0.50 (-3.87)**	FR	-0.09 (-2.45)*
IT	-1.18 (10.02)**	IT	-0.26 (-7.15)**
UK	-0.57 (-4.89)**	UK	-0.25 (-5.60)**
NE	-0.52 (-3.47)**	NE	-0.08 (-2.02)*
DEN	-0.82 (-5.70)**	DEN	0.05 (0.86)
R^2	0.66	R^2	0.30
Number of observations	248	Number of observations	244

t-ratios in parenthesis, based on White's adjustment for heteroscedasticity.
** Significantly different from zero at 1% level (2-tail test).
* Significantly different from zero at 5% level (2-tail test).
+ Significantly different from zero at 10% level (2-tail test).

Table 4.2. Type 2A industries

	1986 mean size		1986–91 change in mean size
Constant	5.41 (10.64)**	Constant	0.24 (4.22)**
MES	0.11 (2.01)*	Initial disadvantage	-0.01 (-0.75)
EU size	0.33 (4.64)**	EU growth	0.41 (2.63)*
Trade penetration	-0.05 (-0.60)	Change in trade pen.	-0.36 (-1.88)+
Trade balance	0.26 (1.95)+	Change in trade bal.	0.31 (0.90)
REG * GE	-0.19 (-0.95)	REG * GE	0.06 (0.75)
REG * FR	0.48 (2.97)**	REG * FR	0.05 (0.51)
REG * IT	0.32 (1.04)	REG * IT	0.14 (1.83)+
REG * UK	0.56 (1.78)+	REG * UK	0.05 (0.49)
REG * NE	0.64 (1.18)	REG * NE	0.06 (0.38)
REG * DEN	0.24 (0.65)	REG * DEN	-0.26 (-4.47)**
FR	-0.34 (-2.03)*	FR	-0.10 (-1.43)
IT	-0.92 (-5.64)**	IT	-0.33 (-4.10)**
UK	-0.13 (-0.49)	UK	-0.26 (-3.91)**
NE	-0.06 (-0.21)	NE	0.22 (1.84)+
DEN	-0.29 (-0.72)	DEN	0.31 (4.48)**
R^2	0.65	R^2	0.70
Number of observations	60	Number of observations	59

t-ratios in parenthesis, based on White's adjustment for heteroscedasticity.
** Significantly different from zero at 1% level (2-tail test).
* Significantly different from zero at 5% level (2-tail test).
+ Significantly different from zero at 10% level (2-tail test).

Table 4.3.   Type 2R industries

	1986 mean size		1986–91 change in mean size
Constant	4.59 (8.75)**	Constant	-0.01 (-0.12)
MES	0.53 (9.96)**	Initial disadvantage	0.07 (2.37)*
EU size	0.24 (3.65)**	EU growth	0.46 (3.14)**
Trade penetration	0.31 (1.49)	Change in trade pen.	-0.14 (-1.24)
Trade balance	0.68 (2.83)**	Change in trade bal.	0.24 (1.58)
PUB * GE	-0.29 (-0.98)	PUB * GE	-0.04 (-0.54)
PUB * FR	0.13 (0.34)	PUB * FR	-0.28 (-1.96)+
PUB * IT	0.71 (2.04)*	PUB * IT	-0.09 (-0.88)
PUB * UK	0.30 (1.02)	PUB * UK	-0.18 (-1.29)
PUB * DEN	0.58 (4.91)**	PUB *DEN	0.05 (0.24)
FR	-0.69 (-3.02)**	FR	-0.15 (-2.79)**
IT	-1.37 (-5.91)**	IT	-0.39 (-5.55)**
UK	-1.15 (-4.35)**	UK	-0.27 (-2.63)*
NE	-1.19 (5.18)**	NE	-0.03 (-0.13)
DEN	-1.08 (4.86)**	DEN	-0.10 (-1.13)
R^2	0.76	R^2	0.47
Number of observations	80	Number of observations	77

t-ratios in parenthesis, based on White's adjustment for heteroscedasticity.
** Significantly different from zero at 1% level (2-tail test).
* Significantly different from zero at 5% level (2-tail test).
+ Significantly different from zero at 10% level (2-tail test).

Table 4.4.   Type 2AR industries

	1986 mean size		1986–91 change in mean size
Constant	1.85 *(1.54)*	Constant	0.15 *(1.32)*
MES	0.22 *(1.50)*	Initial disadvantage	-0.04 *(-0.76)*
EU size	0.80 *(3.84)***	EU growth	0.64 *(1.94)*[+]
Trade penetration	0.54 *(2.62)**	Change in trade pen.	-0.04 *(-0.20)*
Trade balance	-1.03 *(-1.94)*[+]	Change in trade bal.	0.69 *(1.36)*
REG * GE	-1.08 *(-2.85)***	REG * GE	-0.01 *(-0.08)*
REG * FR	-0.37 *(-1.42)*	REG * FR	0.10 *(1.06)*
REG * IT	-0.25 *(-0.73)*	REG * IT	0.21 *(1.65)*
REG * UK	0.87 *(2.38)**	REG * UK	0.09 *(0.55)*
REG * NE	1.78 *(3.16)***	REG * NE	-0.35 *(-1.58)*
REG * DEN	1.33 *(3.14)***	REG * DEN	0.57 *(2.31)**
FR	-1.21 *(2.88)***	FR	-0.11 *(-0.79)*
IT	-1.72 *(-4.50)***	IT	-0.18 *(-1.06)*
UK	-1.75 *(-4.18)***	UK	-0.22 *(-1.15)*
NE	-3.26 *(-4.47)***	NE	-0.02 *(-0.08)*
DEN	-2.45 *(-4.77)***	DEN	-0.24 *(-1.07)*
R^2	0.65	R^2	0.43
Number of observations	38	Number of observations	37

t-ratios in parenthesis, based on White's adjustment for heteroscedasticity.
** Significantly different from zero at 1% level (2-tail test).
*   Significantly different from zero at 5% level (2-tail test).
[+]   Significantly different from zero at 10% level (2-tail test).

4.3. Evidence on EU concentration

Although changes in mean business size may be, superficially, the most directly relevant available evidence on the impact of scale economies, we believe that they can tell only part of the story. This is why, at the outset of this project, we planned to collect information on developments in concentration, observed at both national and aggregate EU levels, between 1987 and 1993. It is to this evidence that we now turn, and we shall argue that these data add importantly to the overall picture in two ways. First, the data themselves are better, in being more up to date and complete than the business size data. Second, and more conceptually, changes in concentration reflect a variety of factors, not only changes in the average size of businesses, and some of these other factors will also depend upon the consequences of the single market.

It should be recalled that there is no official published information on EU level concentration in individual industries. However, in Davies and Lyons [1996], estimates are derived for about 100 three-digit industries for 1987. As part of the current project, using similar methods, these have been updated to 1993. However, this is an extremely time-consuming exercise, involving the careful and meticulous use of primary sources, notably company reports; the original study required four years, the first half of which was occupied mainly with data collection. Given the time constraints of the current project, it would have been impossible to repeat this exercise for the full population with the same degree of confidence as before. Nevertheless, we have succeeded in generating estimates of the output of market leaders for about three-quarters of the population of industries, albeit with rather less cross-checking than would be desirable.

In order to derive estimates of EU concentration, these figures were expressed as a percentage of total EU output taken from *Panorama of EU industry 1995/96* [European Commission, 1996]. Davies and Lyons [1996] put considerable effort into adjusting the Eurostat figures to estimate gaps in the data, cross-check with national censuses, and adjust for the exclusion of small firms from the Panorama database. In this study, we had time only to use our original small firms adjustment. In order to make our concentration estimates comparable, we have therefore re-estimated our earlier concentration ratios using the cruder denominator, and these are the figures presented in this section. They are shown in Table 4.5 as the estimates of CR4 (the four-firm concentration ratio) in grouped form for the four industry types. They should be interpreted as provisional – most importantly because of unresolved uncertainties concerning the accuracy of our source (Panorama) for the aggregate industry sizes (i.e. the denominator of our concentration ratios).

As can be seen, there has been a significant increase in concentration at the EU level between 1987 and 1993. This appears to have been a fairly pervasive trend, but it is particularly strong in industries characterized by high R&D, where concentration has grown considerably.

Of course, this new dataset is of much wider interest than just the current project, and development work will continue. For present purposes however, its main value derives from its advantages over the Eurostat business size data; not only is it more up to date, but also concentration is more immediately responsive to recent events than is the size of business units. In particular, a merger taking place before the end of the financial year corresponding to 1993 should be immediately reflected in the market share estimates from which we have computed concentration. On the other hand, bearing in mind that mergers rarely result in instantaneous rationalization of individual business units within conglomerate firms, one might argue that Eurostat business size data observed in 1991 will almost certainly fail to capture the full restructuring consequences of any merger occurring in the 1990s.[2]

Figure 4.4.   EU concentration changes (%)

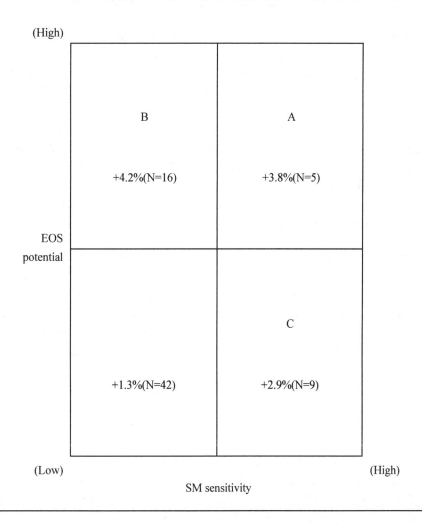

Before proceeding with a deeper analysis of what has driven the concentration changes, we look at how these changes related to EOS potential and SM sensitivity (as defined in Chapter 3, but expressing EOS potential as MES relative to 1987 concentration). The basic results are presented in Figure 4.4, which reports unweighted average percentage point changes in EU concentration. An interesting pattern emerges. Comparing the rows, there has been a greater increase in concentration where EOS potential is high. As we shall see, this has much to do with these industries being Type 2R. A more complex trend is found by comparing columns in the figure. Industries with a relatively low EOS potential have experienced a slightly larger increase in concentration if they have a high SM sensitivity; but SM sensitivity exerts no extra impact where EOS potential is high. Fleshing out this general pattern, in quadrant A, we find

---

[2]   An important difference between the two sources concerns the consolidation of subsidiaries. Our concentration data consolidate into one all firms under common ownership in a given industry. On the other hand, Eurostat data refer to the smallest legally separate businesses.

concentration increases of at least 5% in rail stock, pasta, and insulated wires and cables, and small declines in shipbuilding and wines and cider. In quadrant B, there are significant increases in concentration in man-made fibres, oils and fats and especially in aerospace; but there is a decline in motor vehicles. Finally, in quadrant C, there is a big increase in concentration in electrical machinery (nearly 10%), and small increases (1%–3%) in pharmaceuticals, computers and chocolate and sugar confectionery.

Turning to the interpretation of concentration changes, there are two stages in the argument. First, in any given industry, EU concentration amounts to a weighted average of concentration within individual Member States, allowing for the possibility that some firms may be among the market leaders in more than one Member State.

For example, suppose the EU comprises 12 equal-sized Member States, in each of which there are ten equal-sized firms. Assuming none of these firms operated in more than one Member State, the EU would comprise 120 independent firms in total. However, if each firm operated in, say, four of the Member States, then there would be only 30 genuinely independent firms in the EU as a whole. This idea underpins what Davies and Lyons refer to as their *first core decomposition* in their [1996] study:

$$HEU = HNAT * SPEC * NM \qquad\qquad (1)$$

where HEU refers to EU concentration in a given industry, HNAT refers to the weighted average concentrations in that industry in individual Member States, NM is a measure of the extent of production across Member States by firms (referred to as intra-EU multinationality), and SPEC reflects the distribution of Member State sizes in that industry. All indices are derivatives of the Herfindahl index (although similar decompositions are also easily derived for other measures such as the entropy.) This decomposition tells us that, for a given industry and set of Member State sizes, EU concentration will be higher: (a) the more concentrated is the industry within individual Member States, and (b) the higher is intra-EU multinationality.

The second stage to the argument focuses on concentration within individual Member States, and how it relates to average business size. Any measure of concentration depends on two aspects of the size distribution of business units: their number, and the inequality in their sizes. Concentration will be higher (a) the fewer firms there are (i.e. for a given size of industry, the larger is mean size), and (b) the more unequal are their sizes. In the case of the Herfindahl index, this relationship can be formalized as:

$$H = (s/S).I \qquad\qquad (2)$$

where s is mean business size, S is aggregate industry size, and I measures the extent of size inequalities (more precisely, one plus the square of the coefficient of variation).

Now, if (2) describes the level of concentration in an individual Member State, a weighted average thereof defines the HNAT term in (1).

Re-expressing the two equations in terms of rates of change over a given time period, and substituting (2) into (1), we can write:

$$d(HEU) = d(HNAT) + d(SPEC) + d(NM) \qquad (3)$$

$$d(HEU) = d(s) - d(S) + d(I) + d(SPEC) + d(NM) \qquad (4)$$

where the d(.) notation defines proportionate growth over the period, and s, S and I should now be thought of as (appropriately weighted) averages across the Member States in the growth rates of mean business size, industry size, and size inequalities.

In words, equation (4) tells us that, in a given industry, EU concentration will increase where:[3]

(a)   mean business size grows more rapidly than industry size in Member States;
(b)   business size inequalities within individual Member States increase;
(c)   specialization (by Member State within the EU) increases;
(d)   intra-EU multinationality increases.

This substantiates our earlier claim that changes in concentration provide a richer story than by only examining the size of business units. Since it is likely that only a few very large firms would organize their activities in one industry in one Member State in more than one legally separable unit, our earlier analysis of changes in the size of business unit effectively applies to the first term in (4), d(s). We can now see that there are other forces at work in determining concentration – each susceptible to changes in the other sources of economies of scale, resulting from the competitive escalation of fixed costs such as R&D and advertising.

In order to quantify (4) using the data presently available, we must proxy HEU by CR4 – the four-firm concentration ratio – hardly a major limitation, since most standard concentration indices are highly correlated. More importantly, we do not yet have comprehensive data on the changes in intra-EU multinationality, specialization and size inequalities, although they are on the future research agenda of SPES, outside the present project. Therefore, we shall have to *infer* the likely magnitudes and directions of these changes by observing the typical magnitudes of the observable variables in the identity, and by drawing on specific examples.

Tables 4.5a and 4.5b quantify the components to (4) in the form of averages for each of the industry types. Because of incompleteness in the national data, the coverage of industries and Member States differs across the columns, except in Table 4.5b, where the industries have been paired across the years. Unfortunately, this has been necessary in order to maintain a broad coverage in the face of incomplete Eurostat data, and so the following results should be interpreted cautiously.

For Type 1 industries, mean national business size grew on average by roughly 6%, and as this is only a little more than the growth in average size of industry, we would expect to observe little change in national concentration, unless there were significant changes in (unobserved) inequalities. In fact, typical national concentration *did* stay roughly constant. However, concentration at the EU level appears to have increased a little, albeit from a relatively lower starting point. The implication is that there was a small increase in the extent of intra-EU

---

[3]   Moreover, the first two factors, but not the last, will also increase typical national concentration.

multinationality and/or an increase in international specialization within the EU. Both factors *could* reflect increased exploitation of production scale economies, although alternative explanations are possible.[4]

A different picture emerges in Type 2A. Here, there were quite dramatic increases in the typical size of business units within Member States, and because they easily outstripped the growth in overall national industry size, this implies increased national concentration. This indeed happened, albeit by less than was implied by the size data. This would be consistent with a narrowing of size inequalities, but it is equally possible that our estimates of national concentration, based on only four Member States, are unrepresentative. Turning to developments at the EU level, concentration has increased at about the same rate as national concentration, suggesting little change in specialization and/or multinationality.

In Type 2R industries, mean business size has tended to decline slightly, while industry size has been virtually static; and this is consistent with the slight decline in typical national concentration. However, this contrasts strikingly with the very rapid increase in EU concentration. The reasons, we suspect, are increasing specialization, due to increasing German dominance and (probably more important) substantial increases in intra-EU multinationality.

Finally, in Type 2AR industries, mean business size grew substantially and industry size increased more moderately. This implies the small increase in national concentration which we find. Concentration at the aggregate EU level has drifted up slightly, but not as much as in Type 2R. Davies and Lyons [1996] find Type 2AR industries, on average, to be more concentrated than Type 2R in 1987, and the reversed ranking in Table 4.5b is due to the exclusion of too high concentration in Type 2AR industries. Nevertheless, the modest rise in concentration in Type 2AR tends to support the speculation in Davies and Lyons, that EU integration was already most advanced in 2AR in 1987. By implication, this suggests that 2R may have been catching up on 2AR.

At this stage, and until better data become available, these conclusions are most properly defined as preliminary and provisional. Nevertheless, most of this early evidence suggests that little of the dynamic between 1987 and 1993 can be attributed directly to the effects of increased exploitation of production scale economies. Rather, we suspect that the most striking development that will be detected in further work is an upsurge in intra-EU multinationality, motivated by, among other things, the drive to exploit economies of scale in R&D. For example, in the UK, the 'foreign' multinational share of manufacturing production rose from 18% in 1986 to 24% in 1993. While it is true that a part of this was due to increased Japanese penetration, particularly in electronics, this is offset by a relative decline in US penetration. Most relevant for our purposes is the large increase in the French (and, more latterly, German) shares. Moreover, the number of foreign MNEs in the UK's top 100 manufacturers has risen from 18 to 32 – again, mainly attributable to French companies. It is also clear that this penetration is increasingly associated with leading market shares in individual industries. We do not yet know whether this picture is replicated in other Member States.

---

[4]   Concentration estimates for a number of very low concentration industries (e.g. woodworking), have not been finalized. These are essentially local industries and would probably only dilute the already modest changes observed in Type 1 industries.

Turning to individual firms and/or industries, there are a number of high-profile developments consistent with this story including mergers and/or joint ventures involving Carnaud-Metal Box, GEC-Alcatel, Rhône-Poulenc, Phillips (Osram from GEC), and Daimler-Fokker. Other examples include firms which, although strictly defined as non-EU owned, already have extensive operations within the EU; Nestlé's many acquisitions including Perrier and Rowntree, Philip Morris-Jacobs Suchard, SmithKline Beecham, and Coca Cola-Cadbury Schweppes. Very many of these high-profile examples are most easily explicable as strategic moves in oligopolistic industries characterized by endogenous sunk costs including advertising, rather than driven by the pursuit of pure production scale economies. Less confidently, we suspect that, in a number of industries, size inequalities are widening, with the leading firms beginning to forge ahead of their smaller rivals. Of course, this is often the consequence of the cross-border mergers/alliances just described, but purely national mergers (e.g. Krupps-Hoesch, Daimler-MBB) and/or internal growth (e.g. in margarine and fats, pharmaceuticals) are sometimes responsible. Again, it is unlikely that these are driven by purely production scale economies.

Another potential feature highlighted by the above framework is the impact of changes in the national specialization in individual industries. For example, increased German dominance in some sectors may result in significant increases in EU concentration, even though market shares in Germany remain stable. A thorough investigation of this possibility must await more up-to-date data on national industry size.

Table 4.5a.   Growth in mean size,[1] national level (%)

	Growth in size national level (%)		
	Firm (s)	Industry (S)	Mean national concentration change $(C4NAT)^2$
Type 1	6.6	5.5	-0.3
Type 2A	12.4	5.1	1.3
Type 2R	-4.0	-0.7	-1.9
Type 2AR	12.0	8.2	1.3
All	1.5	3.5	-0.1

[1]   All means are simple (unweighted) arithmetic averages.

[2]   'Mean national' refers to the simple means of Belgium, France, Germany and the UK; for France the time period is 1985–92, for Germany it is 1987–93, and for Belgium it is 1986–91. C4NAT represents the change over the period, not the annual rate of change.

Table 4.5b.   Changes in concentration

	Four-firm concentration ratios, European level (C4EU)			No of inds[2]
	1987	**1993**	**Change**[1]	
Type 1	13.2	14.4	1.2 _1.18_	38
Type 2A	22.3	23.6	1.2 _1.22_	11
Type 2R	32.9	38.9	6.1 _6.08_	15
Type 2AR	30.1	32.4	2.3 _2.27_	7
All	20.5	22.8	2.3 _2.32_	71

[1] Rounding errors (2 decimal places given in corner). Changes in concentration ratios refer to the percentage points.
[2] Data are included for Belgium, France, Germany, and the UK.

4.4.   Conclusion

Our evidence confirms that the EU market was not fully integrated at the start of the single market programme, and that potential existed for further achievement of economies of scale. However, there are important differences between industries. These result from two influences. First, industries have been differentially affected by national boundaries. Second, the competitive imperatives, resulting from differences in the prevailing form of competition, have created qualitatively different types of industrial structure. In our work, the main differences in the achievement of economies of scale have been characterized by separate analysis of four industry types.

The clearest, and most interesting, early effects of the single market programme have shown through in the R&D intensive industries. This is particularly important because it was this group which had caused most policy concern in the mid-1980s, with fears of a loss of European global market share, and which was a major factor in originally inspiring the single market programme. We find that firm size is positively related to specialization in Member States with a comparative advantage, and even before 1992 there was a clear tendency for greater relative structural adjustment in industries which were furthest from attaining full economies of scale. However, as a group, these industries were also experiencing negative industry growth (see Table 4.5a), so this relative effect did not translate into greater absolute size on average.

A great advantage of our research methodology is to show that this is only part of the story. Viewing the industry at the aggregate EU level, we see that firms were responding to the situation by international mergers and acquisitions, with a very substantial effect on EU industrial concentration. Such activity is more likely to have been motivated by R&D and marketing economies than in production, although corporate rationalization may well follow as the internal organization of the merged firms settles down. This, plus further locational specialization, may feed through into production economies. Although not reported upon here, we also have evidence that multinationals which had found it politic to produce in several local markets when selling to the public sector, were beginning to pull back and specialize production in fewer Member States [see Davies and Lyons, 1996, Chapter 13]. This has not yet fed through into the average size data. Thus, underlying the fairly static descriptive statistics of what has been happening at the national level in these industries, we find a complex dynamic picture.

It is not necessary to repeat all the details for each of the other industry types, but a few are worthy of note. For Type 1, we found that public procurement had opposite effects on achieved scale to that in Type 2R (where a policy of national champions, rather than even-handed support, lay behind procurement bias). There has also been a marginal growth of EU concentration in Type 1 industries, which may anticipate further structural change at the national level. Advertising intensive industries have only a weak relationship between business size and production economies of scale. We have been unable satisfactorily to explain the sharp rise in business unit size in Type 2A. This has been quite pervasive, and at least in the short run, undoubtedly has much to do with the strong demand growth in this sector. It has shown through only marginally in national and EU concentration. The Type 2AR industries were already dominated by large multinationals, who were able to surmount most trade barriers, and who were already operating at the largest scale of any industry type.

Finally, we repeat our earlier warning that because of data availability, we are only able to look at the earliest anticipated effects of the single market. Our research methodology could usefully be repeated once more up-to-date information becomes available.

5. Business scale, profitability and costs

In our work so far, we have stressed the impact of the single market programme on the actual size of business units and on industrial concentration. While we have been careful to express these magnitudes relative to potential economies of scale, the previous chapters do not provide an assessment of the actual cost savings due to the achievement of scale, or of the financial consequences. Such assessments are not possible from the data sources exploited so far. In order to gain some insight into these issues, we have had to turn to a quite different database – PIMS. The PIMS data have the advantage of providing more detailed information on costs, especially relative costs by relative size. Against this, it is based on a narrower set of firms, and it is difficult to tie the industrial classification used by PIMS to the NACE we have used so far.

In Section 5.1 we provide a brief introduction to the PIMS data, and show how the profitability of pan-European businesses has changed relative to national/regional businesses since 1985. Section 5.2 highlights some of the reasons that are associated with success, particularly focusing on those factors which are strongly related to economies of scale. In Section 5.3, we try to match the PIMS classification to the NACE, in order to estimate the slope of the cost curve, and thereby the potential for savings due to business size increasing with the single market.

5.1. General approach

In the second scenario explored by Venables and Smith [1988] the SM programme is thought likely to have most effect only if it alters the behaviour and performance of individual businesses. For businesses to use the opportunities provided by reductions in barriers between national markets in order to achieve scale economies, the new market environment must alter the incentives for them to operate in a larger market context.

For the single market to deliver economic benefits in terms of economies of scale, a number of conditions need to be met. One is that businesses which operate on a larger scale should have the prospect of more attractive returns – and thus the ability to attract investment for growth – than those which operate on a smaller scale. If this can be shown to be the case for businesses which define their market as Europe-wide, this may provide evidence that the single market at least provides the conditions in which scale economies are likely to be exploited.

Previous published work on this has provided evidence of 'the costs of non-Europe'. Research by Yip in 1991 using PIMS data found that 'continental scale businesses in Europe performed financially worse than national scale businesses in the period... before the creation of the single European market which would reduce barriers'. This study also found that 'in the United States by contrast, where barriers and differences between regions are much less than in Europe, continental scale businesses performed better than regional scale businesses'. [Yip, 1992]

The definition of 'continental scale' in this work is market-based. It depends upon business managers confirming their presence in the majority of national markets, identifying the same key competitors present across Europe, and adopting a pan-European approach to production, distribution and marketing. The implications of this result are that in most industries incentives for business managers to invest in continental scale businesses during the 1970s and

1980s were low. Possible economies of scale, in production, distribution, development and marketing, were more than counterbalanced by additional co-ordination costs, and by loss of focus on the needs of customers. These problems appeared not to be present in the US.

Despite this overall negative conclusion, the sample contained some businesses which had adopted a pan-European approach and achieved ROCE levels strong enough to attract investment. These businesses shared certain characteristics, which indicated other forms of market barriers supporting their profitability.

In this section we have revisited this work, to check two specific areas:

(a)   to test for any evidence that the performance disadvantages of continental scale businesses in Europe have diminished since Yip's conclusions of 1990/91;

(b)   to identify whether the key success factors, which the more profitable pan-European businesses share, have changed over the same period; and if so, whether the incentives to exploit scale economies have increased.

Evidence has been examined for 128 pan-European businesses which are among the 600 in the PIMS database defining their markets as being 'in Europe'. The unit of observation is a business unit within a company, which supplies a specific set of products and/or services, to a defined set of customers, against a known set of competitors. This definition is almost always drawn at a more specific level than three-digit NACE codes, in terms of a business position in a defined served market.

The 128 businesses describe themselves as operating across the EU, while the rest of European businesses compete in a single country or region. Data on each are captured for a minimum of four years, and they cover cost, margin and capital ratios, market structure variables and competitive measures. A full description of the PIMS data structure, and definitions, is given in *The PIMS principles* by Buzzell and Gale [1987]. An up-to-date summary of PIMS business performance data is given in the report *Building business for Europe* submitted to the European Commission's Directorate-General for Industry by PIMS and the Irish Management Institute in 1994 [Clayton and Carroll, 1994].

Evidence from those businesses which have defined their market boundary as EC or EU over the last 15 years shows that there have been significant changes in the performance of pan-European enterprises since the mid-1980s. These changes appear to have made it less attractive for businesses to position themselves defensively behind market boundaries, and more attractive to achieve greater scale in their European markets. There is evidence on overall cost structure, related to the typology of markets used in Chapter 4 of this report, which supports the conclusions reached from industry level data. There are also data which support the picture from the majority of case studies, of increasing specialization at points within the value chain in enterprises leading to reduced business value added, but at the same time increasing scale in the operation of particular processes. This trend, which in some industries appears as 'vertical disintegration', is consistent with the data on enterprise size which we have seen in Chapter 4.

By splitting the sample of European business units into data covering the period up to 1985, and the period after, we are able to examine how these businesses behave, and how the factors related to profit margins (and hence the ability to attract investment) have changed over time.

For reasons of commercial confidentiality, most of these data are not sector identified, and none are traceable to any individual company.

The business results for ROCE – pre-tax, pre-interest return on historic net fixed assets plus working capital – are sufficiently striking to suggest that the operation of markets for pan-European businesses has changed post-1985. The data in Table 5.1 below are based on four-year average performance, and they confirm the Yip conclusions for the period pre-1985; that businesses which competed on a continental scale in Europe performed significantly worse than those which focused on individual country markets, or on regions within Europe. However, after 1985 the gap almost disappears, because the 'regional/national' businesses perform significantly worse in the later period – close to the level of 'European scale' businesses.

Table 5.1.   ROCE performance of European businesses in PIMS database

ROCE	Pre-1985 (%)	Post-1985 (%)
Pan-European	14.4	13.8
Regional/national	24.5	15.4

As most of the observations are not sector identified, it is impossible to check whether this change in the pattern of performance is due to a radically different sample of business types, or businesses with different competitive strengths. However, we can 'normalize' the sample to check for systematic differences due to share, productivity, quality, and customer bargaining power (which are identified for each and every observation). The basis for this is the PIMS Par ROCE model, based on regression relationships between ROCE and profit determining variables across the whole database. The structure of this model, and statistical relationships underlying its key terms, are set out in Buzzell and Gale [1987]. It provides a means of checking that the changes observed in performance are not due to major changes in the typology of businesses observed.

The results show that differences in fundamental profit-related variables for businesses in the sample do not explain the differences in ROCE performance pre-1985. Nor do they explain the changed position post-1985. Par ROCE values for businesses defined as pan-European are within two points of those defined as national/regional for the pre-1985 sample, and the values post-1985 show only minor, and insignificant, change.

The data therefore support the hypothesis that national market barriers play a much less significant part in determining margin performance post-1985 than before.

5.2.   Performance related factors in European-scale businesses

The results reported above show that a high proportion of European scale businesses pre-1985 achieved ROCE results significantly worse than would have been expected given their market environment, competitive position and productivity. Yip [1992] suggests that these results were due to excess co-ordination costs, and to loss of market focus. In terms of this study, this means diseconomies of scale in production, distribution and administration, and inability (at best) to take advantage of potential dynamic economies of scale in development and marketing.

However, there were around one-third of this sample of businesses which made attractive returns, both in absolute terms and in comparison with the returns expected, given their share position, market attractiveness and productivity. Do these business units share any common characteristics which can provide clues as to the real incentives for investors in European business opportunities in this period? What business types are likely to achieve high ROCE?

Table 5.2.   Significant factors related to high/low ROCE vs Par ROI – pre-1985

	Significance	Strong ROCE	Weak ROCE
ROCE average	****	37%	6%
Scale related factors			
(a) Share rank in market	****	3 or 4	1, 2 or 3
(b) Share of served market	**	20%	27%
(c) Top 3 competitors' share	**	47%	41%
(d) Relative share (b/c)	**	51%	82%
Scope or 'focus' related			
(a) Relative product range	****	Same or narrower	Same or broader
(b) Relative customer types	****	Same or narrower	Same or broader
(c) Relative customer numbers	****	Same or fewer	Same or more
Advertising/sales related			
(a) % consumer products	**	25%	10%
(b) % advertising in marketing	***	7%	2%
(c) Salesforce cost/revenue	**	5.5%	3.9%
(d) Adv & promo/revenue	****	3.3%	0.6%
(e) Total sales & mktng/rev.	****	11.6%	5.3%
Development related			
(a) Leader/follower role	**	Follower	Pioneer
(b) % proprietary products	**	20%	40%
(c) Relative new products	*	Behind competition	Matches competition
(d) Relative quality	**	Above competition	Behind competition
External economy factors			
(a) % from top 3 suppliers	*	47%	40%

Key:
    **** Significant at 99%.
    *** Significant at 95%.
    ** Significant at 90%.
    * Significant at 80%.

As the results summarized in Table 5.2 indicate, strongly performing European scale businesses at this period were:

(a)   less likely to benefit from scale economies, because on the whole they were not European market leaders and more likely to have market shares below those of principal competitors;

(b)   more likely to be focused on a specific segment of a market, with a narrower range of products or services offered, and a narrower range of customer types;

(c)   very likely to have high marketing costs, including the costs of advertising, promotion and selling;

(d)   less likely to be an innovative business, with fewer new products and having entered the market as a follower rather than a leader.

The evidence suggests that the more successful Europe-wide businesses in the early 1980s were 'followers' in their markets. They operated at lower scale than main competitors, and lower relative scale within the European market. This pattern suggests that the more successful businesses tended to be those which were able to occupy a niche of some kind – effectively benefiting from a form of non-geographic segmentation through a specific customer base, or in segments demanding a more limited range of products.

The successful business tended to be in markets where advertising and selling costs were heavier. These are characteristics which are found in Type 2A businesses in the typology used in Sections 4.2 and 4.3, where the fastest rate of firm growth was found, as well as relatively rapid concentration increase. This evidence tends to confirm that exploitation of scale economies in this area on a European scale was well under way before the single market programme.

The successful businesses pre-1985 also tended to be less innovative, measured in terms of order of market entry, ownership of intellectual property, and of new product content. Again this is consistent with the analysis in Section 4.2, which suggests that in Type 2R industries there was, in the mid-1980s, major scope for exploiting unrealized economies in R&D, but it did not happen until later. The PIMS data certainly suggest that the incentives to exploit such economies were weak.

There is, however, some evidence that ability to exploit external economies was a significant success factor in this period. Better performing businesses tended to be more dependent on a few suppliers.

After 1985, the performance gap between pan-European businesses and those which define their markets in national or regional terms narrows. In addition, the key statistically significant factors which differentiate the most and least profitable businesses change.

Table 5.3.   Significant factors related to high/low ROCE vs Par ROI – post-1985

	Significance	Strong ROCE	Weak ROCE
ROCE average	****	31%	-6%
Scale related factors			
(a) Share rank in market	***	1, 2 or 3	3, 4 or 5
(b) Share of served market	**	22%	12%
(c) Top 3 competitors' share	*	39%	48%
(d) Relative share (b/c)	***	75%	26%
(e) Capacity/market value	***	27%	13%
Scope or 'focus' related			
(a) 'Customized' products	***	10%	40%
Advertising/sales related			
(a) % advertising in mktng	**	4.3%	0.8%
(b) Adv & promo/revenue	*	0.7%	0.2%
Development related			
(a) R&D spend/markt. value	*	Increasing	Decreasing
External economy factors			
(a) % from top 3 suppliers	*	59%	47%

Key:
     ****   Significant at 99%.
     ***   Significant at 95%.
     **   Significant at 90%.
     *   Significant at 80%.

The pattern for successful businesses after 1985 tends to be those which:

(a)   are likely to be in the top three suppliers to the European market rather than lower rank, and more likely to have higher scale relative to direct competitors;

(b)   are more dependent on 'mass marketed' products, with little customization, and so more likely to be able to exploit scale economies;

(c)   are likely to be in markets where advertising is a significant part of cost structure, supporting the thesis in Chapter 4 that Type 2A businesses are now exploiting economies of scale faster than most;

(d)   are no longer likely to be 'laggards' in technology development, and may indeed invest more heavily in R&D, which would permit the catch-up growth for Type 2R businesses identified in Chapter 4;

(e)   are even more likely than before to focus on major suppliers for the bulk of their supplies, suggesting that they enjoy additional competitive advantage via external economies.

This pattern suggests that the more successful businesses post-1985 are those which have succeeded in exploiting some economies of scale, either in production, in the development of a better offer to customers, or in the use of marketing resources, including salesforce.

There are differences in the statistically significant factors associated with higher returns on capital employed in pan-European businesses before and after 1985. This evidence suggests that competitive patterns have changed in ways which favour the exploitation of scale economies.

Factors which pre-1985 are associated with strong returns include fragmented or highly segmented markets, lower scale market position, both absolute and relative to competitors, lagging innovation, narrow focus and fewer customers. Businesses with these traits are unlikely to be the ideal candidates to deliver economies of scale gains. By the late 1980s, these factors have disappeared from the PIMS sample of high performing Europe-wide businesses.

They are replaced by a tendency for stronger margins to be clearly associated with larger scale relative to competitors. There is also evidence that successful businesses are those which invest more heavily in assets to support employee productivity – normally evidence for sunk costs.

There are, in addition, data available from these two analyses which confirm to some extent the 'vertical disintegration' hypothesis. The average value added/sales ratio for each group of businesses in 1975 to 1985 has dropped in the post-1985 period.

Table 5.4.   Value added ratios for pan-European businesses

Value added/sales	High ROCE businesses (%)	Low ROCE businesses (%)
Pre-1985	60.6	51.3
Post-1985	53.7	46.7

Thus, it appears that the trend away from vertically integrated chains, from the raw material to finished products, has started to be reflected in the statistics for individual businesses. As 'non-core' functions and competencies are outsourced, to focus on areas of business competitive advantage, it is to be expected that vertical integration falls.

5.3.   The relationship between cost change and output change

PIMS' Competitive Strategy Research Database also contains evidence of changes in costs and output for more than 3,000 businesses over a time span of at least three years. Of these, some 70% are based in North America and 20% in Europe.

In the following analysis we have used two variables:

$\Delta C/C$ The change in cost, deflated by the change in wage rates, as a fraction of the initial cost.[5]

---

[5]   We have assumed that cost inflation is captured solely by wage rate changes at the business unit level (i.e. we assume $(\delta C/\delta w)/C = 1$). Although costs include elements unrelated to employee remuneration, wages are the largest part of manufacturing and other costs, and inflation in non-labour cost elements is likely to be of a similar magnitude.

$\Delta V/V$ The change in value added, deflated, as a fraction of the initial value added.[6]

In the relationship

(1) $\Delta C/C = a + b \cdot \Delta V/V + e$

the interpretation of the coefficients is that:

  b   provides a measure of proportionate rate of change of real cost with real output. In part, this reflects the presence of economies of scale;

  a   in principle, measures the rate of change of real cost independent of output;

  e   is the error term.

We have looked at data up to the end of 1985 for businesses experiencing a change in real value added between -2% and +60% per annum over a three-year period. Businesses with a rapid decline in output were excluded on the grounds that their cost change behaviour could be radically different from that of businesses which are growing.

A regression analysis of equation (1) was undertaken for:

(a)   manufacturing and distribution costs;
(b)   costs excluding purchases, i.e. manufacturing and distribution, R&D, marketing, other costs (primarily administration). A charge on capital was not included.

The results for all businesses in the database within these constraints are shown in Table 5.5.

(a)   For manufacturing costs, the value of 'b' is 0.73, i.e. a 1 per cent increase in output is associated with 0.73 per cent increase in costs. The difference from 1 is highly significant.
(b)   The value of 'b' for costs excluding purchases is significantly lower than for manufacturing costs alone at 0.63.
(c)   Values for 'a' are not statistically significant.

Result 1 is consistent with economies of scale but could be attributed to other causes. If many businesses were operating with excess capacity, real costs would have increased less quickly than real outputs. As a check on this we added a variable for 'beginning capacity utilization level' in equation (1). The coefficient on capacity utilization level was negative, as expected, but not statistically significant.

Result 2 suggests that for marketing, R&D and administrative costs, the propensity to increase costs was lower than for manufacturing costs alone, in the medium term. These costs certainly include a much higher proportion of discretionary expenditures than are found in manufacturing.

---

[6]   Value added is defined as: *revenue less purchases*. Revenue change has been deflated by change in prices; change in purchases has been deflated by change in price of purchased supplies. Both these inflation measures are captured at the business unit level.

Separate NACE sectors were examined, where there was sufficient data, and service businesses were also considered. (Service businesses in the database operate in a range of sectors, including warehousing and distribution, radio and TV broadcasting, banking, insurance, vehicle rental and leasing, nursing and personal care and many others). The general results are shown in Tables 5.6 and 5.7 and are similar to those found for the whole database.

(a)   The median value of 'b' for manufacturing costs is 0.84.
(b)   The median value of 'b' for costs excluding purchases is lower than for manufacturing costs at 0.65. All sectors but one have a value of 'b' less than 1 and in many cases the difference is statistically significant.

We hypothesized that industries with a low 'b' (i.e. a steep slope to the cost curve) would have most to gain from the single market, and so should have increased in size most rapidly in recent years. We therefore tried to relate the estimates of 'b' to changes in business unit size as measured in Chapter 3. No clear pattern was found. Once again, this may be due to the fact that we only have size data up to 1991, but this time we also have the problem of a very small set of observations (so, for example, we could not take account of industry type). Given the lack of a clear pattern, we did not attempt to quantify the cost savings achieved by industries which did experience firm size growth.

However, we have also looked at the performance of those manufacturing businesses in the database that have experienced major technological change, and have contrasted their results with those of all other manufacturing businesses in order to identify significant differences between the two sets.

Business performance measures examined include levels of and changes in:

(a)   profitability,
(b)   relative quality and value,
(c)   market share,
(d)   employee productivity.

Only for change in return on sales and level of employee productivity is the difference between the two sets of businesses statistically significant. A similar analysis undertaken for service businesses produced similar, generally negative results.

Two other variables have been examined:
(a)   real sales growth,
(b)   real market growth.

For these two variables, differences between the sets are extremely significant.

It appears that the benefits to a manufacturing business from major technological change arise not from improvements in internal performance measures, but from relatively rapid sales growth arising from market growth. On this evidence, if technological change does not result in increased market growth, the business is likely to benefit only if it experiences growth in market share.

The causality of the relationship between technology and market growth can be argued both ways – technological change both stimulates and is stimulated by market growth.

Table 5.5.   Analysis of cost and output change

		Value of coefficients		No of Bus's	R Sq	F	Prob
		a	b				
Manufacturing Costs		-0.8	0.73	1003	0.38	622	0
	Std Error	0.5	0.03				
Costs excl Purchs. & Capital Charges		-0.2	0.63	1003	0.42	740	0
	Std Error	0.4	0.02				

Table 5.6.   Manufacturing cost and output change for selected sectors

NACE CODE	Manufacturing Costs		Value of coefficients		No of Bus's	R Sq	F	Prob
			a	b				
327	Other specific equip.		1.1	0.47	13	0.24	3.5	0.09
		Std error	3.5	0.25				
256	Other chemical products for industry		4.9	0.59	38	0.21	9.7	0.004
		Std error	4.2	0.19				
325	Plant for mines		-4.7	1.17	10	0.95	162	0
		Std error	1.9	0.09				
315	Boilermaking		0.2	1.03	9	0.88	51	0
		Std error	1.8	0.15				
	Motor vehicles		-6.1	1.46	8	0.76	19	0.005
		Std error	5.6	0.34				
344	Telecomm.equip.1		0.8	0.48	16	0.09	1.4	0.25
		Std error	4.2	0.4				
372	Medico-surgical equip.		-3.6	1	16	0.77	47	0
		Std error	2.2	0.15				
247	Glassware		-0.8	0.69	10	0.77	27	0.001
		Std errror	2	0.13				
342	Electrical equip.		-3.4	0.84	42	0.67	80	0
		Std error	2.1	0.09				
251	Basic ind. chem.		2.4	0.53	53	0.21	13	0.001
		Std error	3.1	0.14				
493	Photo cine labs		-6.9	1	9	0.78	25	0.002
		Std error	4.6	0.2				
346	Dom. type elec. app.		-3.4	0.78	10	0.47	7	0.029
		Std error	6.5	0.29				
347	Lamps & lighting eq.		-10.9	1.24	13	0.67	22	0.001
		Std error	5.1	0.26				
341	Elec. wires & cables		0.1	0.49	14	0.12	1.7	0.22
		Std error	7.4	0.38				
345	Electronic equip.		-7.8	1.24	15	0.24	4.2	0.061
		Std error	9.5	0.61				
	Services		2.6	0.53	34	0.26	11	0.002
		Std error	2.8	0.16				
61-65	Retail/Wholesale		-2.6	1.02	20	0.26	6.2	0.023
		Std error	5.2	0.41				
	Quartiles for Coefficients							
	Upper quartile		0.8	1.03				
	Median		-2.4	0.84				
	Lower quartile		-4.7	0.53				
	Average		-2.2	0.86				

Table 5.7. Cost (excluding purchases) and output change for selected sectors

NACE CODE	Costs excl Purchs & Capital Chgs		Values of Coefficients		No of Bus's	R Sq	F	Prob
			a	b				
327	Other specific equipment		1.7	0.41	13	0.33	5.4	0.041
		Std Error	2.5	0.18				
256	Other chemical products for industry		3.8	0.54	38	0.25	12	0.001
		Std Error	3.4	0.15				
325	Plant for mines		-1.1	0.99	10	0.89	66	0.000
		Std Error	2.6	0.12				
315	Boilermaking		-1.2	1.05	9	0.90	62	0.000
		Std Error	1.6	0.13				
351	Motor vehicles		-2.3	0.92	8	0.65	11	0.016
		Std Error	4.7	0.28				
344	Telecommunication equipment 1		4.2	0.23	16	0.03	0.4	0.55
		Std Error	3.8	0.37				
372	Medico-surgical equipment		-1.6	0.81	16	0.81	58	0.000
		Std Error	1.6	0.11				
247	Glassware		1.3	0.48	10	0.70	18	0.003
		Std Error	1.7	0.11				
342	Electrical equipment		-2.0	0.66	42	0.66	79	0.000
		Std Error	1.6	0.07				
251	Basic Indust. chemicals		0.1	0.49	53	0.29	21	0.000
		Std Error	2.3	0.11				
493	Photo cine labs		-2.5	0.63	9	0.76	22	0.002
		Std Error	3.0	0.13				
346	Domestic type electrical appliances		-3.2	0.72	10	0.58	11	0.010
		Std Error	4.7	0.22				
347	Lamps & lighting equipment		-6.8	0.88	13	0.78	39	0.000
		Std Error	2.7	0.14				
341	Electrical wires & cables		0.7	0.46	14	0.14	1.9	0.19
		Std Error	6.3	0.33				
345	Electronic equipment		-1.2	0.45	15	0.18	2.8	0.12
		Std Error	4.2	0.27				
	Services		2.7	0.53	34	0.42	23	0.000
		Std Error	2.0	0.11				
61 to 65	Retail / wholesale		-0.5	0.79	20	0.38	11	0.004
		Std Error	3.0	0.23				
	Quartiles for Coefficients							
	Upper Quartile		0.9	0.83				
	Median		-1.2	0.65				
	Lower Quartile		-2.1	0.49				
	Average		-0.6	0.66				

6. Summary of the case study research

As part of this project, a series of sector case studies was undertaken. The reasons for these case studies were three-fold: to examine the influence of the SM on dynamic economies of scale in activities such as R&D, marketing and personnel development; to examine the influence of the SM on external economies of scale and whether this has affected the location of activity; and thirdly to explore some of the practical issues underlying the examination of costs reported in Chapter 5.

The typology of Davies and Lyons [1996] is particularly useful in distinguishing between sectors affected by different types of competition but also by different types of dynamic economies of scale, namely those associated with R&D and those associated with marketing and advertising. As discussed in Chapter 2, investment in both of these areas can be considered endogenous sunk costs; the question is therefore whether the SM has allowed firms which compete in these activities to exploit their investment more fully across the EU.

Davies and Lyons argue that there have been a large number of mergers involving R&D and advertising intensive industries (i.e. Type 2R, Type 2A and Type 2AR industries) since 1987, and these mergers have often been driven by the desire to exploit economies of scale. However, in relation to R&D and marketing, these economies of scale may be as closely related to learning by doing, knowledge transfer and the exchange of personnel between countries as to the establishment of any critical mass (or MES equivalent) in such activities. We therefore also explore this question in the case studies.

In Section 2.5 of this report we discussed the theory of external economies of scale, much of which points to a significant potential impact, in terms of the agglomeration of activity, resulting from the SM. However, it is recognized that there is a large degree of indeterminacy in the locational choice of firms and therefore in the pattern of regional specialization. In the case studies we have explored the question of what, if any, external economies exert a particular influence on the location of activity by firms in the sectors concerned. The particular focus has been on local labour markets and component suppliers.

However, the case studies do not reflect comprehensive research into regional specialization, which is outside the scope of the present project. What they seek to do is to provide some insight into the factors driving exploitation of scale economies in the sectors studied.

Some consideration has also been given to two service sectors in relation to both dynamic and external economies of scale. Full reports on the case studies themselves are given in Appendix A. The sectors covered are shown in Table 6.1.

Table 6.1.   Case study sectors

Type	Concentration quadrant	Sector
2R	A	Rail stock
2R	C	Pharmaceuticals
2R	C	Computers
2A	C	Chocolate confectionery
2A	A/C	Beer
2AR	D	Motor vehicles
1	D	Glass
1	D	Clothing
S	-	Insurance
S	-	Retailing

6.1. Industrial change and globalization

All the sectors examined in the course of the case study research have been the subject of increasing rates of change in terms of industrial structure over the last ten years. For some (as in computers) this change has been profound, while for others (such as beer) the change has been more modest. In each case the nature of the opportunities for exploitation of scale economies has evolved in a way that has been largely independent of the SM programme.

The reason for this is that all manufacturing sectors are experiencing the globalization of production, albeit at different rates. The phenomenon of globalization is not the subject of the present report, but it is an important context in which to place the research. Each case study also places the question of external and dynamic economies of scale in the context of the market trends evident within the EU over the period 1980–95.

In certain sectors (such as rail stock and pharmaceuticals) there has been a wave of M&A activity prompted by the rising costs of R&D. In others (such as chocolate confectionery) a process of concentration has been stimulated by the trend towards global brand marketing, and the consequent exploitation of dynamic economies of scale. As was shown in Chapter 4, the Type 2R industries saw the greatest increase in concentration between 1987 and 1993, and this process has continued in the period since 1993, most markedly in pharmaceuticals.

Both of the service sectors studied (insurance and retailing) exhibit the characteristics of industries which still retain largely national markets, although cross-border activity, including recent M&A activity, is increasing (and re-insurance has been global for many years). In these sectors, the concept of dynamic economies of scale has more relevance than that of external economies of scale, since the development of new insurance products or new retailing formats can clearly be influenced by the extent of current knowledge within the firm and the level of learning by doing, but the exploitation of external economies is minimal. The nature of the local labour market or even the local property market was not considered an influential factor in the location of activity by any of our insurance or retailing respondents.

External economies of scale appear to be most applicable, of the case study sectors, to clothing. However, in all the sectors studied, the role of technological change has been important. For most, this change has been process-oriented, often bringing production costs down but also increasing the rate of innovation. In glass containers, increases in the size of furnaces and machines have contributed to a consolidation of production activity, and in beer there have been technological improvements leading to fewer, larger, faster breweries.

However, in computers and, to a lesser degree, motor vehicles, technological change has also been product-oriented. As the lifespan of new products becomes shorter and shorter, the incentive to sell those products, in common configurations, across as many national markets as possible increases. Removal of non-tariff barriers then becomes more relevant.

The pursuit of Porter's [1980] three generic strategies of product differentiation, cost reduction or focus is clearly influenced by the rate of technological change in any given sector. Brief technological profiles of the NACE sectors considered by Buigues et al [1990] to be most sensitive to the SM are given in Appendix B. In the case studies we have identified the high degree of overlap between product differentiation and cost reduction; in motor vehicles, for example, cost reduction in the R&D process through the introduction of new technology has allowed firms to explore aspects of product differentiation more effectively and quickly.

In the Type 2R industries there has been a general move towards greater focus in terms of product specialization, particularly in the computer equipment sector. In rail stock and pharmaceuticals there are some exceptions to this trend, with an expansion into financial services to customers by one rail rolling stock manufacturer and the development of disease management services by some pharmaceutical MNEs, but in general product development has been more tightly focused, and this has clearly assisted the exploitation of economies of scale. Again, the facility to market such products widely across the EU is important to the return on investment needed in these R&D intensive industries.

The Type 2A industry case studies, chocolate and beer, show divergent trends in marketing, with the former experiencing economies through more pan-European marketing and greater product focus, and the later experiencing increased costs associated with increased marketing on a country by country basis, and expansion of the scope of their activities, i.e. a widened focus in terms of both product range and geographic coverage. Beer also demonstrates the link between process cost reduction and product differentiation through increased innovation.

In Type 1 industries, the introduction of new process technology is obviously critical to competitiveness in terms of production costs. A cost reduction strategy is most apparent in the glass case study, but outward processing in clothing is also driven by cost reduction strategies.

In summary, all three of Porter's generic strategies are evident in the case study sectors, although many of these strategic developments are linked to the globalization of production and technological change within the industry rather than the SM programme itself.

6.2. The impact of the SM: Type 2R industries

In Chapter 4 we discussed the evidence indicating that Type 2R industries have experienced the most significant SM effect in terms of resisting a decline in the average size of business unit where it was initially smallest relative to MES, and in terms of increased EU level concentration, although in both cases there have also been other important forces at work.[7]

There is no straightforward relationship between size of firm and the level of R&D investment, on the one hand, and the rate of innovation, on the other. However, larger firms

---

7   Indeed, the overall size of business unit in the EU, and the level of national concentration have both declined: see Section 4.2.

may undertake incremental R&D activity which might not otherwise be possible, and competitive pressures may force an escalation of R&D expenditure leading to industry consolidation (see Sections 2.4.1 and 2.4.2).

In rail stock, there has been a significant reduction in costs, but for the most part this has not been through increases in plant size. Rather, the opening up of public procurement together with the harmonization of standards, has facilitated longer production runs of standard (i.e. uniform) rolling stock, and consequent reductions in the complexity of product adaptation and marketing. However, this standardization is by no means complete, and liberalization of user markets has not been sufficient for train specifiers not to add their own special requirements and thereby force short production runs.

Knowledge transfer in R&D and best practice with regard to sourcing have had a major impact, and because of the importance of componentry in the total product cost, this has resulted in some significant economies. Although this is already a global industry, the case study research did indicate that without the consolidation that the SM has prompted, the European rail stock producers would have lost their international competitive position.

In pharmaceuticals the level of competition has greatly intensified, and the reductions in some non-tariff barriers have contributed to this. However, a fully integrated EU pharmaceutical market is still some considerable way off and the different Member State policies on pricing and reimbursement are seen as significant hurdles in this respect.

In responding to the intensified competition in the EU, partly prompted by Member States' own drug spending policies, pharmaceutical firms are engaging in more cross-border strategic alliances to gain R&D know-how and local marketing or distribution knowledge, as well as M&A activity. Some benefits from the SM in terms of the free movement of personnel and the possibilities for pan-European marketing are evident in the pharmaceutical industry, but these are emergent only. More significant has been the process of concentration of activity onto fewer sites, which may now include some of the peripheral Member States, but which is driven by global trends in the industry as much as by the SM programme itself.

In computers, the ability to move personnel and assets across borders has assisted in the restructuring of the industry, but European MNEs are perceived to have lagged behind US MNEs operating in Europe in their view of a pan-EU market. This restructuring has led to dynamic economies of scale through greater focus and product/service specialization in R&D. The opening up of public procurement has also favoured this strategy.

Labour costs account for a lower proportion of manufacturing costs in computers than they did in the period prior to the SM programme, but external economies of scale have become significant in relation to the local presence of customer headquarters and suppliers. This has encouraged the recent concentration of manufacturing activity in the UK and Ireland. Government incentives obviously also play an important part in this.

6.3. The impact of the SM: Type 2A and 2AR industries

In some advertising intensive industries, the opportunities for pan-EU marketing are more obvious than in others – where customer preferences are more consistent, or where packaging and labelling requirements are largely common. However, pecuniary gains (through media and advertising production discounts, for example) may still be difficult if, as Davies and Lyons argue, the relevant geographical range of advertising activity is still identified at the national level. The question is therefore whether the move towards pan-European marketing and advertising has been stimulated or facilitated by the SM in any way and the extent to which the difficulties associated with such a move still exist.

In chocolate confectionery, the most significant impact of the SM has been in the elimination of national restrictions on the pricing and supply of dairy and sugar inputs. This has helped to bring manufacturing costs down. However, the scope for production economies of scale may be limited by the Chocolate Directive (73/241/EEC, as amended), which allows Member State governments to set standards for production from their territories.

The case study respondents felt that marketing had become an even more important competitive weapon in the chocolate industry during the period of the SM. There are increasing opportunities for marketing products from one EU factory all over Europe, subject to meeting national labelling requirements, and in rolling out new product innovations quickly across different countries. It is unlikely that such an approach would have been possible without the framework established by the SM, even though much of the investment required to implement such an approach anticipated the actual SM programme.

In beer, there exist major differences between national markets in rates of excise duty and tax, and in the regulations concerning the supply and sale of alcohol. Consumer tastes also differ significantly between national (and even sub-national) markets. However, these latter differences are gradually reducing, affording opportunities for more widespread marketing campaigns. Knowledge transfer in both marketing and R&D is also growing, and with it a greater diversity of products are coming onto the market.

These developments have been made possible in part by the realization of scale economies, which themselves have been assisted by the free movement of both products and capital embodied in the SM programme. Physical transportation is now much easier within the EU, and major intra-EU acquisitions since 1991 have been facilitated by the greater ease of capital movement. The level of cross-border M&A activity has been limited by the over-capacity in the industry, but increasingly firms are looking to sell products into EU markets from their own production facilities (rather than under licence). However, the siting of such facilities is less influenced by the presence of external economies (e.g. in raw material supply) than by the most effective use of expensive production facilities. The growth of the 'international' brewers and the rise in levels of competition in EU markets both have clear links to the SM programme, although the programme may not have provided the initial stimulus for such developments.

In motor vehicles, the process of globalization of production has been a much more dominant force in the restructuring of the industry than has the creation of the SM. Globalization has been linked with the development of lean production methods, and also with the move towards the marketing of vehicles based on common product platforms across as many countries as possible.

Upstream activities such as R&D and component sourcing are also becoming more integrated on a global basis; this process is not a result of the SM although the introduction of Whole Vehicle Type Approval in the EU is facilitating some concentration of regulatory activity.

Downstream activities such as marketing and advertising are still largely undertaken at the Member State level, although the after-market for parts is regionalizing to a certain extent.

The SM does not appear to have influenced the location of vehicle manufacturing operations, although it may have positively affected the ability of component suppliers to trade across the EU. The realization of dynamic and external economies of scale does not therefore appear to have been significantly stimulated by the SM.

6.4   The impact of the SM: Type 1 industries

In Chapter 4 we discussed the fact that in Type 1 industries, in which competition is focused on production costs, firm size depends on production economies of scale and exogenous demand conditions. Public procurement bias obviously affects the second of these factors, but for the purposes of the case studies we sought to minimize this by choosing sectors which are not procurement intensive, namely glass and clothing.

The glass industry can be divided into two sub-sectors – container glass and flat glass – and these sub-sectors are driven by different user requirements and different competitive pressures. Since the early 1980s the branded food and drink companies, to whom the glass container producers are suppliers, have become more European, catching up in this respect with the cosmetics industry. Users of glass containers have tended to reduce the number of their suppliers and to look for more innovation. There are important intellectual property rights involved here, but end-user demand still remains relatively conservative.

Dynamic economies of scale in container glass are generated increasingly through the transfer of operational know-how. Mostly this has been associated with domestic M&A activity (in Germany, Italy and the UK). The transport costs of empty containers still limit the amount of cross-border product movement and hence the level of production and marketing integration within the EU. The principal external economy is related to the advances in process technology made by plant manufacturers, but these advances are global rather than European. Most raw materials are commodities.

In flat glass, market growth has been boosted by EU regulations, particularly those on energy efficient buildings. There has also been some restructuring in the move towards more off-site finishing ('remote processing') and in the emergent export capability of Eastern European producers.

Customer needs for flat glass are converging in the automotive sector, but the buildings market has been nationally defined until relatively recently. While R&D and marketing for the automotive sector can only be structured on an international (or global) basis, that for building products is only now moving towards this, through knowledge transfer between national operations and the establishment of co-ordinating committees within the glass producer firms, particularly the two dominant EU producers (Saint-Gobain and Pilkington).

This internationalization of the flat glass industry has occurred largely independently of the SM, although improved market access and the harmonization of building regulations have probably assisted the process.

In clothing, there is also a process of internationalization occurring, including increased FDI and outward processing by the major Italian companies who were the focus of the clothing case study. New relationships are being established between producers and distributors, with an increase in the level of downstream control and an increase in distributor concentration.

The Italian clothing industry mostly uses domestic suppliers, and can exploit particular external economies in certain regions in terms of local material sourcing and labour. The SM has opened up new market opportunities for the clothing manufacturers, which has had a growth effect on the supplier industry, in the south as well as the north of the country. In particular, the SM may pave the way for more bulk outsourcing to local SMEs, which offer efficiency savings to the manufacturers.

6.5.   The impact of the SM: service industries

The EU Insurance Directives have led to significant readjustment by most of the major operators in relation to a more competitive market environment. The life insurance market has not become more concentrated over the period since 1989, but that for non-life insurance has consolidated and there has been a wave of cross-border M&A activity.

In the non-life sector, common European approaches in marketing and personnel development are now emerging, but these are only due in part to the SM programme; a process of internationalization in the industry was already underway. Nevertheless, dynamic economies of scale have been achieved in terms of improved customer servicing and increased innovation in claims processing. Reorganization of claims processing for certain major operators has taken place on a European basis. In the life sector, on the other hand, different Member State tax regimes have precluded this cross-border approach.

External economies of scale have become available through the increased competition between agents and brokers, but this is not linked to the SM programme. The free movement of capital, as well as persons and services, has allowed insurance operators to work towards a single business structure within the EU, particularly in non-life activities. Market entry in Germany has also been greatly facilitated. But overall, the impact of the directives on economies of scale has been very limited; the establishment of mechanisms for transfer of best practice and the introduction of new information technology have been far more important.

In retailing, there has been a concentration of activity in almost all EU countries over the last 15 years. The level of cross-border investment increased during the early 1990s, but there are still clearly defined national markets, with distinct customer needs and tastes. Strategic alliances are nevertheless becoming more common, with the exchange of market knowledge and operating know-how being a key benefit, as well as (in some cases) increased purchasing power. One respondent saw their membership of the European Council as important to their 'relative learning rate'.

The free movement of products has assisted cross-border sourcing, but food health regulations still limit this in some areas. Beyond this, external economies do not really exist. Expansion into other EU markets by the major retailers may in fact lead to diseconomies through management complexity. Nevertheless, the widening frame of reference for product sourcing and innovation, and for store operating systems, has at least been assisted by the expectations of the SM programme.

APPENDIX A

Case studies on dynamic and external economies of scale

A.1. Rail rolling stock

A.1.1. Market trends 1980–95

Demand for rail stock in the EU has been highly volatile over the period, despite an underlying upward trend; variations in public purchasing patterns have given rise to major 'spurts' in orders at particular points, spread unevenly between EU national markets. However, consumption actually fell in real terms during the second half of the 1980s. Combined with a severe deterioration in the external trade balance, this produced a large fall in output. Steady recovery since then has been built on a strong recovery in apparent consumption, and a more erratic trend in external trade. Net exports, recovering strongly in 1990–91 appear to have weakened somewhat since.

The rail stock industry has always been global, in the sense that European firms have been active internationally throughout their history, and a number of leading EU producers are derived – at least in part – from investment in Europe by major US electrical firms in the early part of the century. A large part of EU output has historically gone to third country markets, in stiff competition with US and other producers. However, the role of third country exports has been variable, with the export:production ratio swinging between 29% and 9% over the last ten years. This is partly because of the volatility of international markets, affected as they are by major contracts, and partly because historic protection brought about by national preference in public purchasing gave rise to excess capacity – which was filled by exports when local demand slackened.

The decline in net exports which has to some extent been evident may reflect increasing sensitivity to local costs, but the EU is still by far the largest producer bloc in the world, including all three of the world's largest producer companies (excluding China, where the valuation of output and estimation of company size is problematic). There has been a major fall in overall employment in the sector, from over 90,000 to under 70,000. Individual companies have seen even sharper proportionate falls.

The industry has seen a dramatic shift in concentration. According to contributing companies to which we have spoken, these changes in European industry structure have been essential to keep it globally competitive; without the changes the participation in export markets would have seen a much sharper decline, and even some of the European based operations could have been under threat of change of ownership. These changes are summarized as:

(a)   1988 merger of Asea & Brown Boveri (part outside EU, anticipating entry);
(b)   1989 merger of GEC/Alsthom, as part of larger restructuring;
(c)   1989 GEC Alsthom acquired most Spanish capacity, and replaced it;
(d)   1994 GEC Alsthom took over LHB;
(e)   1995 merger of ABB/AEG to form Adtranz;
(f)   1996 (since interviews for this study) GEC Alsthom and Siemens agreed joint approach for extra-EU marketing.

Adtranz, GEC Alsthom and Siemens are now the three largest rail stock producers in the world. With world market value around £13–£20 bn (depending on the value placed on output of East European countries and China), producer estimates for the leading company output and shares are as follows:

Company	Sales (£bn)	Approx. world share
Adtranz	1.7	(9%)
GEC Alsthom	1.3	(7%)
Siemens	1.0	(5%)
'Japan Inc'*	1.0	(5%)
GE	0.8	(4%)
Westinghouse	0.6	(3%)
Ansaldo	0.3	
Bombardier	0.3	
Fiat	0.2	

*   Japan Inc represents Hitachi, Toshiba etc., who are effectively seen by European competitors on international markets as a co-ordinated force, operating in consortia with changing composition. Similar Korean groups are coming in behind the Japanese.

These top nine organizations only produce around 40% of world output – which is evidence of a relatively fragmented global supply pattern, in which European firms should have at least some scale advantage. The questions we have explored in our discussions with respondent companies include:

(a)   Has the concentration process in Europe been influenced by the single market?

(b)   Does it bring EU producers any advantage?

Markets for rail stock are changing in character, from domination by large state purchasing organizations (often as few as two per country – one for underground and one for railways) to a wider spread of customers as a result of privatization and deregulation. This process has probably gone furthest in the UK, where there will probably be at least 30 train operators by 1997. These customers will buy train services – rather than trains. Vehicle builders now have to market their output to these customers by finding financing partners, who are able to put 'packages' together to lease products to the train operating companies. These packages can significantly change the relationship between the producer of the train and its operator.

These changing customer needs are altering the cost structure of businesses operating in the rail vehicle market, both in terms of the costs of dealing with a larger customer base, and the need to meet changing customer specifications. Marketing costs are now significant as a measurable cost item for the first time for many years. R&D costs can be up to 3% of total costs; these were previously significantly lower in the UK (almost zero in the case of one of our respondents) but have historically been higher in France, and to some extent in Germany.

A.1.2. Overview of respondents' operations

Both respondents consulted for this study are parts of the 'big three' major European companies. Both have been affected significantly by the acquisition and consolidation process. Both have been transformed from predominantly national operations, and have become parts of pan-European firms with production, design, development and marketing capability in five or more major consuming countries.

One respondent has come from being part of a general engineering group, with sales originally limited mainly to one EU country, plus exports from surplus capacity to international markets. In this situation it had only one operational site, and no R&D capability. It still operates in this way within a large group, but now has access to development and marketing resources and to supply sources across Europe. It operates as an 'integrator', specializing in design and assembly for components produced by others – both inside and outside the larger company. Its number of employees since 1981 has been very variable, reflecting the ups and downs of major contracts, but is currently half its starting value.

This company's view of location for production is interesting. It regards its core competence to be in design, procurement of components and assembly; the location of assembly is only one of the important competitive factors. 'We design a big "Airfix kit" – buy the parts and put them together – and the assembly can be moved.' Local assembly can be important; to some extent in Europe but even more so elsewhere. So a spread of facilities available for assembly (through sister companies) is helpful; 'If you want to be a major supplier in a national market in Europe, you virtually have to be there.' Creating local assembly, through leasing capacity, subcontracting or longer term partnership, can therefore be a highly desirable move in some markets – especially the Far East.

The other respondent was part of an electrical group, which has made major purchases to establish itself as a supplier of complete rail systems, rather than simply components. In doing so, it has quadrupled its turnover, tripled the number of production sites, and doubled the number of employees.

Our respondents included the managing director of one company, and the technical director of the other.

Both respondents regard the merger process which has occurred in Europe as essential to permit the EU industry to remain internationally competitive. 'Without it we would not have been able to keep pace with developments elsewhere.' There has been a steady increase in the scale of economic operation for rail vehicle production, and the number of plants has reduced. The impact of these scale economies, and strong competition, has shown up in the trend of real price reductions – even, for one of the companies interviewed, substantial current price reductions. The average price per vehicle sold (uncorrected for changes in specification) has reduced from over £650,000 in 1980–85 to under £390,000 in 1995.

Ability to take advantage of cross-border sales opportunities and component procurement is still limited by remaining differences in standards, and by the surviving tendency of the remaining national buyers to buy 'one-offs' for their country only. 'They go through the call for tenders, but usually there is a locally preferred supplier who is set up to supply the local specification', and 'There has been important progress on standards harmonization to promote interoperability, but there is still sufficient difference remaining – compounded by power supply differences – to make it possible for purchasers to exercise national preference where they wish to.'

Our respondents have differing views on the role of strategic alliances. One company says that 'We have work to do managing relationships within the larger company, but may be interested in external alliances if they can save us work in the design process, and thus deal with customers faster, giving competitive advantage. This may also apply where partners are very close (geographically). But we only have one "key supplier" arrangement at the moment'. The other manages relationships with three or four external companies – mostly within the same national market as the company's home base, but also across the Atlantic.

A.1.3. Factors driving dynamic and production economies of scale

Importance

Significant changes are in progress in the market factors which influence the effect of scale economies. Although the European market is not yet homogeneous in terms of customer needs, it is starting to converge due to the willingness of non-state buyers to purchase standard units (or units based on standard modules) at lower prices, rather than insist on tailored engineering solutions. As the number of independent train operators grows, and they start to become more concerned with rail travel as a 'high quality' transport mode – able to compete for profitable customers – this tendency is expected by producers to accelerate. As rail operators become more customer conscious, and less dominated by operating company-based teams of design engineers, the scope for design and production economies will grow. One of our respondents claims that its existing order book is already influenced by this trend.

There is a clear lead market for innovation, especially in the HST product area, and it is France; participation in the French market is an advantage for those producers involved, who consider that it gives them significant spin-off, both in product capability and design quality, and in developing new design and assembly processes. For example, one contributor which has a sister company in France engaged in TGV projects, found that a design approach borrowed from the sister company was able to halve assembly time for the main shell of the train.

Respondents confirm that the importance of R&D expenditure has increased at the same time as common standards have taken hold, and the quality of product expected by train operators has improved. One makes clear that in the early 1980s it did virtually no R&D, other than short-term research on how to design to rail operators' detailed specifications. This would no longer be a feasible strategy. Now, as part of a much larger group, it is able to undertake limited research within the operating subsidiary – and more importantly, can now benefit from the substantial research activity of its sister operating companies.

All major competitors are now present in most European countries, usually with the capability for local manufacture, which increases competitive pressures to exploit available economies. At the same time, cost differences in production factors (mainly labour) have increased over time, with the UK having lower input costs. However, productivity differences are probably greater still, and tend to operate in the opposite direction; for example, in 1995–96 UK productivity was lower, but not enough to outweigh lower UK wages.

Free movement of goods and capital may be partially inhibited by differences remaining in technical standards, but in practice the capital movement provisions have probably made the overall consolidation of the industry possible. This has been done by networks of shareholdings across the majority of the largest companies – probably more secure and easier to organize within a single capital market.

Knowledge transfer

Both responding companies have taken steps to improve the transfer of knowledge in their operations across Europe. In one, the process started before 1990, with systems for common reporting of production costs and methods. The process was based on reporting systems already in use in one of the component companies. This then spread through to procurement and development after 1990. It was complemented by external consultant input to develop common marketing, product development and personnel/training approaches.

In the other company, steps to transfer know-how on technical issues have developed since 1990; learning on production processes is well advanced, R&D is shared, and international component purchasing is much more widely practised than it used to be. But development of knowledge transfer was initially held up by reliance on reporting systems, rather than using direct contact and face to face comparisons.

A.1.4. Benefits from dynamic scale economies

Both respondents identify gains in the following areas since 1980–85:

(a) cost reduction – in procurement and manufacturing;
(b) better innovation pay-off from R&D;
(c) access to better quality components, and improved production techniques;
(d) more effective marketing, identifying changing customer needs to be met.

Changes in procurement patterns are covered in the next section, but the impact of European scale competition is acknowledged by both respondent companies. Access to a wider range of markets, and the ability to 'spread' the benefits of new product designs and process advances clearly have made, and are still making, an impact. However, one respondent identified a threat which will arise as standards across the EU continue to converge. 'At present it isn't worth the Americans' while putting the effort into Europe, because they still have a range of specifications and power supply systems to contend with. When there is only one, they will make the effort, and secure part of the market – at the expense of EU producers.'

Diversity and scope of activities

In both respondent companies, the emphasis of commercial strategy in a larger market has been to focus effort at 'the top of the chain', i.e. to be an integrator of either complete rail systems or of complete vehicles. Operational focus has been strongly maintained in both companies in the areas in which each has competitive strengths. Rather than extending the range of products offered, the increase in scope for both has been in the range of financial options and services offered to customers – and in the sale of serviced train capacity, rather than simply vehicle hardware.

The effects of a larger single market permitting scale economies has been different in different areas. One of our respondents, catering for a market in which privatization is well advanced, already sees the impact of simpler specifications made in longer runs – driven by profit motivated train operators who are more interested in train quality than engineering detail. 'If they are happy to leave more of the design to us, we can optimize production.' The other still sees the need to broaden product range to meet different country needs, and probably incurs higher marketing costs as a result.

Influence of external economies

Savings in procurement represent in part the external economies achieved from doing a better job with specific suppliers, rather than simply exerting bargaining power.

Inputs to vehicle building appear to have been highly competitive over the last 15 years. An estimate from one of the respondents shows average vehicle selling price at just over half what it was in 1982 – and approaching 80% of vehicle costs from bought-in components or sub-assemblies. This can only be achieved because input suppliers have achieved major cost reductions. The other respondent estimates price reductions of around 30% in components and in finished vehicles over the period 1981–95.

Access to better (cross company) data on supply sources available across Europe has contributed to these results, and so has – in one respondent company – a programme to identify best suppliers for specific components. For example, a supplier of seats in France has been identified as able to beat others on both quality and cost – and has benefited accordingly, with this information fed to other plants within the group. One respondent used to buy the majority of components within 100 km of its plant, but now goes further afield – including major purchase items such as bodies and bogies from 500 km distance or more – as he now has internal suppliers within the group who are able to offer better quality and prices than were available in the local area.

Both respondents make it clear that intensity of competition among component suppliers has been fierce. This has led in some instances to outsourcing operations which the unit formerly did itself, either as part of the internal rationalization which has occurred as a result of merger or acquisition, or simply by buying in components.

Both respondents confirm that improved innovation and quality have been at least as important in developing external relationships with suppliers/partners as have lower costs. The need to develop designs quickly to meet specific tender opportunities means that speed of response is an important quality of service measure for component suppliers. Developing relationships with identified leaders in specific fields has helped at least one of the respondents to improve its competitive capability in this respect. 'We would like to share development cost and speed up our response to design change needs; if we can delegate part of the design job to a key supplier, then we can deal with customers faster.' But both respondents are looking for the majority of their key supplier or strategic alliance relationships at firms within the country where they have their own main design capability. Proximity is seen to be a factor which helps rapid service and good understanding. As one respondent said, 'We prefer key suppliers to speak not just the same language, but the same local dialect.'

A.1.5. Role of the single market

There is no doubt that our respondents believe the single market measures – mainly harmonization of standards and opening up of public procurement – have had an impact on the operation of the market for rail stock. However, their perception is that these have not been the most important factors behind the drive to achieve production scale economies, dynamic scale economies, and external economies in supply of components – all of which have occurred.

In their view, the pressure to realize economies – both from scale and from more efficient methods of working – has come about primarily because the industry has continued to feel the effects of global competition, in a world market where Europe has for long been leader. The benefits of standards harmonization have been slow to be realized, partly because of the dominant role of national network engineers in setting procurement specifications. Only now, with additional commercial pressures on train operators and purchasers, are train builders able to take the initiatives necessary to achieve all the available design and production economies.

However, it is difficult to accept that an industry which has seen such dramatic real reduction in the prices and costs of its output – at the same time as major moves towards concentration – has not achieved those economies at least to some degree because competition has driven the greater scale of enterprises. Both of the respondent companies are clearly aware of the threat of greater potential – and actual – competition within their main national markets as a result of harmonized standards and more open procurement. They both rate this additional competition within the EU as having the greatest impact in prompting the exploitation of production, dynamic and external economies.

However, as one respondent said, 'The concentration process was essential to enable us to meet international competition. It is certainly arguable that the mergers and acquisitions which made this possible would have been much more difficult to achieve if there had not been a single market to guarantee the free movement of capital, and free movement of people and skills'.

If this view is correct, then by facilitating the mergers which have occurred, the single market programme may have given the rail stock industry in Europe an opportunity to develop its position further. There is still relatively strong competition between EU producers, provided there are limits to further concentration, and the groupings which have emerged are taking advantage of the scope available to learn best practice from their different component parts. Certainly if the structure had remained as fragmented as it was in the early 1980s, EU firms would have found it difficult to respond in a market where both costs of technical development, and the costs of conducting business with a more complex customer base, are rising.

A.2. Pharmaceuticals

A.2.1. Market context

Demand trends

The world pharmaceutical market is dominated by Europe, the US and Japan; however, growth is much higher in the developing world.

Pharmaceuticals companies today are addressing four trends facing their industry: increased world-wide competition largely due to new technology, increased downward pressure on prices and profits from governments reducing healthcare spending, rising R&D costs and increased market harmonization. The two most common strategies for dealing with these trends are acquisition of other pharmaceuticals companies (and expanding into the OTC market; e.g. Glaxo's acquisition of Wellcome, American Home Products' purchase of Cyanamid in the US and the Swiss company Roche's purchase of the US's Syntex) and the acquisition of drug distributors (e.g. Merck, SmithKline Beecham and Eli Lilly – see Table A.2.1), a strategy which is more common in the US.

Additionally, many pharmaceuticals companies are focusing increasingly on the development of self-medication products, responding to the changing behaviour of patients. Some are even producing their own generic versions of popular drugs in order to limit sales losses after patents expire.

Increasing pressure on prices (mostly from European governments and changes in national reimbursement systems) is having an impact on pharmaceutical research. Greater emphasis is now being placed on therapy-oriented medicines which respond to broad medical needs and have a large potential market. In some instances, companies are finding it more efficient to separate their research and development functions.

Until the 1990s drugs companies largely concentrated on providing drugs. This decade's pressure from governments and insurance companies intent on controlling healthcare costs has likewise placed pressure on pharmaceutical companies. Drugs account for less than 20% of the world's $2,000 bn expenditure on healthcare, so pharmaceutical companies have recently been moving into the other 80% of the market by integrating pharmaceuticals with hospital and doctor services. These alliances provide 'disease management services'. The intention is to help co-ordination and continuity of patient care, improve cost incentives for early diagnosis and preventative measures, and make measurement of the quality of healthcare easier. They may also play a direct role in controlling costs in combination with a capitation system of paying for care (whereby healthcare providers are paid not according to the number and kind of treatments performed, but on a flat fee per head of population basis). Disease management packages in areas such as diabetes and cancer could help the setting of that fee by encapsulating all aspects of treating a disease and giving it a single price tag.

This strategy is not, however, being adopted by all pharmaceutical companies. Some have chosen to affirm their future in the discovery and marketing of new drugs (e.g. Glaxo's purchase of Wellcome). It is predicted that the pharmaceuticals industry of 2000 will be split into two camps: research-driven drugs companies and diversified suppliers of healthcare [*Financial Times*, 25 April 1995].

Table A.2.1. The pharmaceutical industry in 2000

Research-driven drugs companies	Research-driven medical products companies	Research-driven healthcare companies	Unreconstructed conglomerates
Glaxo Wellcome	Pfizer	Merck	Bayer
Astra	Sandoz	Eli Lilly	BASF
Amgen	Roche	SmithKline Beecham	
Rhône-Poulenc Rorer	Bristol Myers Squibb	Zeneca	

Source: *FT*, 25 April 1995.

Concentration

Pharmaceutical manufacturers generally do not compete in all therapeutic classes of products; most focus their efforts on a small number of classes, due to the huge resources necessary to cover more than four or five therapeutic classes successfully. There exists strong competition in the pharmaceuticals market both within Europe and worldwide. In the early 1990s no single drugs company had a dominant position in the market: none had a world market share of more than 4%, and the top ten producers had just a 22% world market share based on turnover. In 1991 the pharmaceutical company selling the greatest amount in the EU market held only a 4% share. The second and third largest companies had shares only marginally smaller. Together the three held less than a 12% EU market share. The top ten accounted for under a third. [Johnson, 1993].

Table A.2.2. Market shares of leading corporate groups, 1990

Country	Five leading corporate groups (%)
Belgium	22.9
France	30.5
Germany	19.1
Italy	21.1
Luxembourg	27.5
Netherlands	27.8
Spain	18.2
UK	29.6
Japan	22.6
USA	28.7

Source: Johnson, *European Industries*, 1993.

These data suggest that the EU pharmaceuticals market is not very concentrated in terms of sales. Even in the most concentrated market, France, the top five firms held less than a one-third market share. So neither is there much support for the notion that national pharmaceutical markets are highly concentrated.

Mergers and acquisitions and strategic alliances

Pharmaceutical managers responding to a survey of expectations in 1990[8] expected future consolidation in the industry through mergers and acquisitions of SMEs realigning themselves to prepare for the single market. They did not, however, believe that EU market integration would be the catalyst for consolidation in the first tier of the industry (large multinationals). The results of the study indicated that global trends rather than regional integration was the driver for mega-mergers in the industry.

Since most large pharmaceutical companies dominate only a few pharmaceutical market segments, many are finding mergers or acquisitions increasingly attractive in order to meet the changing market. In addition, collaboration between firms and investment by large pharmaceutical companies in local R&D and/or manufacturing is helping to create competitive research industries. Marketing agreements and other joint venture programmes are providing greater development opportunities for all parties involved. The following table details the largest mergers and acquisitions that have occurred world-wide over the past few years among companies of the same nationality and cross-border.

M&As appear to have been quite common among the multinational pharmaceutical companies. However, Pfizer, the third largest US drugs company, believes it is possible to cut costs and improve R&D without using acquisitions by downsizing across the company, combining financial services through Europe, through Asia and in the US, and rapidly introducing new technologies by surrounding itself with a ring of biotechnology alliances.

In 1994 the chief executive of SmithKline Beecham predicted that another wave of mergers and acquisitions would change the pharmaceuticals industry, as mid-sized companies succumbed to larger competitors better able to compete with developments in the healthcare industries. In consequence, he predicted that many manufacturing sites and hundreds of distribution centres would close as part of restructuring programmes following acquisitions. Purchases would lay the ground for transformation into broad-based suppliers of human healthcare whose customers pay for healthcare, not doctors.

---

[8]   Chaudhry et al, 'The pharmaceutical industry and European integration', *European Management Journal*, Vol. XII, No. 4, Dec. 1994.

Table A.2.3. Mergers and acquisitions in the pharmaceuticals sector world-wide

Bidder	Target	Year	Value £
Merck (US)	Medco (US)	1993	3.8bn
Roche (CH)	Syntex (US)	1994	3.4bn
Sandoz (CH)	Gerber (US)	1994	2.4bn
SKB (UK)	Diversified pharmaceuticals	1994	1.4bn
Hoechst (D)	Marion Merrill Dow (US)	1994	4.6bn
Eli Lilly (US)	PCS (US)	1994	2.6bn
American Home Products (US)	Cyanamid (US)	1994	6.3bn
SKB (UK)	Sterling Winthrop (US)	1994	1.9bn
Glaxo (UK)	Wellcome (UK)	1995	9.0bn
Rhône-Poulenc Rorer (US)	Fisons (UK)	1995	1.7bn
Pharmacia (S)	Upjohn (US)	1995	8.4bn
Ciba (S)	Chiron (biotech, US)	1995	controlling interest
Glaxo (UK)	Affymax (mid-sized biotech)	1995	333m
Novartis	Ciba + Sandoz	1996	

Source: *Financial Times*, various.

Trade

The pharmaceutical industries of the EU differ widely among Member States. France and Germany accounted for 24% of the EU's ECU 67.9 bn market, the UK 18%, Italy 15% and Spain 7% (Remit). The UK and German pharmaceutical industries are largely self-sufficient, carrying out all stages of manufacture, supplying most of their own markets and exporting drugs and active materials. France differs somewhat in that its industry depends more on imports of materials. Likewise, Italy and Spain are major importers of active materials. Other Member States whose pharmaceutical industries are highly export-oriented but also import a high proportion of consumption are Belgium, Denmark, Ireland and the Netherlands.

American companies supply most of what they sell in the Member States of the EU by local manufacture. The US was the leader in discoveries of new medicines during the 1970s and 1980s. By the criterion of number of medicines introduced into major markets of the developed world, the US was still the leader but was followed closely by the EU. The success rate of the UK was particularly high and those of France and Italy quite low.

A.2.2. Overview of respondents' operations

The case study respondents included two executives of a major German pharmaceutical company and an executive of an American pharmaceutical multinational located in the UK. The Germany company maintained 100 sites across the EU responsible for all five of the following activities between 1981 and 1990: procurement, production, marketing, R&D, and training and recruitment. However, between 1991 and 1995 the company embarked on a centralization programme, particularly in the areas of procurement, production and R&D. This has brought the number of sites down to 80. The centralization trend is expected to become even more important over the next ten years and will encompass all five activities. In the past the company did not consider it necessary to have centralization in Europe because profitability was high in all countries. The benefits of economies of scale were simply not necessary. Additionally, national laws made it necessary to be physically present in all markets.

Over the past five years the company has increasingly entered into joint ventures all over Europe. Additionally, it has entered four new markets, including the building of subsidiaries with marketing and administrative functions. The company's alliances in other countries have mainly been driven by the need to market successful products in new markets where the company formerly had no presence. The most important drivers of these alliances have been the need to exploit economies of scale, and reductions in non-tariff barriers to trade. Over the next decade strategic alliances will become much more important, especially in the areas of production and marketing/distribution. Most of these alliances will probably be of a type which will cover several Member States.

The American firm had growth in European turnover of $500 m in the early 1980s, rising to $700 m later in the decade, to $1 bn in the first half of the 1990s. It has had, and continues to have, an R&D presence in every European market. The firm has entered into no new EU markets in the 1980s or 1990s. The company embarked on strategic alliances in marketing and distribution in the 1980s, but this strategy changed in the 1990s when alliances were more in the area of R&D. Today the company is entering into more alliances with SMEs and these asymmetrical alliances are growing in number. The most important reason given for entering these alliances is increased competition in the company's markets. Less important have been higher costs in R&D, and of no influence at all has been reductions in non-tariff barriers to trade resulting from the SM programme.

Factors driving dynamic EOS

In general, a European pharmaceutical company's R&D facilities are widely scattered but its discovery research is highly concentrated in the firm's country of origin. The typical subsidiary centre does local development work or clinical testing. Concentration in R&D is expected to take place slowly, as with production. The SM programme is not thought to have much impact on strategies for innovation – other factors such as scientific opportunities and labour resources are more important. As with production, downward pressure on prices and mergers have had a larger impact.

With regard to economies of scale in marketing and sales, companies have different sales forces for different audiences, e.g. general practitioners versus specialists, and sometimes for different products. If mergers lead to the elimination of overlapping products then sales forces can be reduced as well.

In contrast to the opinion of other pharmaceutical executives, those from the German company cited the most important factors driving dynamic economies of scale as single market effects, including the free movement of capital and people and harmonized technical standards. The liberalization of public procurement has not been a factor. Other minor factors include homogenous market needs and common marketing approaches.

The factors of highest significance driving dynamic economies of scale for the American multinational have been increased competition and increasing minimum scale for R&D. Of lesser significance, but still factors, have been scale economies in R&D driven by common customers, and economies in marketing from common marketing approaches. Another market driver has been increasing minimum scale for marketing/advertising. Cost drivers in the form of country factor costs differences and communication/personnel efficiency differences have been somewhat important in driving scale economies in R&D. The single market effects have been important in the area of economies in personnel organization through the free movement of people. Scale economies in marketing have been driven by harmonized technical standards to a certain degree.

Knowledge transfer between operations in national markets has occurred in the areas of production and marketing for the German company. Between 1991 and 1995 external consultants and internal facilitators have assisted in this transfer in the area of production. During the same time period, external consultants, internal facilitators, common datacommunications and shared training have all helped in the area of marketing, particularly in market research.

For the American multinational, knowledge transfer has occurred in many key activities. In procurement this has come about through reporting systems to transfer development ideas. In production, knowledge transfer has come through internal facilitators, reporting systems and common IT systems. In marketing it has occurred through shared training, and in personnel and training it has come about through reporting systems.

The scope of activities of the German company with regard to marketing approaches and channels, technical diversity, range of products/services and skills of new or newly trained staff did not change in the survey period.

The American multinational, on the other hand, has indeed changed its scope of activities. In its range of marketing approaches and channels used, the company has narrowed its focus. In the area of technical diversity and range of products/services offered it has also narrowed focus on fewer therapeutic areas due to increasing global competition and reduced pharmaceutical spending at national level. With regard to the range of skills of new or newly trained staff, however, the company has increased its range with 'less people doing more' facilitated by the increasingly important role of IT.

The benefits of dynamic economies of scale reaped by the American multinational have been cost reduction in procurement, production and personnel development, better quality in procurement, production, marketing and R&D development and greater innovation in marketing, production and R&D development.

Influence of external economies of scale

The German company has not experienced any input cost changes, nor did it therefore report any benefits gained from increased external economies of scale.

The American multinational's cost structure changed between the first half of the 1980s and the first half of the 1990s. Marketing and selling costs increased from 28% of total cost to 30%, and R&D increased from 10% to around 15.5%. However, some unit input costs have declined. Costs of agents and distributors in the EU declined 20% between 1981 and 1986, and declined a further 6% by 1991. Local labour costs have also dropped – by 10% during the early 1980s, and by a further 5.6% during the late 1980s. Driving these changes has been increased competition among suppliers and distributors. Of somewhat lesser importance have been reductions in non-tariff barriers to trade resulting from the SM programme, and increased geographic proximity of suppliers and distributors to the company's operations. Increased scale and buying power in the company's own operations has been of some importance, but not a great deal.

The greatest benefit the American multinational has gained from increased external economies of scale has been market penetration via strategic alliances, closely followed by innovation in products/services and processes, also through alliances. Of some but lesser importance have been cost reduction of minor inputs, increases in product and service quality and more efficient geographic location of activity.

Role of the single market

In 1995 EAG provided financial support for a follow-up survey of pharmaceutical company executives along the same lines as the 1990 survey reported in Chaudhry et al [1994]. This survey asked participants to identify any strategic issues related to regional integration that have affected the pharmaceutical industry. Some of the strategies mentioned which also encompass the possibility of reaping greater economies of scale included monitoring the potential for vertical and horizontal integration of wholesale distribution in the EU, seeking R&D synergies with other firms, rationalizing production facilities, changing the organizational structure of the firm (i.e. to restructure the firm from a decentralized to centralized approach), developing more co-marketing and co-licensing agreements, and creating one pan-European tradename.

The single market programme's reductions in non-tariff barriers will mean increased competition for the German company, which plans to cope via intensive use of strategic alliances in future. Other factors which will become increasingly important, although they have not been in the past, include homogeneous market needs, common customers, common marketing approaches, increasing minimum sale for production and R&D, country factor costs differences and public procurement liberalization, all of which the SM programme is expected to facilitate.

The single market programme has been of some importance to the American multinational in the areas of personnel organization (through the free movement of people/skills) and in marketing (through harmonized technical standards). Pan-European marketing has improved the competitive performance of the company, and increased production efficiency has come about through opportunities for rationalization which the SM programme has afforded in reductions in non-tariff barriers.

Numerous non-tariff barriers to trade in the EU formerly resulted in a highly fragmented European pharmaceuticals market. Differences in marketing authorization rules and different classification systems among Member States created technical barriers which have been eliminated through the single market programme. A fully integrated EU pharmaceutical market requires, however, the further harmonization of national health systems, which today have different levels of price controls and reimbursable products. With the elimination of these market distortions many more pharmaceutical companies will respond to the SM, particularly SMEs. Large companies have responded to globalization trends through M&As. But increased EU harmonization is likely to increase cross-border alliances within the EU among medium-sized pharmaceutical companies.

Additionally, peripheral Member States are expected to become increasingly important as investment locations. Production facilities are expected to decline in number as companies gain the benefits of increased scale economies through fewer production sites. Factors which may impede this outcome are unfavourable local reactions at a time of relatively high unemployment, and national health systems which are still in a position to express their displeasure through cutting prices, refusing price increases or insisting on low prices for new products.

A.3. Computer equipment

A.3.1. Market trends 1980–95

The radical change in the market for computer equipment over this period is from a supply situation dominated by relatively few international producers, for whom equipment was the primary source of revenue and profitability, to one where competition for hardware is much more fragmented, and leading producers are attempting to make service and systems integration their major source of income. As one company contact said, 'We used to give software and service away to sell the equipment; as the hardware becomes more competitive the priority has been learning how to market and create value from them'. Leading equipment suppliers now derive a substantial part of their income from sales and service – in some cases over 50%.

Although total EU output of equipment has approximately doubled in current prices over the period, employment has remained within 15% of its starting position, and has – over the last couple of years – fallen below the level of the early 1980s. Real output is difficult to measure, because of the fast changing nature of outputs, but an industry 'rule of thumb' since 1990 is that the price of computing power has halved every 18 to 24 months. While exports have increased, the net trade balance has become steadily more negative as more equipment has been sourced offshore, in large measure by EU-owned firms.

Within the growing market total, there has been a strong swing away from large systems (where demand is in absolute decline) to mid-range 'open' systems and personal computers. There has also been a significant increase in the datacommunications component of sector demand, reflecting the increasingly blurred boundary between computer equipment and telecommunications.

As the sector has become larger, more closely related to telecommunications and increasingly dependent upon service, the strategic response of most producers has been to focus on the market sector, or the part of the value chain, in which each has competitive advantage. Concentration in each European national market where data are available – measured as the share of the top ten vendors – has steadily declined through the 1990s.

The competitive position of companies active in the European market is, of course, dominated by the global marketplace. Product standards in most sectors of the hardware market are effective world-wide (led from North America), and most large international competitors are US based. US dominance of the world market is less pronounced than it was in the early

1980s, being partly shared now with Japan. However IBM, HP, DEC, Unisys, and their suppliers and partners still exercise a strong hold on the global market, and account for the major part of EU production.

A.3.2. Cost structure and scale

Computers and office machinery is an industrial sector where the PIMS database contains sufficient observations to draw conclusions on cost structure and its sensitivity to scale. The evidence – taken from markets world-wide rather than limited to Europe – shows that:

(a)   there are significant scale economies in manufacturing costs, and in process development costs, as a proportion of total business cost and per unit of output;

(b)   there are strong positive correlations between relative scale and the proportion of business cost devoted to product development, to advertising and salesforce, and to business co-ordination.

Production and process scale economies have helped to achieve the continuing fall in output prices mentioned above. The fact that larger companies undertake a disproportionate share of marketing and R&D suggests that, normally, it is the larger enterprises in a competitive arena which are better able to bear the costs of product development, and more likely to incur the costs of bringing the results of such development to market. This is *prima facie* evidence for the importance of dynamic economies in this sector on an international scale. Since sales/marketing and R&D costs typically account for up to 20% of sales revenue for businesses in this sector, they also have the potential to benefit from simple scale economies.

However, the market evidence is that concentration is declining, for the EU as a whole and in each national market. This suggests that the dynamic scale economies achieved through specialization, as the range of applications in the market proliferates, are more important than straight production economies of scale.

A.3.3. Overview of European operations

In the early 1980s, the European IT market was dominated – as it still is – by US companies, and a limited number of European national challengers. American companies were usually organized on a pan-Europe basis, with manufacture of specific modules located to take advantage of development subsidies provided by governments, and to optimize operating costs across Europe. Typically the American competitors' European operations were vertically integrated (or linked), co-ordinated across Europe, and active in all application sectors.

At the same period, in the early 1980s, all European-owned competitors were focused heavily on their national markets. Copying the American majors, they also tended to be vertically integrated, to manufacture at a number of sites mostly within their 'home' countries and to offer a range of products to all sectors of their national markets. Activity outside their domestic bases was limited. Public sector procurement was what most of them depended on for the bulk of their profitable sales.

In the early 1980s the competition from truly international companies on innovation and costs – led by IBM, which was globally at least ten times the size of the largest European – began to force a number of changes. European 'national' companies made operating losses because they could match neither the rate of new product development nor the production economies of scale. They began to realize that they must grow or specialize – preferably both. ICL in the UK, which had been formed by merger during the 1970s, chose early to specialize. It identified that it could not remain a fully integrated producer, and exited from chip production and printer manufacture. However, in order to sustain a position in the PC sector it acquired the PC and network operations of Nokia Data, mainly in Scandinavia, in 1990. Siemens of Germany, on the other hand, remained in almost all sectors, and became European leader in peripherals, acquiring Nixdorf in the late 1980s.

At the same time, our respondent companies reduced costs as fast as they were able, in order to compete. One achieved a 30% reduction in employees over the period 1981–86, partly by outsourcing whole operations and partly by efficiency improvement in manufacture and R&D. It also, at the same time, began restructuring its marketing operations into a 'vertical market' approach, specializing in specific products and customer types where it had a strong position in its home market – and looking for ways to internationalize these strong positions. It entered most European national markets, but not for every product. Having set the target of achieving at least 50% of its revenue outside its domestic base, it had – by 1995 – achieved effective presence for its 'world leading' sector products in all but two EU markets.

However, the tests which the business applied to its strategic objectives in this period were not specifically related to European presence. The competition standards were set by global companies, based in the US. For this reason, at least one of the company's international businesses, with the majority of its sales in Europe, is headquartered in the US to give it a window on US market trends and technology.

Structural changes in the 1980s in the companies we have spoken to were largely aimed at achieving 'critical mass' and at focusing on areas where competitive advantage could be achieved. In addition, there was a great deal of attention paid to removing low level cost, with some functions – including standard product manufacture – moved offshore. In the 1990s the pressure for cost competitiveness has continued this process – for example, IBM has outsourced all property management activity to a specialist company – but has also forced more sharing of high level cost.

ICL has, for example, formed strategic alliances with Microsoft on security software development, and with Sun Microsystems on open systems development. It has, in addition, set up its contract manufacturing organization, D2D, as a stand-alone entity, capable of being floated off from the rest of the company. Since D2D also supplies other vendors, this represents a form of 'internalized' external scale economy. IBM's separation of its disk drive subsidiary Xyratex, again supplying other system vendors, represents a similar phenomenon, permitting scale economies in production of modules to be realized despite the increasing fragmentation of vendors present in the IT market. However, it is worth noting that one group of lower level 'module subcontractors', the producers of assembled printed circuit boards – which expanded significantly in the late 1980s – has found the market increasingly difficult as higher value module producers have become more active in the market.

A.3.4. Factors driving dynamic economies of scale

Importance

In terms of hardware standards, the market has been transformed over the 15 years since 1980. In the 1970s European producers 'lived grace and favour of the American majors', in the words of one of our respondents. With proprietary hardware and software systems, the large integrated producers had a substantial advantage in setting the competitive framework for smaller players. The arrival of open systems, and the work which the European Commission carried out to lead the way in setting standards for products, was important because it 'created a product area in which scale was less important', and where smaller equipment and software suppliers could compete on a common hardware platform, specializing in a specific area to gain advantage. Without the lead taken by the EC, with European producers on open systems in the early 1980s, it is likely in the view of one of our respondents that fewer EU-owned companies would have survived to the 1990s.

In virtually all other areas covered by our questionnaire, the pressures for exploitation of scale economies are driven at a global level rather than within Europe. Market factors are approaching global scale. Customer needs for hardware are more or less homogeneous, except perhaps in the public sector and certain sectors of the consumer market; large companies tend to adopt purchasing strategies for IT which are at least European if not global, and marketing approaches are similar across the world.

Competitive forces are also global; in application markets, such as retail systems for example, there are national 'lead' markets in which it is essential for major global suppliers to be present. These are the countries in which retailers are developing new approaches, and set the standards for point of sale systems elsewhere – even though retailers are for the most part not global customers. Production scale for most 'boxes' is set globally, although modular specialization enables sub-global scale vendors to compete in many areas. And most markets are now developed to the stage where global leaders in each application or product segment are present in the majority of markets. There are still significant EU producers which have over 50% of their revenue in their original 'home base' national market, but this is usually supported by major outsourcing of components and modules to third countries.

Country factor cost differences within Europe are relatively small, certainly smaller now than the 1970s and early 1980s when capital subsidies and low wage rates made some countries (e.g. Ireland) particularly attractive. The wage rate content of manufacturing plant costs is now significantly lower than it was then. What is more important, according to respondents, is the ability of managers to use people and assets flexibly, to provide good service and to respond quickly to innovation.

There is some indication that dynamic external economies determined by capability in these areas have begun to develop in the EU's two most IT intensive economies – Ireland and the UK. These two countries have also probably benefited from another external economy – shared language with the world's largest IT market in the US, which has made them a more attractive site for work on software and data processing. This advantage is now threatened by the Indian sub-continent.

Knowledge transfer

There is no doubt that the response of all European-owned manufacturers in taking advantage of the opportunities from scale economies in the 1980s lagged behind that of the American – and even the Japanese – producers. The Europeans were too concerned with national market structures, and with defending positions in specific niches – including public procurement monopolies. The 'outsiders' were able to set up organizational structures which reflected the existence of a single market, to exploit scale economies, transfer know-how from their home base and also between operations in different EU countries. The UK was, for example, the international base of IBM's transaction systems business from the 1970s right through this period, transferring knowledge to operating units around the world, on an organizational model developed to deal with the large single market of North America. IBM's declared strategy in this early stage of single market development was for Europe to be operated as one organization, with production located in the best place to take advantage of local skills and resources, with units supplying the whole continent.

European-based firms, by comparison, left it relatively late to set up organizational structures which were truly European, transferring knowledge and best practice from one centre to another. ICL's programme to train a European cadre of managers did not begin until 1985, and it has taken until the mid-1990s for the majority of 'line of business' managers in the company to come from outside the UK. In addition, organizational structures for pan-European business units to ensure coherent marketing approaches did not evolve until 1993. Other EU-based companies are probably less well advanced in terms of coverage and systems.

Benefits from dynamic scale economies

One respondent identified the impact on R&D costs of scale through focus and specialization as very significant; a reduction from the mid-1980s to the mid-1990s from an average 12% of revenue to around 6% had been achieved. This was partly due to sharing with a much larger international partner, and partly by focusing on specific product and market segments. It was also assisted by acquisition, using know-how from an acquired EU company to extend capability at relatively low cost in a specific market at the same time as acquiring share.

There have also been savings made through vertical market focus by some vendors in sales and marketing costs. In any event, the commoditization of much equipment has left some producers unable to recover these costs in their prices. But in the majority of companies, there has been a clearer focus of sales and marketing effort on vertical end use markets which has helped to improve the value of this effort to end users. In this sense, the benefit of focus has been realized through a better quality package of service surrounding the product.

The process through which technical sales people have been transformed into specialist consultants has been important for a number of IT companies. In many cases they have changed their marketing organizations from a salesforce incentivized on value of equipment sold, to consultants supplying value added services through systems integration – often buying in 'boxes' from other manufacturers.

Both IBM and ICL undertake major projects in which their systems integrators have supplied solutions with no own-make equipment involved. From the impressive growth and strong performance of some of the specialist IT service companies, it seems likely that economies of scale spanning the marketing of services and the marketing of equipment are relatively limited.

Diversity and scope of activity

The trend away from integrated IT equipment supply has already been described. Even where a company, such as IBM, retains virtually full range capability as a vendor, it has still set out to specialize its delivery units within the organization. Specialization in equipment and software development, and in the consulting service which accompanies it, is essential to efficient and effective development.

For the European producers, most of whom are working from much lower scale – both absolute and relative to their target markets – specialization is essential, both in end-user needs targeted and in the technologies which each company chooses to retain as its core competence. Without such focus, minimum scale for development and marketing would not be possible for them.

A.3.5. Influence of external economies of scale

As discussed above, the industry has generated its own external scale economies through 'spinning off' module manufacture from the main computer equipment companies, and also through shared component suppliers. In a number of component areas, effective production and dynamic economies of scale are very great indeed, with one or two suppliers managing to defend global market shares in excess of 50%. But these economies are available on a global basis, not just in Europe.

The 'silicon glen' phenomenon in Scotland and its equivalent in Ireland, initially created by government incentives and cheap labour, has begun to create and feed on external scale economies. Following the establishment in Ireland of assembly plants by most of the PC manufacturers, including Apple, Dell, Gateway, DEC and others, Ireland has become the preferred base for a number of other outside investors entering Europe. This preference is based not just on the fact that customers and suppliers in the IT industry itself are close at hand, but also on external economies in sectors such as packaging, since packaging and logistics make up an important part of the cost structure of PC assembly.

In addition, the establishment of Intel and Microsoft – the key component supplier and the most important software systems developer – in Ireland has strengthened the country's position. Microsoft in particular requires packaging and logistics expertise, and it uses the same type of customer support mechanisms – help lines and call centres – which are used by PC suppliers. With lower cost telecommunications, Ireland and Scotland are both becoming increasingly important centres for this type of support operation.

Role of the single market

In the view of our respondents, the impact of the single market on European producers has been significant, but it was felt relatively early. It is certainly argued by some of them that without the prospect of a single market the American suppliers who treated Europe as one from the 1970s onwards would have found it more difficult to apply North American business models across the EC. This example – and the competition – set by the inward investors eventually led the more conservative and nationally focused European companies to follow suit.

However, the market pressures which have been exerted on European producers – both indigenous and those owned by the US and Japan – have been essentially global. The last area of the market to free up its purchasing behaviour from protectionist tendencies, the public sector, has certainly been influenced by single market legislation, but the first moves were felt in the UK very early in the 1980s as a result of GATT principles being applied early by the national government.

The product area in which the EC has played a leading role, and made a significant impact on the development of the European IT industry, is open systems. The BISON group in the early 1980s, and the Esprit programme, led to joint definition by experts and producers of the elements of open systems, which informed the Commission's work on standards in this area. As one respondent said, 'This agreement gave the European producers who were prepared to enter the open systems market a breathing space – a short period in which they could compete on equal terms with companies which would otherwise have a major scale advantage. The experience showed us how important it was to share development costs, to be more open and solve problems together'.

A.4. Chocolate

A.4.1. Market trends 1980–95

The European market for cocoa and chocolate products has grown steadily in real value over the period, apart from a small decline in value in 1992 which was recovered by 1994. Production volume, however, has increased year on year both in the EU as a whole, and in its biggest market, Germany. In the next largest, the United Kingdom and France, production has also increased significantly, although statistics for the UK are complicated by changes in definitions affecting chocolate covered biscuits. A major growth area for chocolate producing companies in Europe over the last six years has been Eastern Europe, which has absorbed both a large volume of exports and considerable investment in production capacity.

In none of the EU countries, except perhaps Portugal, has there been any indication of a sustained decline in production. Nor has there been any closing of the 'consumption gap' between southern country markets – exemplified by Spain and Italy – where per capita consumption is less than 2 kg per annum, and northern countries – Germany, Scandinavia, the UK – where consumption is typically over 6 kg per annum.

The chocolate products market in most countries is relatively concentrated, at its highest in the UK where Cadbury, Nestlé and Mars account for over 80% of consumption. Other major companies, including Ferrero and Jacob Suchard/Philip Morris, hold somewhat less concentrated positions in France and Italy. Only in Germany is there a significantly more fragmented structure, partly due to the stronger position of private label brands. In the smaller markets, particularly those which are more recent EU members, the typical position is of a few local producers competing with two or three international companies in a relatively concentrated market structure.

During the late 1980s and early 1990s the effect of competition from the large scale brand owners has significantly changed the structure of the market. The acquisitions of companies whose chocolate sales are focused on one or two countries, by European or American owned firms with a continental approach to the market, have continued. The larger firms are attempting to secure their position in a concentrating European scale market for globally marketed brands; at the same time acquisitions by smaller regional firms seek to bolster their positions in defensible national markets with specific tastes.

During the last three years, in addition to this process, there has been accelerating investment in acquisitions in Eastern Europe, and further afield. In 1993/94 the top five chocolate producing firms – Nestlé, Cadbury, Suchard/Philip Morris, Mars and Ferrero – made over 20 acquisitions, of which nine were in former Communist countries, and four were in the

Americas. Not all of these acquisitions were in chocolate. Some reflected the increasing interdependence of the chocolate and ice cream markets, following the launch by most producers of chocolate bars, in the early 1990s, of ice cream bars under the same brand names and aimed at the same consumers.

The extension of brand names in this way reflects the impact of international marketing campaigns, particularly aimed at younger consumers. High levels of TV advertising have started to change the consumption patterns of younger consumers, even in some of the smaller national markets with more differentiated traditional products.

Although the spread of strongly branded products has continued to concentrate national markets, the scope for production economies of scale may be affected by the existing Chocolate Directive (73/241/EEC, as amended). This permits national governments to set standards for chocolate recipes for production in their territories – so that a Mars bar made in Germany may not have the same composition as one made in the UK or the Netherlands, and the scope for replicating production practices may be constrained.

The respondents in this case study cover a large producer with global brands and a strong presence in most European national markets, and a strong regional firm in one of the countries which has more recently acceded to the EU. In both cases the respondents were consultants who had worked inside the companies on strategic issues over a considerable period. One was an employee–consultant, the other independent of the firm.

A.4.2. Overview of respondents' operations 1980–95

The 'European' scale firm

The firm with European scale had begun the period with some form of operation – manufacturing or a marketing organization – in almost every EU country. Manufacture in Germany/Austria was added in the late 1970s, bringing the total to five chocolate manufacturing sites. Over the period production has risen by around 40% in volume terms, while the total number of employees has reduced by 20%, a physical productivity increase of around 70%. This increase in output has been achieved by increasing the number and capacity of lines at selected sites. Some technology changes have helped increase line output, and capital productivity, by way of improved process control; but some parameters of chocolate lines – particularly those determined by physical heating and cooling rates – constrain possible advances.

Product selling price per tonne for the firm has moved in line with inflation in the largest EU markets. Over the period the number of principal sites involved in chocolate production in the EU has remained unchanged, and the major expansion of capacity at new sites has occurred in eastern Europe. Despite lower labour costs in the east, this has not been a significant factor in determining production location because factory labour costs account for such a small proportion of total costs for this firm. The organization of sales and distribution has been largely unchanged – with national selling teams – and the location of R&D has not significantly changed. The only aspects of the organization of production which have changed over the period are centralization of procurement to fewer centres, and the establishment of a European graduate recruitment and training cadre.

The reason for this relative stability is that the firm set out during the 1960s and 1970s to build its organization on a European basis, with common products where possible (although this was sometimes hampered by the legacy of acquired brands). It also had significant in-house expertise in plant design and construction, which tended to make it both self-reliant and co-ordinated in its approach to products and capacity.

During the late 1980s and early 1990s the firm organized itself more explicitly on a European basis, with pan-European reporting structures – but without changing the location of many of its activities. Thus, for example it now has a single R&D structure in Europe, but R&D is still located in four countries. In a number of functional areas the evidence available within the firm suggests that co-ordination costs have shown some increases as a result of these changes.

The 'regional' firm

Volume for the firm has been more or less static since the late 1980s. Production was originally based in three countries, then four (all western European but not all within the EU), and now the firm has reduced the number of plants. It has also made an acquisition in one of the 'near east European' countries – both to secure a base in the local market and to gain access to lower cost production capacity. Its procurement has moved from being strictly national for each plant to a European basis, and major economies on input prices for sugar have been achieved. The firm's marketing activities have continued to centre around its strong brands in its home markets but have also expanded into one or two neighbouring markets, particularly into the German supermarket brand area. It has also created and retained a position in distribution to airport and duty free outlets across certain parts of Europe.

Prices in its home markets have been significantly affected by the opening-up of tariff barriers and deregulation after accession to the EU. The very substantial premium which existed over large EU markets such as Germany and the UK – for some products, over 50% – have been quickly eroded by competition from producers of the major international branded products. While penetration of these products was at first relatively slow during the 1980s due to 'taste barriers', increased levels of advertising have changed buyer behaviour – and therefore much of the market growth has gone to these imported brands. The single market has therefore delivered substantial price reductions to consumers in these markets, and the profits of regional producers (including our respondent) have suffered accordingly.

A.4.3. Dynamic economies of scale

Key drivers and changes over the period

Although the European market for chocolate is far from homogeneous, the degree of similarity between national markets, the marketing approaches and the products offered, is much greater in 1996 than it was in 1980. In part this is because consumers are more mobile, and subject to more uniform lifestyles. But advertising, packaging, and the needs of retailers have also had an important impact. Advertising programmes for some products now have a common European format, sharing images between different countries and varying the soundtrack. Packaging for a significant range of products is also designed for a European market, with labelling in most EU languages, and meeting the different standards of national regulations on composition of chocolate. This permits identical images to be used in adverts. Since advertising for a pan-European producer typically accounts for around 5% to 8% of product value, and other sales and marketing costs for 4% to 6%, the impact of cost sharing in advertising and marketing can be significant.

Packaging approaches have also been used to increase the attractiveness of products, and economies of scale in creative approaches are available here. The impact of better pack design for Rowntree products after the acquisition by Nestlé was an important part of the added value from the takeover. In addition, the use of new packaging films and techniques has improved the shelf life and handling qualities of chocolate products from the retailers' point of view. The ability of producers to innovate in these areas, and to spread the benefits of such innovation across a number of national markets, is an increasingly important aspect of competitive advantage.

Retailers have made initial steps towards pan-European sourcing of chocolate products, some through operations in a range of countries, others through shared activity in international buying groups. The importance of store brand chocolate products in Germany – the largest single national market – reinforces this trend. The sourcing arrangements now permit retailers to ship products to take advantage of arbitrage between national markets, or to exert bargaining power to force price parity. These are the forces which have removed the price premiums in peripheral EU national markets which used to be protected.

There is no 'lead market' for innovation in the European chocolate industry; national tastes are still sufficiently different for new products to develop in various ways. However, innovations are probably more likely to occur in the 'high consumption' markets of the north, and some product transfers from the US appear in the UK first, perhaps because of shared language.

Increasing production scale has been brought about through stronger European competition between major companies, and costs have been reduced by increasing the number of lines per plant. As noted above, marketing and advertising costs have not increased as a proportion of sales value for the pan-European producers – but the absolute level of spend by these companies has increased as their share has grown. The threshold scale for effective advertising has therefore risen, and this is reflected in the increasing burden reported by smaller regional companies in matching the impact of the multinationals.

The pattern of competitive activity across Europe is certainly not uniform. Most of the big six are present in the majority of national markets, but the UK is a significant exception, since Suchard/Philip Morris and Ferrero are so far behind the other three.

Knowledge transfer

There are no significant factor cost differences or major efficiency differences which mark out specific areas or countries as cost leaders. Leading companies tend to exchange information between their national operations to take advantage of skills acquired and developed. Our pan-European respondent has had systems in place to achieve this since the early 1980s; reporting systems for procurement and manufacturing, internal facilitation systems for marketing, and the more recently developed European management cadre. In regional firms there seems to be no problem in exchanging skills between plants in different countries, as shown by the ability of our respondent to move products between plants without major problems.

Benefits from scale economies

We have already referred to scale economies in procurement and production achieved by our pan-European respondent, and similar – though less dramatic – economies have been available to regional producers. Both have benefited from liberalization of the sugar market, and those for other ingredients; both have increased their output per plant quite substantially – one by a 40% volume increase from the same number of plants, and the other from a reduction in the number of plants with constant output. Scale economies in costs at the plant level consist, according to our respondents, of a sharing of fixed administrative and logistics costs over a larger volume; this is usually achieved by grouping more lines in each plant.

The increase in competitive scope has increased MES, but because of the variety of products in the market, and the lack of homogeneity remaining between countries, an estimate of how much MES has increased, or of its level, is extremely difficult. For plants which are involved in production only, supplying private label products to supermarkets, high volume efficiently run plants are essential; but firm size can be much smaller as it does not have to maintain a critical mass of advertising and marketing expenditure.

Dynamic economies of scale in production – through intersite learning and transfer of practices – are reported by both our pan-European respondent and the regional firm, although for the latter it is relatively recent as a formal system.

Advertising and marketing economies are clearly significant in determining the strategies and the performance of respondent firms. It is important to recognize that advertising is only the visible half of costs in this area, and that for fast-moving consumer goods (FMCG) firms the costs of maintaining a sales and marketing organization to support in store display and distribution is usually just as important. Advertising is what prompts consumers to take the product from display; sales and marketing effort to put the product on display is a complementary – but equally expensive – activity.

Work recently completed (and as yet unpublished) with a dozen European FMCG producers on salesforce operation shows that economies of scale in salesforce costs·are very significant within countries, but not yet across national boundaries. The costs of operating a salesforce in a country are to a considerable extent fixed, and so salesforce cost as a proportion of total cost shows a strong negative correlation with output. None of these companies (which included our chocolate respondent) were yet able to operate truly automated sales order handling or customer service systems which crossed the important national boundaries. However, a number of them were very interested in being able to do this once a single currency was in place.

Development costs are quoted by our pan-European respondent as an area in which significant dynamic scale economies have been achieved over the last ten years. The ability to roll out new products across a number of markets, either simultaneously or in quick succession, has given the continental scale producers the scope to derive the maximum impact from R&D activity. It has become much easier to undertake innovation as a result of a unified structure, and particularly to take the big steps in new product introduction which are needed to gain advantage in market position.

A.4.4. Diversity and focus

Our two respondents provided a classic contrast in the position of high and low share businesses in response to this question. The regional company, since the opening up of the single market and stronger interest in its domestic market by pan-European firms, has concluded that it can no longer afford the marketing cost to support its full, pre-1990, range of products. It has therefore reduced its product range to focus on brand positions which are stronger, and which are proportionately cheaper to support. In addition, it has sought to develop its position in confectionery materials, as a supplier to other branded and catering product manufacturers. At the same time, it has sought to develop routes to market for finished consumer products which are less marketing intensive, including distribution to duty free shops, and expanding its presence in the store brand market. Having been affected by the eastward push of other large-scale European firms, it has had to strengthen its efforts in the east.

There are, by contrast, 'brand owners' in the market which are able to assemble relatively small, focused positions of premium products into major international businesses. For example Leaf, originally of Finland – which operates in other confectionery markets in addition to chocolate – has a range of brand positions, including Elizabeth Shaw, and a substantial US business. It is headquartered in the Netherlands and claims to be one of the top ten global confectionery companies. Leaf is an example of a type of consumer marketing company found in other product markets, built on a core competence in marketing, innovation and developing premium positions. Such skills are often transferable from one market to another irrespective of market barriers, because they do not necessarily depend on the physical movement of products. They do, however, depend upon the free movement of capital and people, and the effective protection of intellectual property and brands.

Our pan-European respondent, by contrast, shows a different pattern of behaviour, although at first sight there are some similarities. In the latter part of the 1980s the firm spent time and energy on simplifying and consolidating its product range, and on simplifying its marketing approaches to major retailers. This appears in part to have been a 'deck clearing' exercise to prepare for later expansion in other areas.

Since 1990 the firm has launched a major brand extension into ice cream, using the 'pull' advertising for chocolate products to assist the launch. Although there were various difficulties associated with this product diversification, mainly to do with access to channels of distribution, it has provided a significantly broader base over which to spread brand advertising costs. The firm has also pursued very strong geographical diversification into all the markets of eastern Europe, based on its European/global brands. The strength of these pan-European/global brands has given the company major advantages in media advertising, particularly given the spread of satellite media which cover larger areas, and the growing importance of brand exposure through international sporting events.

In the view of our respondent, ability to innovate successfully is the most important competence for the competitive performance of the firm, and the role of the single market has not changed this. However, the integration of European markets has increased the importance of marketing effectiveness relative to production efficiency. The responses given on behalf of the regional firm support this view of the increasing importance of marketing costs and capability, and the necessity to have strongly positioned, focused, brand positions.

External economies

In this area, our respondents are agreed that significant benefits have been achieved. In the early 1980s each country manager in our pan-European firm would find local partners for the supply of key materials, reflecting local regulations on chocolate recipes and local market conditions. Since 1994 a European approach has been adopted for the procurement of sugar and of dairy products, with some benefits to pricing, to process control, and to the control of working capital – although it is too early to judge the overall trade-off between operational benefits and co-ordination costs. The regional respondent has seen significant savings in materials costs – around 30% – as a result of a more open and deregulated market.

The approach of the two companies to strategic alliances to achieve economies is somewhat different. The pan-European firm has pursued a number of avenues, focusing on suppliers closer to its plants, using the scale and buying power of its operations, and also contracting out certain non-core operations. It has, for example, made more use of 'co-packers' as subcontractors for certain packaging operations. Its approach to packaging suppliers has also become significantly closer, with the expectation that producers of packaging material will take greater responsibility in the value chain, and retain ownership of the wrapping film until the point where it enters the packing machine. This transfer of responsibility can only be managed effectively if the firm concentrates on a limited number of suppliers.

For the regional firm, downstream alliances are more important. Focusing on specific outlets to market, either via store brands or duty free outlets, has been important in securing reductions in marketing costs.

A.4.5. Role of the single market

Our respondents are agreed – from opposite perspectives in the market – that the single market, together with deregulation, has achieved a significant reduction in the cost of materials for the chocolate industry, and that it has increased the importance of marketing as an international competitive weapon. The increase in producer scale has not reduced marketing costs as a proportion of total costs, but it has raised the ability of major internal suppliers to promote and benefit from strong brand positions.

The ability to sell products made in one factory all over Europe (subject to meeting national labelling regulations) has increased the ability of firms to achieve site economies of scale in production, although in practice our pan-European supplier which makes use of this ability double-sources most of its major products to ensure security of supply and flexibility in logistics. The remaining barrier to uniform products, in the shape of the Chocolate Directive which allows national governments to set recipe limits, may constrain companies, but not enough to hinder their ability to roll out product innovations across Europe with minimal delay.

Although the perspective of our pan-European respondent is that the single market programme has had relatively little effect on their operations, this is in the light of a strategic approach in which 'trade barriers are not seen as important to investment, and the structure of the European business is based upon an integrated approach'. Whether such an approach would have been possible without the framework provided by the movement towards a single market is more than questionable. Much of the company's European structure was put in place before the single market initiative, but on the assumption that the framework for movement of capital, people and products would be developed over the succeeding decade.

This pattern of pre-emptive investment in anticipation of being able to operate in an increasingly open market is observable in other product areas within the EU, and is now clearly visible in the near eastern European markets. Particularly in products where strong brand positions are an important driver of profitability, the need to enter markets ahead of the competition, to secure share and brand awareness advantage, has led to investment behaviour ahead of the measures which are designed to promote it. For our pan-European respondent this seems to be true; a European approach to manufacturing and marketing predated the 'official' single market programme by ten years. It is arguable that such pre-emptive investment was easier for companies which are the owners of global brands than for companies building up from, or amalgamating, national positions.

For our regional respondent, the impact of increased competition has forced the reduction of internal costs – partly through plant scale and partly through efficiency gains, as well as a critical re-examination of marketing costs. The strategic impact has been to encourage specialization on those products and market positions where customer preference is more clearly expressed, and on parts of the value chain where smaller scale is not a disadvantage.

A.5. Beer

A.5.1. Market trends

Demand trends

The market for beer in Europe is a relatively stable one, with overall volume demand growth of around 0.3% p.a. between 1980–93. Within this relatively static market there have been some national markets – particularly those where wine has traditionally been the dominant alcoholic drink, such as Spain – where beer demand has been faster than average. Others, such as Germany which is predominantly a beer market, have shown absolute decline of up to 3% p.a. In this sense the pattern of demand for alcoholic drinks across Europe has become marginally more homogeneous over the last 15 years, but very large differences remain.

Common patterns across the EU in terms of changing consumer behaviour include the move towards selling beer through retail grocery outlets as opposed to bars or specialist retailers, the shift towards lighter beers (including low alcohol beers) for health reasons, and the increasing role of 'fashion' beers such as those from South America and those imported from elsewhere. Thus, although overall demand in the EU has been virtually static, imports into ten out of the 12 national markets showed increases in volume terms over the period 1990 to 1994.

Exports, on the other hand, increased from every single national market except Luxembourg, reflecting the strong performance of EU producers not just in intertrade, but also in net exports to the rest of the world. Extra-EU exports increased by over 60% during the period, but still account for less than 10% of production.

Technology impact

Technology changes in the beer industry have shown effects in two areas. Firstly, the improvements in process control, which have made the operations of larger breweries more efficient – but have not necessarily increased the minimum economic scale of brewing operations since they have also, to some extent, benefited smaller units. There has been a reduction in the number, of breweries through a shift to larger scale in most countries, but a bigger reduction in the number of people employed per brewery.

Secondly, there have been significant changes in the technology used for packaging and distributing beer. Faster filling lines for bottles and cans have made it more economic to use these types of packaging, partly in response to the increased demand for products through supermarkets for home drinking. There has been substitution of these packaging and distribution methods for barrels and tankers in many countries.

Structural changes

In virtually every country there has been some degree of concentration over the period since 1980. However, the concentration pattern, and the share of the leading producer, varies enormously from country to country.

Table A.5.1. Producer pattern by national market

Country	Number of breweries	Production (mhl)	Growth p.a., 1980–89 (%)	Share of largest firm (%)	Market scale of largest firm (mhl)
Belgium/Luxembourg	102	14.7	-0.16	68	10.0
Denmark	17	9.5	1.25	53	5.0
France	27	20.8	-0.29	48	10
Germany	1281	115.4	-0.04	9	10.4
Greece	7	4.5	4.60	75	3.4
Ireland	7	6.9	0.95	60	4.1
Italy	19	11.7	2.50	39	4.6
Netherlands	16	20.4	2.00	33	6.7
Portugal	8	6.6	4.80	55	3.6
Spain	27	24.3	1.50	27	6.6
UK	95	56.7	-1.00	30	17.0
Total	1606	291.5	0.26	6	17.0

Sources: *Panorama of EU Industry*, ELRA, PIMS estimates.

As can be seen from the above table, the leading players in most countries enjoy a substantial domestic share of total national production, but the leading European producer (Heineken) only accounts for around 6% of the total beer market in Europe. Industry estimates suggest that Heineken now sells about 17 mhl of its beer throughout the major European markets. They are estimated to sell 5 mhl in Holland, 6 mhl in France, 4 mhl in Spain and 2 mhl in the UK. Interestingly the newly formed Scottish Courage now sells around the same volume of beer in Europe but almost all of this is in one country, the UK.

The major changes brought about through acquisitions have not been uniform across national markets. Companies such as Heineken (NL), Interbrew (B), Carlsberg (DK) and Danone (F) have been particularly active in developing their European positions. Over the period 1984 to 1996 Heineken's European sales have increased from around 12 mhl to 17 mhl, with some 12 mhl of this final volume in EU countries other than the Netherlands. In contrast the major brewers in the UK and Germany have been almost totally focused on sorting out their own national market structures.

Looking at the leading European companies gives a revealing picture. As can be seen from Table A.5.2 below, the top ten brewers in Europe account for around 42% of the market. Against this, on average, the top three companies in each country (Germany excepted) account for between 60%–75% of their own national markets. However, the total European market is starting to slowly concentrate as Heineken, Carlsberg and Interbrew develop their positions across national boundaries. It appears from our contact companies' perspectives that this trend seems likely to develop more rapidly. It may even start to show effects in Germany, up to now the most fragmented and isolated market in Europe.

Table A.5.2.   Production pattern by major firms

Company	EU output (mhl)	EU share (%)	% sold in 'own' market	% sold outside 'own' market
Heineken	17	5.8	29	71
Scottish Courage	17	5.8	94	6
Danone	15	5.1	66	34
Bass	12.5	4.3	92	8
Guinness	12	4.1	33	67
Interbrew	12	4.1	66	34
Carlsberg	12	4.1	42	58
Brau & Brunnen	10.5	3.6	86	14
Maerz	9	3.1	89	11
Whitbread	7	2.4	93	7

Source: PIMS estimates.

Trade and globalization

The rationalization of national markets is beginning to have an impact on the ways in which global brands are managed, and the competition between large world players develops. The early stages of this process are illustrated by a comparison between Heineken, the largest European-based brewer, and Anheuser Bush (AB), the largest North American brewer. Unlike the chocolate or computer markets, the powerful American beer producer AB has been unable to use its production scale or know-how to build a strong position in Europe.

Even as the largest world brewer with 100 mhl production in North America, AB has been unable to penetrate higher than brand position No. 20 in a major European country, or to do well in many non-US markets. Heineken, on the other hand, has put together a series of market positions and is much better placed to transfer know-how internationally. Either there are barriers to entry in the form of consumer tastes, access to distribution channels or strength of local competition which have kept the US companies out (but which some Europeans have overcome), or the US companies were doing too well at home to take Europe seriously.

A.5.2. Overview of respondents' operations

Our contact companies in this study, interviewed at director level, were a 'big five' company in the UK, and a leading premium beer company in Germany. They operate in very different market conditions, with different strategic objectives, but have interesting common views on the effects of the single market on scale economies.

Location and scope

Both of our contact companies had their main brewing activities concentrated in a single national market in 1995, as in 1980. In this sense the single market has not encouraged them to invest in production facilities across a wider spread of countries. The German firm, after focusing on developing a single site for many years, acquired an existing brewery in the east for complementary beers. It has doubled its output, roughly doubling the number of its employees at the same time. The UK firm has seen its production volume show marginal decline over the period, and its number of breweries halved from over ten to around five. Its number of UK employees in the same time has reduced by 33%, and the sales value of its output from brewing has increased only marginally. In both cases scale economies in production have been achieved, helping to absorb the impact of input cost increases.

The UK firm has centralized procurement of materials, and also marketing, from former regional structures, but has not taken any similar steps with regard to recruitment and personnel development. The German firm, with expansion by acquisition into additional beer types and into soft drinks/mineral water, now has three operations in each of these areas where it formerly had one.

The importance of these factors in the cost structure of typical firms has changed for both our respondents, with an increase in marketing expenses (advertising, promotion and selling) both per litre and as a proportion of the selling price. One firm reports that its costs, apart from production, include:

Element	% sales value	Trend
Marketing/selling	12%	up from 8%
Distribution	6.5%	down from 8%
R&D	0.8%	up from 0.5%

The German respondent estimates that its advertising and selling costs have increased from 6 ECU/hl to around 24 ECU/hl over the ten years. 'We have achieved substantial production scale economies, and virtually all these savings have gone into additional marketing to maintain growth of the business, and our differentiated premium position.'

New market entries

Distribution costs have fallen for our contact firms, and marketing costs increased, because of the fact that they now have supported brand positions in a wider range of markets, both in the

EU and elsewhere. For example, the UK firm has entered France and Spain, while the German firm now exports to most EU markets, and has also entered Eastern European countries in a major way. However, it has done so without forming its own sales organization in each country, relying on agents and partners on the ground.

Mergers and acquisitions/strategic alliances

Both companies have been involved in acquisitions – the German company by acquiring a firm in former East Germany, and bringing its marketing and commercial skills to bear on its output. The UK company has long been involved in acquisitions and mergers, some of whose brewing capacity has been closed in the period to achieve production scale economies. In addition, it has bought new beer brands where these are strong enough to stand up in an increasingly competitive and advertised branded market.

As has become the practice in the UK market, acquisition of brands has been linked to long-term supply arrangements with former 'tied house' outlets, which in other industries might be regarded as a form of strategic alliance. In the UK beer industry, however, the changes have been enforced by local competition policy which has required major breweries to divest large numbers of owned pubs. The effect of this change has been to make the market for branded beers more like the markets for other consumer non-durables. It has accelerated the pace of concentration in brewing and increased the advertising spend in the industry, and is currently being reconsidered because of its impact on choice and prices.

A.5.3. Factors driving dynamic economies of scale

Customer convergence

There are few common distributor customers for beer across national boundaries. Bars and retailers have so far been predominantly national. However, major retailers and wholesalers are increasing their activity by sourcing internationally. This is not helped, however, by major differences between national markets in duty and tax, and by regulations concerning the supply and sale of alcohol. There have grown up, particularly in the UK, large differences in duty rates – more than trebling in the last ten years – which have induced large scale 'inward smuggling', disadvantaging local retailers as well as beer producers.

Consumer taste differences, as a cumulative result of local tradition, climate, social practices and availability of materials, are still very significant in much of the EU. In the view of our German respondents, the market is still in the process of moving from local tastes and preferences to a national market with strong national brands. There is still relatively strong local brand loyalty among consumers, so Germany is not as open as other markets. However, German producers have found it easier to export, and the larger producers – including our respondent – are part of an international market in that sense.

The increasing role of imported brands in every national market clearly shows that consumer tastes are moving together in some areas, particularly among younger drinkers who are more influenced by television advertising. Advertising programmes are used for some brands to present messages which are consistent across national boundaries; this is particularly true for international brands belonging to Heineken, Carlsberg and Interbrew.

'Lead' markets

There are no 'lead' markets for beer in the EU in the sense that innovations are launched predominantly in one country and then 'rolled out' elsewhere. New products are often borrowed from other markets rather than invented from scratch, although the newly arrived set of alcoholic cordial drinks aimed at younger drinkers – some of which qualify as brewed products – are genuinely new. Innovations of this type tend to come from the markets with the loosest regulation, often the UK, while the scope for 'borrowing' brands seems to be greatest from countries with the lightest beers.

Innovation to meet the needs of retailers through new and high quality packaging approaches is probably best advanced in the UK. New bottle designs for supermarket brands and the development of high image glass packaging for exotic beers and ciders have both moved ahead faster in the UK than in other EU markets.

Our UK respondent considered that the competitive rivalry in the UK was stronger than elsewhere in Europe, because there are still four large brewers who are competing on roughly equal terms for a large but declining market. He also considered that the structural changes imposed on the UK market had increased competitive intensity, because it had forced each of the major producers to set long-term strategic targets and go for them. The importance of innovation in this market to preserve market share, and the tendency for new ideas from outside Europe to be marketed here first because of shared language with the US, both have an effect.

Movement of products and capital

The movement of brewed products has certainly been aided by the development of trans-European transport networks, as evidenced by the responses of both our companies on transport costs. There have been acquisitions involving transnational capital movements, including since 1991:

(a)   the acquisition of Cruzcampo (Spain) by Guinness (Ireland);
(b)   Heineken (Netherlands) purchases in France and Italy;
(c) . Interbrew (Belgium) acquisitions in the Netherlands and elsewhere.

But the movements towards national concentration have been just as significant, including consolidation in Germany and the acquisitions between the former 'big six' brewers in the UK. So have acquisitions in the east, such as Interbrew's moves into Hungary and the former Yugoslavia.

One of the factors inhibiting transnational investment – or any new investment – is the existence of overcapacity, estimated by our respondents as around 15% in excess of EU demand plus net exports. Such investment as there has been in higher capacity units, which are much more capital intensive than traditional brewing processes, has tended to make the overcapacity problem worse; and so links between companies have often attempted to seek mechanisms to use spare capacity, through mergers, alliances, or licensing arrangements.

Brand licence arrangements have been more significant than the movement of products or capital. In many cases, within the EU and elsewhere, a brand is launched into a national market on the back of a local licence agreement for production, or for production and marketing. The original brand owner is usually not required to find the capital to support its exploitation in a new market, but finds a local partner, with brewing capacity and access to local channels of distribution to do this for him. Our UK respondent has been involved in a number of arrangements like this, but the German firm has declined to license products – either as licensor or as licensee – in order to retain its differentiated premium brand position.

There are signs that this pattern of market entry is no longer the preferred route in all cases. For example, our UK respondent has launched English brands in France and Spain from UK production, and Anheuser Bush is in the process of switching its Budweiser operation in Europe from a licensed production approach to one where it takes over a brewery from a UK company. Movements of products and capital appear to be on the increase. The single market framework makes these new directions in company strategy possible, but does not of itself make them happen.

It was also clear from one of our respondents that even the remaining influence of national governments over health, safety and information regulations is seen as waning. 'Up to now we have relied on national government contacts to influence what is going on in setting standards for the industry, but we can see that the people we really need to talk to are in Brussels.'

Knowledge transfer

Both of our respondent companies have adopted systems for the transfer of know-how within their operations in order to build competitive advantage. The UK firm adopted a common IT system to secure scale advantages in production as long as ten years ago, something which was not required in the German company until 1992. The UK firm used external consultants to centralize procurement, while the German firm used external advisors to boost marketing.

But in both companies the overwhelming majority of work to transfer know-how on marketing, development, and production is done by internal staff. These areas give some scope for cost saving, but significantly more for additional value to be created. The truly international firms – Heineken, Danone, Guinness, Interbrew, and Carlsberg – are focusing on these areas, and setting the standard for others to meet.

One interesting example quoted of knowledge transfer was in the area of managing brand positions in different markets. Some companies have discovered that in moving from one market to another, brands can be repositioned much more profitably. The case of Stella Artois, which is a standard product in Belgium but is marketed as a premium brand in the UK, using pan-European brand images, showed how lessons on brand introductions had been learned – and then repeated in other markets. Whether this was in the consumer's interest was a good philosophical question!

Benefits of scale economies realized

Both respondents agreed that there had been benefits achieved via dynamic economies of scale, as a result of stronger competition. Apart from the expected – and agreed – benefits of cost reduction in procurement, production and distribution, both identified innovation as a gain which had come from greater scope of competition. The German firm also believed that quality benefits in marketing and production, as well as a number of other functional areas, could be substantiated. Because of its greater scale, and the need to compete in a more innovative market, the German respondent had invested in a small R&D brewery able to produce short runs of production scale varieties, to increase the company's ability to introduce new products. In association with this, the transition to national competition across Germany had led to better and more professional marketing approaches to take advantage of new ideas.

However, neither respondent was prepared to credit the single market with the achievement of these gains. They were seen as being part of the global development of the industry, and partly a natural evolution from the purely local competitive structures of 20 years ago. In Germany the major opportunities for growth were seen to have arisen from events in the east, and in the UK the major upheavals associated with the split of distribution from brewing were the most obvious driver of market change.

Despite this it is arguable that German market liberalization through abolition of the 'Deutsches Reinheitsgebot', even though penetration has been limited since it happened ten years ago, has had an impact on firm behaviour by encouraging German brewers to look at competitive structures in other markets. It is also very clear that the international strategic approach of Heineken, Danone, Carlsberg, Interbrew and Guinness is understood by those major brewers – in the UK, Germany and elsewhere – who are still focused on a single major domestic market. They expect structures in their markets to change in the not too distant future as a result of the international players, even if the past has been relatively stable. They recognize that their own strategies will need to adapt in order to meet this challenge.

Diversity and scope of activities

Both our respondent companies confirmed that the impact of a larger market had induced them to diversify the scope of their offer to customers, either through a broader product range, or through marketing via a more comprehensive range of distribution channels. Tailoring containers or delivery systems to customers' needs had made production somewhat more complex, and a greater range of IT and customer service skills was required from employees to meet new market needs.

Our German respondent has retained a very focused approach to branding, attempting to maximize the impact of the brewery name and image – in effect, taking advantage of scale economies in advertising and promotion. It has altogether avoided blurring its distinctive position in the market, and has refused to become involved in production of store brand beers. But it has introduced to its range a dark beer, low alcohol beers, and a mineral water product.

A.5.4. Influence of external economies of scale

Both our respondents gave a surprisingly low rating to the importance of external economies relating to purchased materials. Since value added as a percentage of revenue is relatively high in the brewing sector, the costs of materials – which are in large part commodities – is less important than effective use of expensive plant or than achieving the right price position in the market. Input cost changes in the sector have not been excessive, and most producers continue to use mainly local materials. The German respondent commented that its own growth has given it more purchasing power, with benefits in its procurement process for materials and distribution services. Price increases have been limited by a larger potential supplier group. 'But we already have close relationships with our suppliers, and our aim is to get the best quality from them – which they know how to give us.' There is a large incentive for a premium position business like this to avoid jeopardizing its quality reputation, and this has constrained the search for alternatives.

A.5.5. Impact of the single market

Although our respondents do not regard the single market as a determining factor in their own international development strategies, the freedom of movement for products and capital is starting to affect the way in which the brewing industry operates. Products, particularly premium brands of higher value, are travelling further as firms base market penetration strategies on own production. Investment in own capacity outside a company's domestic base is starting to be a preferred option to licensing of marketing operations and/or production.

The growth of international brewers has accelerated markedly in the last five years, with Heineken, Danone, Interbrew, Guinness and Carlsberg all now having between 30% and 70% of their business activity outside their domestic markets. It is noticeable that none of these companies is based in the three biggest national markets for beer, suggesting that each of these companies has been forced to expand outside its domestic base to generate returns for its shareholders. The ability to move products and capital between EU national markets has facilitated this type of expansion, not caused it. The test of whether this process has genuinely improved the international competitive capability of EU brewing will be the success of these new international companies in extending their activities outside Europe, to compete in wider markets.

There have been gains in procurement, in restraining prices for materials, but this is seen by our respondents as a second order benefit. The benefit which is noted as more substantial is the incentive for innovation which companies have experienced. In both the UK and Germany innovation has also been prompted by regulatory changes affecting domestic market organization. Disentangling the effects of these changes is at best difficult, particularly since the German regulatory change was implemented in order to meet requirement on movement of products. But it appears to be the case in the UK that radical changes in distribution structure have reinforced the pressures for innovation which the single market has brought.

A.6. Motor vehicles

A.6.1. Market context 1980–95

EU manufacturers of motor vehicles are only now recovering from the worst recession in their industry since 1945. The drop in sales in 1993 alone was far worse than that induced by the oil crises of the early 1970s, and resulted in major layoffs across almost all Member States. Pressures to cut costs were felt all the way along the supply chain, and many businesses reorganized extensively in order to compete in the global marketplace. 1994 sales in the EU recovered to 11.2 million units, an increase of 4.6%, but the market is far from being fully restored.[9]

Sector employment also dropped off in the early 1990s, from 1.23 million (1990) to 1.02 million (1994). This decline has been faster than that in the manufacturing sector as a whole, and while falling demand was largely to blame, productivity improvements and industry rationalization/restructuring also contributed.

---

[9]   European Commission [1996], *Panorama of EC industry 1995/96.*

The EU as a whole runs a consistent trade surplus in motor vehicles, which in 1994 amounted to 18.5 MECU. However, extra-EU imports have been rising faster than imports in recent years, reflecting the fact that the EU has now become the world's largest market for automobiles, and therefore the principal commercial battleground for the major global manufacturers.

Competitive pressures have therefore forced the EU-based industry to adopt the lean production techniques with which Japanese firms in particular have been so successful. This re-engineering of the production process involves *inter alia* a more vertically fragmented industry, and a more co-ordinated approach to product and process design. This might therefore be expected to offer scope for the realization of dynamic and external economies of scale. Attributing this shift to the SM is questionable however, for while the re-engineered processes might be broadly characterized as 'European' in location, the competitive pressures are global.

Indeed, the next few years may finally see the emergence of the 'world car' as global producers focus their resources on producing a variety of model types from key product platforms in their network. These platforms are in turn served by the globalizing automotive component industry on a just-in-time delivery basis.

A.6.2. Overview of respondents' operations

A full survey of the motor vehicle industry is beyond the scope of this case study, but we have sought the opinions of major industry leaders, notably the Chairman of Ford in the UK (and president of the UK motor vehicle trade association[10]) and Toyota Motor Europe, which is one of the 'transplant' industry leaders in lean production techniques. We also examine the changes made by Fiat, one of the EU's long-established carmakers, as reported in a parallel study on the effects of the SM on this sector.[11]

These firms represent a range of manufacturers in the motor vehicle sector. Ford is one of the oldest automotive businesses in the world, and one of the few approaching a genuinely global identity. Ford of Europe was established back in 1967, as even then the company recognized the value of a pan-regional identity. The company has a presence in five EU countries, including two major manufacturing sites in the UK, one in Germany, one in Belgium, one in Spain and a Portuguese factory that produces Ford's multi-purpose vehicle.[12]

In contrast, Toyota has only become a truly global manufacturer comparatively recently, but their arrival in the sector had an immediate impact, particularly in the US. It has now established a major manufacturing facility in Derbyshire, UK, and also has a spare parts distribution centre near Brussels, Belgium. As in the US, part of the rationale for establishing a manufacturing 'transplant' in the EU was to overcome the increasing antagonism that the high level of imports was causing in Toyota's major markets.

---

[10]   The Society of Motor Manufacturers & Traders (SMMT).

[11]   European Commission [1997], *The Single Market Review*, Vol. I:6, Impact on manufacturing: Motor vehicles.

[12]   The MPV is produced in collaboration with Volkswagen.

Fiat represent one of the EU's oldest established carmakers, who have had to restructure their operations significantly to respond to global competition. They have continued to maintain their core manufacturing in Italy, but have shifted some operations to the more southern regions of Potenza and Avellino, where costs are lower and where the company is eligible for a range of developmental assistance. Major new investments outside Italy have tended to be in emerging markets, such as Poland and Brazil, where Fiat sees future growth potential through the development of its 'world car', the Palio.

A.6.3. Factors driving dynamic economies of scale

According to Ford, globalization is leading to the exploitation of dynamic EOS with respect to R&D. The integration, through technology, of Ford's various research centres is leading to increased returns on R&D expenditure (measured in terms of new innovation) and a reduced time to market for new models. This is part of the Ford 2000 programme, which is gradually superseding the regional division of responsibility, represented by Ford of Europe. Essentially, Ford 2000 seeks to identify world-class expertise across the company wherever it is found, and project it onto Ford's global markets. This will lead, for example, to a concentration of R&D for smaller vehicles in Europe, which is perceived to be particularly strong in this respect, with the US taking responsibility for larger vehicles.

Although these models are increasingly (although not entirely) the same across the world, Ford brands them and makes changes to the specifications for each national market. Consumers in each Member State of the EU are still viewed as having distinct requirements, and Ford still has to vary the product and marketing strategy to account for the different tastes and local competition.

For their part, Fiat have extensively reorganized their operations in order to respond to the more competitive environment in the EU. The *fabbrica integrata* (integrated factory) project takes the Toyota model of lean production and attempts to apply it to Fiat's Italian operations through a functional integration of the various processes associated with production, in order to give greater flexibility, productivity and cost savings.

In the experience of Fiat, advertising has become very much uniform throughout Europe allowing for some scale economies to be realized. Major institutional marketing (designed to raise and enhance the profile of the Fiat marque) is run from the Italian headquarters, but targets what is clearly seen as a European consumer. The emergence of this marketing identity is clearly a long-term phenomenon, on which the SM can have had only marginal impact.[13]

With respect to the distribution of motor vehicles throughout the EU, the Block Exemption under Article 85 of the EC Treaty was considered by Fiat executives to have favoured dealers ahead of producers and consumers. The new agreement allows multi-franchising with some restrictions: different brands must be kept in different showrooms under legally distinct corporate entities. Some cost savings are likely to be achieved by the economies of scale and scope possible through common servicing arrangements.

The creation of Toyota's parts distribution centre in Belgium is in part a reflection of the fact that the SM allows free movement of automotive components, so that Toyota can provide

---

[13]   European Commission [1997] op cit.

after-care to its dealerships from a central EU location in a way that would clearly not have been practicable from Japan.

A.6.4. Factors driving external economies of scale

There is a noticeable overlap between dynamic and external EOS in the automotive sector. For example, technology is enabling the re-engineering of business processes whereby key service inputs can also be externalized to an outside supplier as part of the lean production strategy identified above. The parent (assembly) firm still retains a close, symbiotic relationship with this specialized service supplier, which often has been spun-off from the parent firm, which recognizes that this new entity (the service supplier) is better able to supply these services as part of its core business, in a way the parent company never was.

The best-known example of this phenomenon is the creation, development and subsequent disposal of EDS by General Motors in the US. EDS has since become a world leader in the provision of IT and consultancy services. In effect, internal economies of scope have been replaced by external economies of scale.[14] Since almost 50% of the value of a vehicle now consists of bought-in products and services, this can lead to a significant reduction in overall costs.[15]

In the continuing shake-out of the motor vehicle industry, it is also clear that even as firms de-layer their own organizations, a new hierarchy is emerging in the wider industry. The leading assemblers have indicated a clear intent to reduce the number of suppliers they source from and then build up strategic, long-term partnerships with these firms. Fiat, for example, have reduced the number of suppliers they purchase from to 380 from around 1,200 in 1987. This has come about in spite of the increasing proportion of the total cost of the car accounted for by bought-in components.

These so-called 'first tier' suppliers will in turn depend on 'second tier' manufacturers to provide components for sub-assembly into, for example, the engine, before this is delivered to the vehicle assembler. The traditional concept of external EOS, in which firms locate near to abundant labour and established sources of supply, no longer appears valid. The availability of low-cost labour remains an important issue, and provides the rationale for Ford's Portuguese plant, not least because such areas often qualify for development grants. However, the buying power of global motor vehicle assemblers is such that the suppliers will relocate near to them, if only to guarantee the just-in-time delivery of components.

Other EAG research has noted the tendency of component suppliers to agglomerate around their major customers, the assemblers. This may in part be due to the outsourcing through disposal of some input functions, but it is also clear that new investment is attracted to the area.[16] Scott identifies a circle whereby vertical disintegration (externalization) leads to

---

[14]   Coffey and Bailey [1991], 'Producer services and flexible production: an exploratory analysis', *Growth & Change*, Vol. 22.

[15]   Rhys, G. in Johnson, P. [1993].

[16]   For example, the north-east of England after the Nissan investment and now southern Italy for Fiat's new production facilities.

upstream agglomeration (geographic concentration of suppliers) which in turn encourages the process of vertical disintegration.[17]

Strategic outsourcing goes beyond subcontracting a specified intermediate task in the production process, in that partner firms are expected to be creative and pro-active. This sort of partnering carries responsibilities on both sides: Fiat identify this process as *crescita guidata* (assisted growth) which they have employed since 1991. Toyota, too, have long been known for the specialist knowledge and problem-solving expertise they transfer to their strategic partners, in contrast to the more conventional practice of jealously guarding such crucial intellectual property. In terms of Porter's paradigm, the modern, global automotive value chain is only as strong as its weakest link.[18]

In their traditional home market of Japan, Toyota's intellectual property would have been protected by the *Keiretsu* network of equity-crossholdings, which ensured that both supplier and assembler were dependent on each other, logistically and financially. In the EU however, where different market structures prevail, this has been more difficult to get off the ground, but is now clearly observable.

A.6.5. Role of the single market

Because of the motor vehicle sector's high political and economic profile, the creation of the SM was always going to be a delicate exercise. This is reflected in the various exemptions granted to automotive producers under various international trade agreements, including the GATT and the Treaty of Rome.

As one long-time observer of the EU motor vehicle industry has noted: '... the motor industry was already one of the most European of industries and had done much to anticipate 1992. It has long regarded Europe as one market and already operates on this basis. It is not fanciful to say that a transnational company like Ford had achieved its own 1992 when it created Ford of Europe back in 1967.'[19]

Nevertheless, some significant developments did occur as part of the SM programme. The major elements are as follows:

(a)   the reduction of fiscal trade barriers stemming from large intra-EU variations in indirect taxes;
(b)   the removal of physical non-tariff barriers which impede the free movement of motor vehicles (quotas, customs regulations, etc.);
(c)   the development of EU-wide technical standards and product specifications, such as the Whole Vehicle Type Approval (WVTA).

It was generally expected that the benefit of these measures would be felt primarily in the production and distribution functions, and could potentially lead to unit cost reductions of

---

[17]   Scott, A. [1986], 'Industrial organization and location: division of labour, the firm and spatial process, *Economic Geography*, Vol. 62

[18]   Porter, M. [1980], *Competitive strategy*.

[19]   Rhys, G. [1993], in Johnson op cit.

around 5%.[20] The WVTA, for example, was thought to offer economies of scale through the standardization of vehicle specifications across the EU.

Research has shown that the WVTA is indeed one of the most important ways in which the SM is contributing to cost savings for motor vehicle manufacturers through the realization of dynamic EOS. These come from reducing the number of testing procedures from 15 to one (which is then recognized by all other Member States), and the consequent reduction in the time to market. The direct saving has been valued at around ECU 1–1.5 million for each model launch, with further indirect savings of almost ECU 30 million.[21]

The evidence presented above suggests that upstream activities, such as R&D, testing procedures and supplier purchasing, are becoming more integrated and concentrated, thereby enabling some firms to realize dynamic economies of scale, but this process is not a result of the SM programme. However, opinions vary with respect to downstream activities such as marketing and advertising, which are still largely undertaken at the Member State level, although the after-market for service and parts has to some extent been regionalized.

The automotive component industry is also responding to competitive pressures through globalization and concentration. Assuming key product segments remain competitive, external economies of scale are potentially realizable for assemblers of motor vehicles, as cost savings are passed on from their suppliers. Evidence as to whether this has actually happened is extremely difficult to find because pricing matters remain highly confidential within the industry. However, the removal of physical barriers to trade may have allowed more component suppliers to trade across the EU and thereby contributed to the scale of their operations. (The removal of such barriers was not considered important by the vehicle manufacturers in the case study, as they already made special provisions for customs clearance, etc.).

As has been noted previously, earlier work on economies of scale did not directly address the issue of dynamic and external EOS. We have found both non-production EOS to be important in this sector, but the link with the SM is tenuous at best. The SM does not appear to have influenced downstream activity or the location of manufacturing operations. The EU motor vehicle industry has clearly intensified its co-operation at the regional level in a way which supports the exploitation of EOS, but this was never seen as an alternative to globalization in order to meet world-wide competitive challenges from more efficient producers in Japan and North America.

A.7. Glass

These case studies cover two applications sectors of the European glass industry, container glass and flat glass, and are based on interviews with leading companies in each. Only one major European company competes in a leading role in both sectors, and the two have different end-user and immediate customers, and different competitive pressures. For the most part, they will therefore be treated as separate case studies in this analysis.

---

[20] Emerson et al [1988b].

[21] European Commission [1997], op cit.

The large producers, and their involvement in applications sectors, are as follows:

Company	Approx 000 employees	Containers	Flat	Tableware	Fibre	Special
Saint-Gobain	96	****	***		**	*
Pilkington	40		***		sold	*
Schott	18					***
Glaverbel	9		**			
Waterford	8			***		
Gerresheimer	6	***				
Rockwool	5				**	
PLM	3	**				
SIV	2	**				
BSN	2	**				
Rockware	2	**				
United Glass	2	**				
Owens Corning	1				*	
PPG	1		*			

Cost structure, from international data

There are enough observations on the glass industry in the PIMS database to draw some general conclusions – across segments – on the scale sensitivity of costs. Glass is an industrial sector in which manufacturing costs make up a relatively high proportion of sales revenue for the majority of businesses, reflecting the fact that most firms in the industry add a high proportion of value – and cost – to very basic raw materials. It is also a relatively fixed capital intensive sector.

The available data suggests that sales, marketing and R&D costs in most businesses in the sector are low, but that:

(a)   there are significant production scale economies, measuring scale in terms of relative share;

(b)   it is the larger scale producers which appear to invest more heavily in product and process R&D, as well as in aspects of marketing;

(c)   larger scale producers tend to have higher process stocks, which may be related to their greater involvement in off-site processing (see Section B.2).

A.7.1. Containers

Market trends 1980–95

Container glass amounts to around 15 million tonnes of the total EU glass output of 23 million tonnes. Its composition in terms of end use varies between national markets, but is composed mainly of wine bottles, beer and cider bottles, bottles for spirits and alcohol, food jars, cordials and mineral waters, toiletries and cosmetics, and in the UK, milk bottles. Some of these applications are in steady decline over the long term, and some – such as pharmaceutical containers – have now been almost completely substituted by PET. Soft drinks and larger beer bottles are now largely blown from PET, except for premium brands, and for applications where hot sterilizing is required. Mineral water bottles are mostly substituted by PVC, and more recently by high quality PET whose superior finish makes it a further threat to glass.

In the early 1980s glass container demand in Europe fell rapidly by around 5% p.a., as substitution by PVC, PET and cans took over many applications in beer, soft drinks and mineral water, and as cartons took over in milk. In the late 1980s total container demand stabilized, mainly because growth in spirits and premium beers was starting to compensate for continuing losses elsewhere. Since 1991 growth of around 2% p.a. has been achieved overall, but the pattern from year to year, and across national markets, has been irregular.

For lower value glass containers there has been increasingly fierce competition from Eastern Europe, but there is still a small positive overall trade balance in tonnage terms. Much of the growth in EU value added has been in higher value products, in custom designed bottles for soft drinks and mineral waters, for premium beers and ciders, and in toiletries and cosmetics.

The bulk of EU demand is satisfied by production relatively close to the point of filling, because the cost of transporting empty containers is high. The exceptions to this general rule are in higher value branded products, spirits and premium beers, where containers may travel farther. The only application in which there is a genuine European scale market for glass containers is in toiletries and cosmetics, where global brand owners of the final products buy on a European scale, and co-ordinate procurement, production and marketing at this level. Since the package is a vital part of the brand image for such products, innovation and design, consistency and guaranteed quality, and the ability when required to provide short runs and flexible service are crucial in this sector.

Overview of production facilities

Production economies of scale in glass containers exist at three levels:

(a)   the number of furnaces per factory, which permits sharing of overheads and logistics;
(b)   the size of glass furnace, which shows the normal 'cube rule' for process plant;
(c)   the size and number of bottle making machines on each furnace.

Changes in technology over the period 1980 to 1995 have permitted two main developments. The maximum furnace size has increased from 400 tonnes per day (tpd) to 500. The maximum machine size has increased from '10 section double gob' which can make 20 bottles simultaneously, to '12 section quadruple gob' which can make 48. Most major producers now have at least one machine of maximum size, but not all have maximum furnace size. The maximum number of machines per furnace is five, limited by the problems of assembling and managing a varied order book. Clearly big machines are best suited to long runs of simple products, such as standard wine bottles or food jars, in single colours.

Structural changes in the industry since 1980 have reflected the changes in plant scale:

(a)   In Italy a number of producers came together to form AVIR.
(b)   In France, BSN absorbed UMC, and Saint-Gobain and BSN took over much of the previously independent Spanish capacity.
(c)   In Germany, Weigan became part of Niewburger, and Testaur, Wistoff and Gerresheimer came together.

(d)   In the UK, United Glass acquired CTG, and Rockware acquired the Co-operative business, before itself being acquired by BTR. PLM acquired Redfearn.

BTR's view on acquiring Rockware (based on Australian experience) was that a single furnace plant, with 400 tpd furnace plant feeding two machines could compete effectively in the European market, but that the load it would require to compete was important. This is because such a high proportion of the plant labour cost is tied up in finishing and packaging, and outbound logistics. Only about 15% of plant labour cost is typically in the 'hot end' making bottles; the other 85% is in inspection, decoration, finishing, packaging, warehousing and despatch. But as 80% of capital assets are normally in the 'hot end', this is where management attention on technology focuses.

Automation in finishing has also advanced over the last ten years, particularly as standards of inspection and product precision have tightened. Bottling plant speeds have increased substantially, putting greater strain on the product and leaving less room for flaws. In addition, final product liability has lessened the tolerance for foreign material in bottles – or of harmless discoloration in the glass. Automatic testing and handling has therefore become more important.

Marketing and sales costs in the container sector typically account for less than 2% of sales revenue, because most sales organizations are focused on a single country. Producers have agents outside their domestic base, but the bulk of sales are to a relatively concentrated customer base in one national market. Distribution costs within a major market usually amount to 5% of sales revenue, and up to 10% for longer distances or a sea crossing. R&D for most producers is around 0.5% of sales revenue.

Relatively few producers had sites in more than one country until the 1980s. Saint-Gobain and BSN's presence by acquisition in Spain started the trend, continued by PLM's acquisitions in the Netherlands and Germany, and of Redfearn in the UK. Australian ownership and influence over Rockware was the first 'outside' presence. Most major producers now have at least three or four production sites – more for St. Gobain, which is the world's largest glass container company. Where possible each site tends to specialize in a particular market segment or product type, in order to maximize the output of furnaces and machines, and to keep the problems of finishing and logistics manageable.

There is still a role for smaller producers, left by the increasing scale of the larger plants. For example, in the UK Lax & Shaw have grown significantly – and profitably – as a small scale bottle maker, specializing in short runs and miniatures which are unsuited to large plants. And Rockware has 'spun off' its toiletries and cosmetics plant, which it could not operate successfully within a large organization, to a small management buy-out which is better able to direct attention to quality and service.

Factors driving dynamic economies of scale

Competitive factors driving the glass container industry are much less European than those which are shaping the production of other packaging systems. Cans, PET bottles and cartons all have somewhat greater homogeneity in production systems, in the supply of technology and in applications across Europe than do glass containers. Bottles and jars tend to be related to more traditional products where national differences in taste persist, and there is less market homogeneity. Ability to exploit scale economies depends to some extent on national differences in demand structure; high output machines are more likely to perform well where there is demand for long runs of standard products, such as wine bottles in France, or milk bottles in the UK. According to one of our respondents, who worked as a planning manager in a UK container company in the late 1980s, the pursuit of scale economies through volume by extending product range was undertaken by more than one company at that time, and turned out to be a major strategic error.

Common customers are present across national boundaries in greater numbers now than in 1981, as food and drink branded products companies become more international. Cosmetics companies have been international in this sense since the 1960s. Insofar as there are lead markets for innovation in glass containers, the UK leads for food and drink, while for cosmetics it is Italy/France. However, innovations in design, and in trends such as 'lightweighting' the glass content of bottles to reduce costs and handling effort, tend to be copied across international boundaries relatively quickly. The R&D costs of keeping abreast of the product and process innovations which do occur, however, are increasing. This factor, which may also affect customers, may be one reason for the increasing tendency of packaged goods manufacturers to reduce the number of suppliers they use regularly. If they focus on a few bottle suppliers, they can develop closer relationships, speed up the process of producing new packaging solutions, and contain development costs.

Factor cost differences between countries within the EU are not large enough to overcome transport cost barriers for many products, but labour costs in eastern Europe – and their likely levels over the next few years – are certainly low enough to influence investment decisions. Efficiency differences between countries are much more dependent on company know-how than they are on local factors.

Know-how and inter-site learning certainly does occur in the industry, through a number of routes. Some companies have developed management approaches, for selection of business and management of the planning process, which appear to give them worthwhile cost and commercial advantages. There are also proprietary technologies, held by major glass companies and licensed to other producers. The application of such know-how in the glass industry reinforces the tendency for specialization in market segments, and is not specific to the container sector. For example, Pilkington's recent sale of its fibre business to Owens Corning – while unlikely to present opportunities in the short to medium term for production scale increases – has permitted the acquiring company to implement management and reporting improvements developed in other European plants, and in North America.

There are also important intellectual property rights affecting the glass container industry held by the main suppliers of bottle-making machinery. Plant suppliers have an important role in transferring knowledge of what is going on in the industry, and determining the rate and direction of technological advance. At least one of them operates a 'benchmarking' information system, by which individual plants are able to plot their achievements in productivity against others world-wide. The two main plant manufacturers, Owens and Emhart, are both American-owned.

Benefits from dynamic scale economies in the glass container industry are almost entirely attributable to gains from transfer of operational know-how, and they owe relatively little to the single market. The gains certainly exist – but they are identified only through internal studies undertaken by companies in the industry to track differences in productivity and plant performance. Most of the benefits have been realized by in-country mergers (in Germany, Italy and the UK). The notable exceptions are Saint-Gobain's move into Spain, and PLM's presence in Sweden, Norway, the Netherlands, Germany and the UK – built up before Sweden's entry to the EU.

Scale benefits are reported in one of our responding companies as a direct result of acquisition within its domestic base, both through improved labour productivity and increased capital productivity. The arrival of Australian management know-how with BTR's entry via acquisition in the UK market is also reported to have provided the framework for significant reductions in overhead costs.

Marketing gains are limited by the heterogeneity of market demand between countries, due to the fact that there is still a large base of container users who operate only in one national market, and by the transport costs of empty containers. For Saint-Gobain, the market leader, the achievement of marketing economies is also perceived by competitors to have been slowed by the vertical split between production and marketing which existed in the organization for much of the period.

Influence of external economies of scale

While container suppliers provide external scale economies to their customers by closer relationships and shared development costs, the scope to do this in the glass industry is very limited. Most of the raw materials are straight commodities. They are affected by issues of quality control, but the main focus is on price and delivery. As a respondent said, 'We can buy these materials from a range of suppliers, except for soda ash where in most European countries there is one local monopoly supplier – but it still isn't worth the cost of importing'.

The main external scale economy in this industry is in plant development, where virtually all producers benefit from the process control advances of two plant manufacturers. However, the framework within which this happens is world-wide rather than European. Owens technology is used by United Glass, Gerresheimer, BSN and BTR/Rockware, while Emhart technology, which is somewhat less capital intensive, is used by Saint-Gobain. Development and comparison learning tends to occur within these groups – and their international partners – rather than between them.

Role of the single market

In terms of the main dynamic cost elements, it is clear that the impact of the single market on the glass container industry has been limited. While cross-European competition has been much more evident in other packaging media, three factors have tended to keep market boundaries relatively local for glass: the relative conservatism of much of end-user demand, the short geographical range of individual plants, and possibly the burdens imposed on producers by process capital intensity.

The most international producer, PLM, which has a manufacturing presence in five European countries, is not the largest container producer in Europe, nor is it the largest producer in the majority of its market – only in Scandinavia is it a clear leader. However, this entire position was built up in advance of the accession of PLM's home country to the European Community, and it is difficult to argue that the single market has a strong influence on behaviour.

A.7.2. Flat glass

Market trends 1980–95

Flat glass has shown significant increase in EU consumption and production over the period, driven by the demands of the construction and automotive industries. Since construction is a commercial investment market, and automotive demand is strongly related to consumer confidence, both applications are cyclical. Sustained growth in demand throughout the 1980s was halted by the 1989–92 recession, with production falling in 1991. Since then, there has been some recovery in market demand.

The two main areas of the market are radically different in the way that purchasers behave. The automotive sector is global, with customers who seek to buy at least on a European level, possibly wider. The major customer's R&D effort in automotive is led from North America, and manufacturers' strategies have attempted in most cases to add value – to deliver to automotive customers a complete module ready for the assembly line. Building, on the other hand, is primarily a set of national markets. Glass sheet is made at float plants, fabricated into double glazed units by processor/distributors, then sold to builders.

Today's European market demand is around 4.6 mtpa for building, and 5.7 mtpa for automotive, but average auto prices are significantly higher than for building glass. Shares of the major suppliers across Europe are roughly similar in each segment.

Market growth has partly been boosted by EU regulations, particularly those on energy efficient buildings (see Appendix C). Double glazing is now mandatory under building regulations in many countries, which has increased glass demand, and also the market for glass processing.

Overview of production operations

According to the managing director of one of the major European producers, who was involved in technology development at the beginning of our review period, the basic technology has not changed significantly in 15 years. There have been improvements in refractories and process control, but the physics of heat removal from floating glass, and laminar flow, impose limits on maximum plant size which have not altered. The optimal plant has two lines, each consisting of furnace and float tank of around 5,000 tonnes per week; there are no real economies in common furnaces as there are for glass containers. However, the refractory and process improvements have lengthened the life of furnaces, as much as halving the depreciation charge per tonne of glass produced.

The real limits on plant scale economies are in logistics. Firstly, transport costs are significant, as transport costs are around ECU 0.1 per km. 500 km is the normal 'catchment' area of a float plant, and beyond 1,000 km it becomes impossible even to cover variable costs, with today's price/cost structure. Secondly, the complexity of the order book has a major influence, and here there have been major changes.

In 1980 it was normal for a float plan to finish most of its glass on site, to cut to size, polish and fabricate products sold to the builder or auto manufacturer. Now much of this work is done off site, either by the producer or in the market by independent finishers. Under this arrangement standard sizes are shipped out of the float plant, using in-plant packaging. Capital requirements at the plant are significantly reduced by the removal of on-site finishing, as well as the number of employees and the complexity of the operation. But it has required investment in intelligent cutting machines in local finishing/distribution centres.

The economic effect of remote processing is significant, because it has led most major producers to take significant downstream stakes. Rather than sell unprocessed glass to processor/distributors, Saint-Gobain processes/distributes over 80% of its output in France, while Pilkington processes between 50% and 70% in the major markets of Germany and the UK, and PPG and Guardian are also involved in distribution. This trend has also made the market more accessible to imports of unworked glass from third countries.

There are some areas of downstream processing, particularly in the automotive sector, which generate enough value added to justify significant transport costs and plant specialization. For example, the manufacture of windshield modules is undertaken at a processing plant in Sagunto, northern Spain, using unworked glass imported from the UK. This is then sent in bulk each day to Opel in Germany. Similarly, Pilkington have a plant in Finland which specializes in replacement windshield units, and which supplies the whole of Europe.

Pilkington's pattern of float plants across Europe has changed little in the last ten years, except for the 1995 acquisition/integration of SIV in Italy, and the replacement of major lines in the UK. It now has 11 lines in five countries, with the main concentrations in the UK, Italy and Germany, but no presence in France or Spain. Saint-Gobain is present as a float producer in most major markets except the UK and Scandinavia. All main producers have float plants in Benelux/Germany, or at least within range of the major part of these markets. Both major producers, Saint-Gobain and Pilkington, have processing plants in almost every national market in Europe. Pilkington have entered Spain (1980), then France (1988–91) in this way. The objective of most producers in penetrating markets is to build up a base load through processing plants which can eventually be used to support a float plant.

Float plants are now beginning to be considered in Eastern Europe as economical suppliers to the EU markets. Poland in particular is attracting investment because its wage rates are 10% of those in neighbouring Germany, and it has both a strong local skill base in glass technology, and relative political stability. Some investment projects are underway, in the knowledge that sooner or later a significant part of the output of the plants will come back to compete with EU producers.

Factors driving dynamic economies of scale

Our respondent rated three factors as most important in determining the exploitation of scale economies in process and product development, and in marketing:

(a)   the increasingly homogeneous character of customer requirements, especially in the automotive sector;

(b)   the 'balance of power' which requires major producers to be active in all markets in order to service Europe-wide customers and retain parity of market presence;

(c)   the need to be abreast of developments which take place in the most advanced markets, and to transfer them to others.

In addition, the increasing imbalance of factor costs in Germany, which can add as much as 60

ECU/tonne to the labour cost of glass production there, is beginning to force all producers to look carefully at their Europe-wide production pattern.

Homogeneous customer needs have the strongest impact in the automotive sector. The largest auto customers in Europe are strongly influenced from North America, and Saint Gobain has suffered strategically from not being present in this market. At the time of writing it was negotiating for the purchase of Ford America's ageing glass plant to fill the gap. Within Europe, the lead markets tend to be Germany and Benelux, which have a concentration of sophisticated car makers. All glass producers approach the automotive market through key account sales organizations, at a European level.

In building products the markets were almost entirely nationally defined until 1994. For most producers selling is still organized on country lines, but converging demands by building companies have prompted at least one company to develop products aimed at specific segments, rather than tailored for national markets. The commercial aim of the strongest companies is to develop differentiated solutions for target segments of the markets, as well as to contain costs. Harmonization of building regulations, and the increasing importance of international construction companies have brought about the change.

Co-ordination and knowledge transfer are becoming increasingly important in the flat glass industry. One respondent company now has internal European co-ordination for procurement of raw materials – until recently a purely local activity – as well as for plant loading and logistics. In addition it has a world-wide manufacturing board, since the scope for learning is global.

The same company also has a marketing database to cover the Europe-wide requirements of its customers in the building sector – where sales activities are still predominantly national. Development work for the automotive sector can only be structured on a world-wide basis, with lead customers. In the building market, development activity takes place under the guidance of a group co-ordinating committee, in order to ensure focus on target segments.

Development in the company is led from a US base for automotive products, from the UK for melting and coating, and from Germany for building products. Its personnel and training activities are mainly national, except for a cadre of managers identified as top management potential, who are trained and planned on a world-wide level.

Benefits from scale, or knowledge transfer across European markets are acknowledged by respondents. Cost reductions are claimed through co-ordinated procurement, through distribution planning between float plants and processing centres on a European basis, and on marketing. Overall sales and marketing costs have declined from around 6% of sales value in the early 1980s to around 4.5% today, over which period the selling price per tonne of the products has hardly changed. R&D costs, on the other hand, have increased over the period from around 2% to about 2.5%. In one major company the incentive for national organizations to take full advantage of shared R&D is maintained by ensuring that each pays a standard 'levy' towards group effort, and is encouraged to access results without further cost. It reports several instances in which solutions to problems in one market had been easily transferred to others.

The effects of scale economies are difficult to disentangle from the impact of general efficiency improvements, but taken together they have been substantial. Despite the doubling of labour costs, increases in silica and soda ash costs, and the volatility of energy prices, producers have managed to live with virtually static money prices. To achieve this they have doubled output per employee, improved material yield from 60% to 80%, and doubled thermal efficiency from 100 therms/tonne to around 50 therms/tonne.

Influence of external economies of scale

Scope for external economies in materials supply has been relatively limited over the period. Most inputs, as in the case of glass containers, are bought commodities whose prices are determined in national or local markets. The only significant exception is lamination material for windscreens, where one major glass producer has selected a single strategic partner to help it meet the development needs of the auto manufacturers.

External economies in marketing and distribution are an essential part of the change which has taken place, described in the section above. Finishing operations remote from the float plants have permitted operations to be greatly simplified, and reduced the costs incurred in production. However, this has only been possible because of reliable, relatively cheap transport links between float plants and finishing plants. And while the description focused on the in-house remote finishing operations of the major companies, the independent glass finishers and distributors have benefited from the same type of investment in intelligent cutting machines. In the view of one respondent, the effort needed to set up the logistics and co-ordination to match float and independent finishing operations often represents investment in a strategic partnership.

Role of the single market

Just how much internationalization of the European flat glass industry would have taken place without single market measures is debatable. The industry in the EU is dominated by two strong European firms, with a positive impact on net trade. Both have become increasingly European in their approach to marketing, development and planning, and both now have finishing operations in each national market. The pattern of float plant centres and finishing operations which has been created across Europe certainly relies on the permanence of access to all national markets, but that access predates the single market measures in most cases.

Harmonization of building regulations has probably had the greatest positive impact on the process. Without this it would have been more difficult to simplify production patterns at float glass plants, because the number of sizes and specifications for the building sector could not have been reduced. It would also have been more difficult to organize logistics if product standards for the output of finishing plants had not become compatible across national boundaries.

Standardization of products, and a European approach to float production and finishing, would probably have occurred even without single market measures – given that the automotive industry had established itself on a European scale in response to global competition.

A.8. Clothing

A.8.1. Market context

In general, Italian textile and clothing (TC) companies would appear increasingly European minded, i.e. more inclined to take advantage of new opportunities offered by the EU market. This is confirmed by the high level of exports towards the EU: in 1994 EU TC exports was 58% of total exports, 66% when also including EFTA countries; conversely, in the Italian manufacturing sectors as a whole the corresponding shares were 51% and 60% [Ice, 1995].

Due to the development of big pan-European distributors, the degree of concentration in the distribution channels is going to increase [Steele, 1995]. This evolution will mainly affect Italy, where the concentration degree of retailing is lower than in the EU as a whole: in Italy only 10% of TC sales comes from big distributors, whereas about 50% of exports are towards big retailers.

This implies, on the one hand, a greater attention among Italian exporters towards big pan-European distributors, and on the other hand, more opportunities to export for SMEs without a direct distribution chain. The first opportunity has been exploited by Golden Lady (774 employees and LIT 301 bn sales in 1994), where large retailers account for 70% of exports to France and 50% to Germany.

One of the SMEs that exploit the second opportunity is Igeat (LIT 10 bn sales in 1994), which deals with Galeries Lafayette, Printemps, etc.; Igeat's first market is not Italy but France, and the second is Germany. To avoid the competition coming from extra-EU imports Igeat produces fashion, customized and creative products, and proposes a different collection to each big customer, in order to give them the idea of exclusiveness and customization.

The Italian firms that try to pursue this strategy are making huge investments in high technology plants, based on CAD-CAM systems, automated cutting lines, automated warehouse, etc., in order to design and prototype such a very wide range of collections.

Another notable example is the Bic Puglia Sprint consortium in Bari which exports to large EU distributors. EU funds were used to subsidize international services to ten SMEs to export to EU markets using a common trade mark (named F. Ranieri) throughout the product range [*Largo Consumo*, 1995].

The opportunity to deal with pan-EU distributors is enforced by the penetration of big foreign retailers within the Italian market. The arrivals of Auchan, Continent, Markant and Carrefour enable SMEs to have contacts with EU retailers in their own city or country (without travelling abroad, shipping sample collections, visiting fairs, etc.).

Unlike the upstream relationships, large companies stand to benefit from the concentration of EU retailing. Of course, the weight of this distribution channel is relatively lower in big groups: Gft (1,492 bn sales 1994) and Marzotto (2,430 bn sales 1994) trade with Marks & Spencer for a low percentage of their total revenues. They prefer to control the demand evolution using their own direct distribution chain in the EU.

The relationship between SM completion and retailing concentration implies a new definition of 'ideal EU product', as the EU consumer's taste and, especially, EU distribution needs are different from those in Italy.

Firstly, big EU retailers need exclusive collections, such as Gft provides for Marks & Spencer in the high segments, or customized products, as Igeat (10 bn sales 1994) for Printemps (F) and Tamigi (20 bn sales) for El Corte Ingles (E) do in the medium-low segment.

Secondly, big EU retailers ask for big orders and delivery schedules: large companies and SMEs use outward production also for this scale (Igeat has 12 direct and 100 indirect employees).

Thirdly, the ideal product for big EU retailers is medium-high quality, but not the very high quality product usually destined for boutiques. According to this evolution some big groups are going to substitute brands having status symbol with brands having quality-and-reliability symbol. The goal is to maintain the same high unit margins in a lower price item.

Fourthly, big EU retailers require a lesser number of versions of the same collection than the usual mix asked by the Italian market. For example, Lubiam (LIT 60 bn sales in 1994) has 150 different sizes for each model; Gft had reduced that production complexity only a few years ago. The reduction of production complexity is a good economy, if we consider the high cost of design and prototype process: roughly 5–10% of total sales.

A.8.2. Overview of respondents' operations

During the last decade the foreign direct investments (FDI) of Italian companies have been increasing, in terms of number of plants and number of firms involved. During the 1990s even SMEs were involved in FDI abroad [Cominotti, Mariotti, 1994]. The aggregate data confirm this evolution: the stock of foreign employees in the 1991–93 period increased by 30% in the apparel industry and 11% in textiles; on the contrary the total industry average was 6%. The share of foreign employees out of the total TC employees doubled from 4% to 9% over the same period.

The corporate data show a similar pattern: Marzotto had no foreign employees in 1989 and 23% in 1993, and Gft increased from 23% to 36%. Within that trend, the importance of TC foreign employees located in Central and Eastern Europe has been increasing from about zero (early 1980s) to 40% (1993). The share of the total Italian industry accounts for 17% [Cominotti, Mariotti, 1994].

However, FDI in the EU was highly relevant in the 1980s, but has become far less important in the 1990s. Thanks to the abolition of tariff and non-tariff barriers, the EU is a domestic market for large companies, and a quasi-domestic market for SMEs.

The location factors for Italian FDI in Europe were:

(a)   labour costs in southern Europe, such as Spain (Zegna, Miroglio, Benetton, Gft), Portugal (La Perla) and Greece (Miroglio);
(b)   product-distribution relationships (i.e. Benetton in France, or Miroglio in Germany);
(c)   EU common trade marks (i.e. Marzotto and Gft in Germany);
(d)   good raw materials (i.e. Benetton in Scotland);
(e)   tailoring-skilled blue collars (i.e. Zegna in Switzerland).

The reduced importance of the EU within Italian FDI is confirmed by the aggregated data. In 1991 the foreign apparel employees in the EU and EFTA declined to 48% of the total foreign employees, and 52% in the textile industry; in 1994 the same percentages reduce to 28% in both sectors [Cominotti, Mariotti, 1994].

Another aspect very close to the SM completion is the penetration of foreign firms within the Italian manufacturing system. It is noteworthy to consider the role of extra-EU companies, that usually acquire an EU firm in order to take advantage from the SM programme. Within the TC Italian industry there are very few cases of US and Japanese-owned firms.

The completion of the SM, the higher European competition and the new commercial agreements with CEECs (Central and East European Countries) are going to increase the Italian outward processing trade (OPT) with Asian countries and, especially, with CEECs: Italian share of EU OPT was 6% in 1988 and 15% in 1993; the OPT counted for a mere 1% of total TC imports in 1988, but 10% in 1993.

We have to consider that international sourcing is likely to be used in standardized contracts, big consignments, and programmed orders (10–12 months in advance). This is why larger European distributors are going to be increasing their use of international sourcing.

The completion of the SM is likely to affect the product-country specialization of Italian sourcing, as follows:

(a)   Asian countries, as far as low quality, big shipments, long noticed orders are concerned (higher quality could be obtained using Japanese high price tissues);
(b)   Mediterranean Rim, as far as products using Italian tissues, small consignments, quick orders are concerned (higher quality is obtained using Italian technicians travelling abroad);
(c)   CEECs are in the middle of these situations (higher quality is obtained using Italian technicians locally resident) even if some cases of 12 days' orders have been registered in Romania [*Tecnica della Confezione*, 1995].

The level of international sourcing in the Italian TC industry as a whole is not dramatic: only 14% of the apparel and knitwear production [*ModaMarketing*, 1995]. Of course, in labour intensive production that share is higher (apparel 24%, shirt 22%) and in the highly automated sectors it is lower (knitwear 6%, stocking 1%). In another study the international sourcing in the total TC and footwear industry is less than 10% [Brusco, 1995].

The devaluation of the Lira has induced a slackening in international sourcing. In 1995 Simint (LIT 202 bn sales in 1994) of the Armani group relocated in Italy 90% of its former foreign production. Miroglio (1,400 bn sales 1994) is going to build a 400-employee plant in Taranto; in 1995 Benetton (2,751 bn sales 1993) doubled the production capacity of Castrette plant; Polli is building a new plant in the 'Mezzogiorno' area.

Economies of scale are more important in the downstream relationships than in the upstream or horizontal ones. The case of horizontal inputs reflects the absence of strategic alliances in the Italian TC industry.

Over the period 1985–94 the external growth in the TC industry was mainly based on non-equity agreements (45% of total operations), followed by majority acquisitions (30%), joint venture (15%), and minority acquisitions (10%) [Osservatorio acquisizioni e alleanze, 1995]. The main characteristic of these operations is the role of non-TC companies as partners of TC firms involved in agreements and joint ventures. Within the TC industry the cases of horizontal alliances between competitors in the same product are rare and not significant for the company's growth strategy. The attitude towards co-operation with non-competitor partners derives mainly from the small entrepreneur's culture, very suspicious of competitors' behaviour. Even in the TC industrial districts this seems to have happened when the relationships are not intermediated by local institutions, such as consortia, chambers of commerce, etc. On the whole SMEs try to increase their vertical integration in an indirect way, using non-equity agreements in order to save financial efforts.

A.8.3. Factors driving economies of scale

As a result of the increased competition prompted in part by the SM programme, Italian TC companies have reinforced their investment efforts in relation to the control of distribution channels and the relationships between producer and retailer.

(Other typical endogenous sunk costs, such as advertisement and R&D are not considered here: the data on advertising show a clear relationship with the economic cycle, and not with the structural data of the internationalization process; the data on R&D are affected by design and prototyping efforts, considered in the firm's accounting schemes as R&D investments.)

As far as the new relationships between producer and distribution channel are concerned, it is notable that producers' main efforts are aimed at reducing the market power of distribution channels. In this context, Italian manufacturers are making big investments in product-service relations, i.e. in the content of service within the manufactured goods. These investments are directed to:

(a) changes in the production cycle, in order to reduce time-to-market. Using information technology firms can substitute serial stages by parallel stages, and reduce time-to-market for designing and prototyping suits from 26 weeks to 19 weeks [Texco, 1991];

(b) increase the quick response production (10–15 days), at the expense of the traditionally planned production. For example, Lubiam ships only 50% of its total orders at the beginning of the season, and the remaining according to the sales cycle;

(c) just-in-time service for retailers (for example, Lubiam has a 48-hour consignment from a 2,000-products catalogue);

(d) increase out-of-season orders: due to the high volatility of modern demand, retailers place a minimum order at the beginning of the season waiting for the best kind of article in comparison with the demand. In response to this, manufacturers have to replay to short notice orders of 2–3 weeks [Largo Consumo, 1995];

(e) implement information technologies that link producer/distributor organizations. Thanks to Electronic Data Interchange (EDI) all the daily sales are transmitted from retailer to manufacturer, in order to plan shipments just-in-time. EDI is present in Lubiam, Max Mara, Gft and Benetton, among others;

(f) provide information service to the retailer, using free-phone numbers, selling-out training, consulting for window dressing, etc. [Confezione, 1995];

(g) service the final client through the retailer: for example, in two weeks Zegna provides a suit to measure (fitted at home, in the office or in the shop), and the price includes season washings, tailoring modifications (up until one year from purchase), and insurance against theft or loss. The customized suit by Lubiam is made up in two weeks, and represents 5% of total sales [Confezione, 1995];

(h)   provide financial service to retailers, organized by big groups with a strong financial position: for example, during the economic recession of 1991–93 Benetton granted deferment payment to retailers; Miroglio is now organizing a weekly payment on the basis of the weekly units sold, that allows the retailer to balance cash-flow [*Tecnica della confezione*, 1995].

If high quality production has greater opportunities to face EU competition and extra-EU imports, the future of Italian high quality firms is to increase the worker's skills by a continuous training effort.

Even though the relationships between product performance and skilled workers are clear, we do not find such training efforts in the Italian firms. Neither in the big groups nor in the SMEs does training play an important role.

In a (biased) sample of 37 TC firms, only 14 among them trained some workers in 1994. Several companies organize training meetings with franchisee vendors, and with the employees in the direct-owned shops. Max Mara and Lubiam are good examples of this attitude. The blue-collar workers were relatively less involved in training than white-collar workers: the former account for 31% of the number of trained people, the latter for 62%; the former account for 20% of the number of trained hours, the latter for 70%. The top management accounts for the residual share.

The evolution of firm organization at manufacturing plants or distribution channels affects the recruitment policy too: instead of looking for skills derived from experience, acquired in other companies, the interviewed companies are interested in open-minded workers, i.e. in persons having the right flexible mind for adapting themselves to the different production stages, to sustain the hard stress of quick response production, to work in teams, and to learn to use different machines and plants in a short time. In general, firms train new workers for a two-week period, but this period is considered too short by employees [Sda-Bocconi, 1995].

The strong competition between EU companies has also affected Italian industrial relations. In the last (1995) collective wage agreement, trade unions agreed to a very flexible working time organization. The TC firms can choose two different kinds of working time, according to production needs: the first one is a 6 hour-6 day organization, where three or four turns can be done; the second one is based on 8 hours-5 days, with a shifting idle day (Sunday is a fixed idle day) and six full days of production using two or three turns.

As far as the degree of the producer's power on the distribution channel is concerned, on the basis of our interviews several strategies appear to be possible:

(a)   some companies invest in direct distribution channels, or in franchising channels, both in Italy or abroad (see Table A.8.1);

(b)   some companies predominantly use agents, who put them in touch with boutiques, small retailers or wholesalers: for example, Gft (250 agents that determine 99% of total sales), Marzotto (where agents account for 80% of total sales), and Golden Lady (50% of total sales);

(c)   some SMEs deal with big distributors, using private label production, or with big department stores, opening small corners. The share accounted for by this channel is more than 90% in Mantel (LIT 11 bn sales), Maglificio Morga (26 bn sales), Igeat (10 bn sales).

Table A.8.1. Ownership of distribution channels

Selected Italian manufacturers			
Company	Sales (bn LIT)	Franchising outlets	Directly owned outlets
Benetton	-	7,000	40
Stefanel	508 (in 1993)	1,026	124
Max Mara	1,043 (in 1994)	130	58
La Perla	379	100	-
Prenatal (Chicco Group)	260	160	180
Zegna	250	-	46 (23 corners, 60 shop-in-shop)
Irge	32	92	20

The selling strategies are composed of a mix of different channels, according to the market characteristics. In the US, where department stores and big distributors determine three-quarters of total sales, all the interviewed companies have relationships with these channels, from which they acquire corners or shops-in-the-shop; but even in the US market, Italian firms usually pursue traditional strategies, opening directly-owned boutiques. In Japan, Italian firms are usually in touch with local trading companies, even when they try to open directly-owned points of sales.

A.8.4. Influence of external economies of scale

The Italian sourcing process is mainly organized within national boundaries. Conversely, in the other European textile and clothing (TC) industries, the sourcing process refers to the international level; with outward processing trade (OPT) and delocalization sourcing in the CEEC (Germany) or Asia (UK) or the Mediterranean Rim (France) [see *Textile Outlook International*, 1994].

In the Italian case we can find three different kinds of sourcing: within the 'district', at the north-south level, and as part of the relationship between small and large firms.

In the first case, the area of sourcing is so limited that relevant external economies are born: the industrial districts of Carpi (13,100 employees in TC industry in 1991), Prato (48,000), Como (17,300) and Biella (29,000) derived by strong relationships between customers and suppliers of the same filiere [Brusco, 1995].

The second and the third case are based on the high gap in the salary and in the flexibility of labour existing in the dual Italian economy. Some data confirm this:

(a)   in the Italian TC industry as a whole, the blue-collar labour cost of a less-than-10-employees firm is 78% of that of a more-than-500-employees company;

(b)   if we compare northern and southern firms of the same size, the gap is higher: the labour cost in the southern SMEs is 66% of that in the northern company [Brusco, 1995].

The characteristics of the Italian dual economy affect the role of the SM programme within the TC industry in several ways.

Firstly, the salary gap is higher in TC than in the other Italian industries, because of the diffusion of 'black jobs' in the TC filiere [*Politica ed Economia*, No. 5, 1995]: the 'black economy' accounts for 10% of total TC employment [*Il Sole 24 Ore*, 1995].

Secondly, due to the high quality of Italian production, there is a high weight of labour cost in TC firms: in the 352-firm sample by Centrale dei Bilanci [1995], labour cost is 68% of value added of the apparel and footwear industry and 18% of total sales over the period 1982–93. The importance of labour cost gives priority to labour savings.

Thirdly, the 1992 Lira devaluation has increased the competitiveness of Italian production. Northern large companies now also base their operation on outsourcing towards southern small firms.

Within the Italian industry, the most important case of external EOS is likely in relation to downstream input, and refers to the transaction costs. On the basis of our interviews we can estimate cost savings due to a higher concentration in distribution channels, from which higher orders and higher shipments follow. All the interviewed companies declared that orders coming from pan-European distributors are, on average, six to ten times bigger than the average order from Italian customers.

The savings are likely to be realized in the following ways:

(a)   cost saving in the acquiring of raw materials, due to the quantity of unit consignments and the early time of orders that the planned organization of big distributors permits: less 20% of raw material costs;

(b)   cost saving in the outward and inward production thanks to the reduction of complexity and volatility of production, and the bigger orders: less 20% of direct manufacturing costs. The complexity of production affects not only the workshop, but also the design and prototype process (the latter costs account for 5–10% of total sales);

(c)   cost saving in the distribution channel, due to reduction in the number of agents, number of contacts with distributors and advertising: less 30% of selling costs (we have to remember that the agent's profit is 10% in retailing and 5% in wholesale contacts);

(d)   cost saving in financial costs, thanks to the higher credit rate of big distributors within the credit bank discount, and to the lower client failures (irrecoverable credits): less 25% of financial costs on commercial credits and 90% of irrecoverable credits;

(e)   cost saving in general costs: we have received no estimations from the interviewed firms because of the difficulty of analysis (in any case, it is a minor percentage).

According to the distribution of costs, where raw materials' share is roughly 30% of total sales, manufacturing is 30%, selling is 25% and financial cost and irrecoverable credits are 7%, we could estimate a cost reduction of roughly 25% of total sales. If we compare the cost saving with the discount in price that big distributor usually claims, less 10–15%, the final result is an economy of at least 10–15% of the total sales.

As far as the role of big retailers in Italy is concerned, it is important to note that:

(a) big retailers have taken a rising share of Italian TC sales in recent years, from 9% in 1988 to 14% in 1993;

(b) big retailers are giving more importance to TC sales within their consumer goods: in specialized supermarkets, TC is 80% of total sales of Coin and 70% of Rinascente; in popular supermarkets, TC is 50% in Upim and 16% in Standa; in hypermarkets, TC is 10% in Continente, 8% in Coop and Città Mercato-Sma, 14% in Euromercato, and 7% in Auchan [*Largo Consumo*, 1995];

(c) within those shares, the weight of private label is massive: 90% in Coin (it owns Sirema, a manufacturing TC firm with LIT 43 bn sales 1993), 80% in Rinascente, 85% in Standa, and 95% in Upim;

(d) a special characteristic of the Italian system is that only 26% of the total private label comes from extra-EU imports, chiefly from Asia. On the contrary, in the EU this share is significantly higher [Ginzburg, Simonazzi, 1995];

(e) although the share of total sales directed to big distributors has been increasing in the last decade, it has still only reached a low level: at Marzotto it increased from 0% in 1985 to 20% in 1995, at Gft from 0% to 1%, and at Golden Lady from 10% to 35%. The 1995 share at Maglificio Bellia is 10%, at Lovable 15%, at Garda 10%, and at Zegna 10%.

A.8.5. Role of the single market

The completion of the SM programme affects the following aspects of the growth strategies of Italian firms: the role of suppliers, at national and international level; the role of EU markets, as far as product characteristics and distribution chains are concerned; and the role of human resources.

Within these aspects the important impacts are on:

(a) the external economies of scale, that could be exploited upstream, in connection with big suppliers, or downstream, in connection with big pan-European distributors, or by horizontal relationships in strategic alliances;

(b) the investment efforts of Italian firms, mainly those having the characteristics of endogenous sunk costs and the goal of facing European competition.

The SM has affected the traditional growth strategy pursued by Italian TC companies and favoured a high level of investments.

The main investment needs stressed by the firms we have interviewed are the following:

(a) Inward production: the new Italian plants that Miroglio, Benetton and Polli are going to build indicate good expectations in the TC future and in the SM programme.

(b) National outward production: the increase in the north-south links has been possible thanks to new forms of organizations, both in the north and in the south. In the northern companies, the main effort of the network company is in CAD-CAM systems, automated cutting lines, automated warehousing, etc., in order to design and prototype a very wide range of sample collections and to control the outward laboratories' outputs.

In the southern firms, the main investments are in new production capacity, machines and skilled workers.

(c)   International outward production: in the effort to invest in CEECs, SMEs try to use indirect controlling forms as non-equity agreements, and low levels of invested capital. This aspect implies a greater use of OPT.

(d)   The new relationships between small subcontractors and main producers, or between small producers and big retailers, force firms to invest in information technology systems, such as EDI, and in just-in-time organization.

(e)   The relationships between SMEs and pan-EU distributors force firms to invest in export consortia, trade marks, and quality management systems.

(f)   The changes in the production cycle force firms to invest in the reduction of the time-to-market process, using information technology firms that substitute serial stages by parallel stages of design.

(g)   The increased importance for promotion and corporate advertising force firms to have free-phone numbers, and to provide other services to final clients or retailers (such as selling-out training, consulting for window display, etc.).

(h)   In order to improve the producer's control of the distribution channel, a large number of companies make huge investments in direct-owned points of sale or in franchising channels, both in Italy and abroad.

Although our evidence is by no means conclusive, the completion of the SM may pave the way for bulk outsourcing, both at national and international level. On the basis of our interviews, we found several 'hollow companies' in the apparel filiere, such as Diesel (LIT 550 bn sales in 1994), Stefanel (316 bn sales), Belfe (125 bn sales) or Textura (71 bn sales), that design the product, acquire and cut the material, and organize the 'kit' to be assembled by external and small (<10 employees) laboratories. The distribution chain is, of course, controlled by the 'hollow company'.

The aggregated data suggest this evolution: the outward production increased from 59% in 1983 to 72% in 1992, and a low part of the latter (8%) is at the international level [Brusco, 1995].

As far as the SM impact on national sourcing is concerned, we could say that the higher competition induced by the SM has increased north-south sourcing – the new employment created in the southern TC industry in 1987–91 is higher than the new employment created in the remaining southern manufacturing system [Birindelli, 1995] – and has shaped a new organization. Usually, the northern company (e.g. Versace, 146 bn sales 1994) has no relationships with local southern SMEs, but only with its main subcontractor (e.g. Manifatture Ittierre, 329 bn sales). Also Tamigi (20 bn sales) has no relationships with Albany's SMEs that produce for Tamigi's main subcontractor in Puglias. This means that a new kind of firm is becoming more and more important: the intermediary firm that puts in place the so-called hollow company and the manufacturing system (even at the international level).

The structure of southern industry is going to be shaped according to the northern needs: high level of blue-collar labour, as the manufacturing aspects are more important than design and distribution; low level of exports, as the international relationships are a northern prerogative (except the links between Puglias and Albany).

Another aspect of the SM impact is the new opportunities for SMEs to become suppliers to European producers or, more likely, big pan-European distributors (today only 5% of TC SMEs have international customers) [*Tecnica della confezione*, 1995].

By contrast, the opportunities for large companies to find new suppliers in the EU industrial system are less important. Even if large companies could gain lower transactional costs through a reduced number of suppliers, we have to remember the low level of sourcing or acquiring of semi-finished product in the EU: that process mostly involves extra-EU countries or southern Italian firms. The main relationships between Italian and EU industry are undoubtedly within the downstream area, rather than upstream.

Other research on the impact of the SM on distribution channels predicts an increase in the degree of concentration, through the development of big pan-European distributors [Steele, 1995]. This forecast is overwhelmingly true in Italy's case, where the distribution system is very fragmentary:

(a)   in 1992 Italy had 30% of EU points of sale but only 24% of total TC consumption [Texco International-Roland Berger & Partner, 1991; Federtessile, 1995];

(b)   the small retailing sub-sector has a strong importance (67,000 points of sales in the TC), but a decreasing trend: it represented 79% of total TC sales in 1988, 70% in 1990 and 68% in 1993;

(c)   even the wholesale sub-sector is composed of relatively small and inefficient firms (6,000). This channel accounted for 45% of total sales in 1993;

(d)   large retailers account for 14% of total TC sales, where the EU average is more than 30% [Federtessile, 1995].

The completion of the SM is going to shape Italian distribution according to the EU model: on one hand, the big Italian retailers (such as Coin) are becoming bigger and bigger; and on the other hand, the entry of foreign big retailers (Continent, Auchan, etc.) in the Italian market will change consumer and producer habits, and reduce the protection of the Italian market.

A.9. Insurance

A.9.1. Demand trends

The insurance industries of EU countries differ considerably in many respects. Those in the Mediterranean countries have generally been growing much faster than in the northern Member States, although premium per capita is much higher in the north. National markets differ in their structure as well and, with the exception of reinsurance, remain largely national in the scope of their operations. Nevertheless, there are a number of trends common to the industries of all countries.

The EU Insurance Directives have resulted in the insurance industries of most EU countries readjusting to a more openly competitive environment. Insurers in those countries that formerly regulated premiums and contracts can no longer rely on selling standardized products at prices set at levels which support inefficient producers, with competition based solely on service and the control of distribution channels.

A major social change currently taking place within Western society which will have a significant impact on the insurance industry is that the dependency ratio (i.e. the proportion of the population of working age to those too young or too old to work) is rising, and will continue to do so over the next 20 years. Expectations of living standards in old age are also changing while the traditional family unit is increasingly breaking down. Changes in the dependency ratio and the resulting pressures on the Welfare State in Europe will provide a long-term stimulus to personal savings, which increasingly comes in the form of insurance (such as pensions policies).

Expenditure on insurance tends to increase at a faster rate than GDP and as GDP is growing, expenditure on insurance should rise faster. These economic features are similar across Europe. Furthermore, continuing deregulation and harmonization of the EU market is expected to provide opportunities for increased cross-border trade in insurance.

While consumers have historically spent more money on insurance as GDP grows, they are also putting increasing pressure on insurance companies to provide them with better value products and higher standards of service. The consumer is partly responding to changes in the marketplace and partly driving those changes. Over the last ten years the market has been stimulated by the development of new forms of competition, including the following:

(a)   Direct writers (i.e. those not using intermediaries) have demonstrated that they can achieve considerable competitive advantage by adopting a new approach to the market. In the UK they have 25% of the personal motor insurance market and a growing share of the household insurance market, and have begun to sell basic life and savings products.

(b)   Banks and building societies have tended to concentrate on the life sector. In the UK their market share has grown from 7% to 19% over the last five years. The bancassurance concept is based on the extensive contact that these organizations have with the public; salespeople should be more productive because they operate from 'warm leads'. Dramatic growth, however, has come largely from banks and building societies breaking ties with insurance companies and establishing their own operations (see Figure A.9.1). Bancassurers have so far shown limited interest in underwriting general insurance business, although they are important distributors of these products.

(c)   The last few years has also seen non-financial services companies entering the market, either with a retailing or consumer brands background. Their marketing and customer service expertise in the insurance sector is expected to influence the market's character.

The rapid emergence of direct writers over the last five years has forced general insurance companies to examine their approaches. Many established companies have started their own direct writing operations, but they are also transforming their intermediary-based operations. Duplication is being eliminated by the development of 'preferred partners' and the creation of networks fully automating data transfer.

Life companies are also examining new distribution techniques with the aim of boosting productivity. Remuneration structures for sales forces are being overhauled and companies are focusing on their core strengths and eliminating peripheral distribution outlets and products.

The brokerage sector is also experiencing enormous change, with a move away from commissions to fee-based advice. Some larger commercial brokers have disclosed that almost half their business now takes this form. Fees bring with them greater focus on value added.

Many insurance companies and intermediaries now face the need to rationalize activities and concentrate on chosen markets to generate higher productivity and simplify administration. This will still allow a diversity of approaches ranging from the supermarket approach and one-stop shopping, to large specialist providers and niche companies. The successful companies will be those which match their product and distribution strategies to customer needs and preferences.

The potential market for long-term care, health insurance and income protection products is enormous. Similar opportunities exist across Europe which, alongside the continuing deregulation of the market, will provide further opportunities for strong insurance companies. However, harmonization of tax, marketing practice contract and road traffic legislation are still many years away. The Third Life (92/96/EEC) and Non-Life (92/49/EEC) Directives merely mark the start of a single market in insurance.

A.9.2. Concentration

Over the ten years 1982–92 there has been a trend in the EU towards greater premium income in life business compared with non-life business. In 1982 life had 40% and non-life 60%, but in 1992 this had changed to 49% life, 51% non-life [CEA, 1993].

Concentration in the life market has not been high over the past decade; in certain cases (Spain, Ireland, Italy, Greece, UK), the opposite trend has occurred, as illustrated in the table below.

Table A.9.1.   Market share of the five largest life insurance companies, 1989 and 1994

Member State	1989	1994	% change
Belgium	56.0	55.4	-0.6
Denmark	62.4	70.0	7.6
France	47.4	47.6	0.2
Germany	33.3	30.9	-2.4
Greece	76.1	68.2	-7.9
Ireland	70.0	55.7	-14.3
Italy	64.5	46.1	-18.4
Netherlands	52.9	55.7*	2.8
Portugal	45.7	53.0	8.7
Spain	58.3	46.6	-11.7
UK	36.1	28.0	-8.1

* 1993.
Source: CEGOS.

In contrast, the non-life market shows significant concentration trends, notably in the northern European markets (Belgium, Denmark, Ireland), as the following table shows:

Table A.9.2. Market share of the five largest non-life insurance companies, 1989 and 1994

Member State	1989	1994	% change
Belgium	32.0	39.0	7.0
Denmark	47.2	60.0	12.8
France	41.5	40.8	-0.7
Germany	24.4	23.5	0.9
Greece	51.4	38.7	-12.7
Ireland	49.1	50.5	1.4
Italy	36.2	33.8	-2.4
Netherlands	31.8	44.0*	12.2
Portugal	55.8	53.7	-2.1
Spain	19.5	19.7	0.2
UK	51.9	28.7	-23.2

* 1993.
Source: CEGOS.

A.9.3. Mergers and acquisitions and strategic alliances

Most of the M&A activity, as well as the purchase of minority interests and strategic alliances, has involved the larger European insurance players. A prime example is Germany's Allianz which has made the following acquisitions: Deutsche Versicherung (the former East German state monopoly), the UK's Cornhill, 25% of Münchener Rückversicherungs-Gesellschaft, Rhin et Moselle (France), Riunione Adriatica di Sicurta (Italy), and companies in Spain, Hungary and the US. In 1991 it became the first European insurer to be authorized to form a subsidiary in the non-life sector in Japan. Generali of Italy is also an acquirer of foreign firms due to the fact that its domestic expansion in Italy is constrained.

Over the past decade British companies have been takeover targets because of the relative ease of acquisition in the UK. The following are some examples:

(a) Cornhill by Allianz (1986),
(b) Equity & Law by Axa-Midi (1987),
(c) Sentry by AGF (1988),
(d) Chandos by Sirius (1989),
(e) National Insurance & Guarantee by Skandia (1989),
(f) Prolific Life by Hafnia (1989),
(g) Pioneer Life by Swiss Life (1989),
(h) Victory Re by Nederlandse Reassurantie Groep (1990).

Other major alliances include:

(a) Marketing agreement between Allianz and Dresdner Bank (1992),
(b) J Rothschild Intl. acquired by Scottish Amicable (1994),
(c) Anglo-American acquired by Zurich Re (UK) (1994),

(d)   Cheltenham & Gloucester Building Society acquired by Lloyds Bank (1994),

(e)   Groupe Victoire acquired by Commercial Union (1994),

(f)   Provincial Insurance acquired by UAP (1994),

(g)   Swiss Re's European direct insurance acquired by Allianz (1994),

(h)   Sun Alliance and Royal Insurance unveiled a £6 bn merger to form the largest composite
        insurance company in the UK, the first such merger in more than a decade (1996).

Mergers are often less expensive than acquisitions. The Netherlands' fourth largest life
insurer, Amev, merged with its biggest savings bank, VSP Groep. One of Europe's biggest
bank insurers was created in the Netherlands in 1991 with the merger between Nationale
Nederlanden and Postbank. Share swapping is also used. In France, the largest insurer, UAP,
swapped 10% of its shares with BNP.

Joint ventures are also common in the EU. In the UK, Commercial Union and Midland Bank
formed a joint life-assurance undertaking, while NatWest formed a joint venture with Clerical
Medical. Scottish Equitable is linked to the Royal Bank of Scotland. Standard Life bought
35% of the Bank of Scotland in 1986 and has a tied agency with the Halifax Building Society.
In fact, insurers have links with eight of the top ten building societies. In Italy, TSB Life and
France's Caisse Nationale de Prévoyance set up a joint venture with Cariplo, the largest Italian
savings bank.

Some of the smaller companies in Europe sought to protect themselves from hostile takeover
by seeking mergers with companies established in other EU states. This had the additional
benefit of extending the geographic scope of their activities and thereby providing better
European service for their commercial policyholders. Other companies entered into more
formal groupings, setting up joint-venture companies as the vehicle for expansion of their
European operations. In addition, co-operation agreements were arranged between national
agricultural mutual companies and co-operative movement companies to provide local
servicing arrangements for clients throughout the EU.

The pace of such restructuring activity has now slowed down, and some groups are
rationalizing their European operations by withdrawing from markets where they feel that
either they do not possess a critical mass, or their long-term prospects are poor. Nevertheless,
the restructuring of national industries can be expected to continue, with the major pan-
European groups increasing their market shares and many of the smaller companies ceasing to
exist as independent entities. The industry will enter the 21st century concentrated on fewer
companies overall, and with a small number of large groups represented in most Member
States.

A.9.4. Trade

There has generally been a movement away from trade restriction since the mid-1980s towards
trade liberalization on both regional (EU) and global levels. That movement culminated in the
conclusion in December 1993 of the Uruguay Round of the GATT, which for the first time
embraced trade in services, including insurance and reinsurance.

Although the basic framework is now in place, the creation of a true single market has been
delayed by differences in tax regimes, judicial systems, road traffic and other legislation,
culture, market practices and language barriers. Acquisition of local companies therefore

remains the most practical approach for many in the short term. Others, such as direct writers, are establishing new operations through which they can apply their expertise, but in a form which they hope will be attractive to foreign markets. Some insurers have found that certain functions can be performed in their home country (such as claims processing and risk assessment) but that certain other functions require some local representation (such as claims handling). This poses some limitations to the full exploitation of scale economies (discussed below).

During the 1980s the introduction of mini- and micro-computers with links to a central computer enabled insurance companies to distribute to their branch offices first routine administrative work and later more complex tasks, and to supply them with ready access to customer and other information. Companies then extended their networks to independent intermediaries and tied agents, which, besides providing them with full functional support, also presented opportunities for cost savings by the elimination of tasks being performed by both the company and its intermediaries.

Work being undertaken by a joint task force set up by LIMNET (a UK market network), RINET (a Brussels-based reinsurance network) and two American bodies, Brokers and Reinsurance Markets Association (BRMA) and the Reinsurance Association of America (RAA), could lead to a global network connecting brokers and insurers/reinsurers world-wide within the next decade. Although purely screen-based trading is unlikely to replace physical face-to-face contact between brokers and underwriters for the placing of large, complex insurance and reinsurance contracts within the foreseeable future, screen-based trading does have important implications for the structure of European markets. It will facilitate the placing of risks across national frontiers with insurers or reinsurers located anywhere within the EU.

Central and Eastern Europe and the former Soviet Union are also gradually opening up to foreign brokers and direct insurers. More recently the focus of attention has moved to Asia, which has enormous potential in terms of population and economic activity. The eventual opening of China and Vietnam to London-based and other western insurers is being anticipated by the establishment of representative offices by several companies and brokers. Another vast market, India, is also expected to be reopened when the process of insurance denationalization is completed. Figure A.9.2 shows how UK general insurers have changed the distribution of their overseas business.

A.9.5. Overview of respondents' operations

There were five respondents in this case study: a trade association, three insurance companies (two composites and one non-life company – all three are among the largest British insurers) and a health insurance company. All are UK organizations.

One of the composites and the non-life company have non-life operations in many EU Member States. These foreign operations have responsibility for claims processing, marketing, new product development, and training and recruitment. Despite the fact that it has operations in seven states, the non-life company has not entered into any new EU markets between 1981 and 1995.

The composite company has life operations in five Member States (Denmark, Germany, Italy, Netherlands and Spain). This company also moved aggressively into Scandinavia in the 1990s. The company's direct and retail business made a greenfield investment in Germany in 1995; it also acquired a French direct insurer that year. Most of the company's underwriting and claims handling is done in local markets, which is now possible on a branch rather than subsidiary company basis. This means less export of capital is needed for market entry. The company has been aiming for less centralization, to establish stand-alone, self-sustaining operations in each of its markets. The company has partnerships with intermediaries in the area of personal direct insurance. It is also pursuing opportunities in direct insurance in Germany and France which are not as advanced in this area as the UK or the US.

The other composite insurer's life business operates in just two EU Member States, with two sites in the UK and more recently (the early 1990s) one in the Netherlands. Both sites undertake claims processing, marketing, new product development, and training and recruitment. The company's non-life business (just over one-tenth as large as its life business) has two sites in the UK which have responsibility for the four main functions. It has not opened any new business in any other EU Member State.

The health insurance company has two European sites responsible for claims processing, marketing strategy, new product development, and training and recruitment. The sites include one in the UK and one in Spain set up by acquisition in the late 1980s.

A.9.6. Factors driving economies of scale

The respondents unanimously said that the opportunity to exploit new economies of scale, either through entry to new EU markets or geographic concentration of activity, were not due to single market factors; although one composite insurer said that concentration was facilitated by the free movement of people and capital.

In the cases where insurance companies have been able to reap greater scale economies, the factors they designated as most important were a convergence of consumer demand in Europe, closer focus on the customer (niche strategies), a need to be more cost-efficient and a need to be more business development driven.

For the non-life insurer, common approaches in marketing and training and recruitment were developed in the early 1990s. The group reorganized along regional structural lines with two European divisions: UK and Ireland, and continental Europe. Increasingly broad policy issues and strategic initiatives, especially in marketing and IT, are now considered at regional level and validated at group level rather than locally. This has not been influenced by the single market as such but more by the expected convergence of consumer demand in Europe.

This company has increased the range of marketing approaches and channels it uses over the past decade, including direct distribution in the UK and Ireland. It says this was done as a result of a closer focus on the customer. There has been a narrowing of focus in the diversity and range of products/services offered. Again this has not been driven by the single market but as a result of greater focus and niche strategies, mainly local rather than regional. There has been no change in the range of skills of newly-trained staff, but the company does anticipate multi-tasking in future.

The company has achieved dynamic scale economies in the area of claims processing in terms of better service quality and greater innovation. In its marketing strategy benefits have come in the form of cost reduction; and in the area of new product development, benefits have arisen in cost reduction, better service quality and greater innovation. The company said that further improvements will arise from best practice transfer into and between local operations.

In one of the composite's life operations, common approaches in IT systems have been implemented in the Netherlands in the areas of claims processing and training and recruitment; but it said that the single market had not significantly influenced any of these introductions.

Where changes have occurred for the other composite's life operations, the most important driver of the increase in its range of marketing approaches has been common strategic approaches. In the area of product and service development the driver has been common customers. The respondent said that his company had taken standard UK products and made them available to EU clients.

There has been an increase in the range of marketing approaches and channels used as the company has moved from broker distribution to include direct distribution in the UK. It has also utilized some EU (non-UK) brokers in addition to UK brokers. This strategy, the respondent said, was not driven by the single market. There has also been an increase in the range of products and services the company offers. Retail financial products have been introduced into the UK, and new UK products are being sold outside Europe. Lastly, there has been an increase in the range of skills of new or newly-trained staff due to a re-engineering of UK processing to its present single point of contact for customers.

The benefits derived from dynamic economies of scale for this company have been in the areas of claims processing, new product development and training and recruitment. They have come in the forms of cost reduction, better service quality and greater innovation.

The company has moved from being cost conscious in the late 1980s to becoming more profit oriented in the early 1990s – or business development driven. In non-life operations, strategic marketing is now given much more emphasis largely due to business process re-engineering.

The health insurance company said that in the areas of claims processing and training and recruitment, IT harmonization has taken place between the company's UK and Spanish sites with provider policies in the area of claims processing and human resources. The company's respondent said that more input has been derived from non-European sources than from all interchanges within the EU.

There has been an increase in the range of skills of new or newly trained staff in that the single market has provided for greater opportunities for UK/Spanish cross-training. This change has been driven by a common strategic approach. The company has not seen any evidence of significant increases in economies of scale except the possibility of economies in the area of IT, but it anticipates these will not be specifically European.

A.9.7. Influence of external economies of scale

Both the non-life company and one of the composite insurers (in both its life and non-life operations) said that with regard to drivers of input costs, they believe that increased competition among agents and brokers has been influential in changing unit costs over the period 1986–91, despite the fact that they did not reveal whether unit costs had increased or decreased.

For the life business of another composite, changes in costs of agents and brokers increased by 5% between the early and late 1980s, and increased by another 5% between the late 1980s and early 1990s. In contrast, changes in labour costs declined by 20% between the first and second periods and declined by a further 25% between the second and third periods. They attributed labour cost reduction to process re-engineering. Increased scale and buying power in the company's operations, and increased contracting-out of certain operations, have been of only minor influence. The company believes that neither cost changes were driven by the single market.

Over the period 1986–91, the company's external relationships have had a high impact on cost reduction. They have also had significant impacts on product/service quality, product/service/process innovation and market penetration. They have had no impact on the geographic location of activity. The company representative said that external economies of scale relate to the expense problem in the insurance industry generally, and that to address this the company was outsourcing its mainframe application. He also believes that there are no external economies of scale to be had through labour supply in terms of country divisions, but perhaps in regional locations within countries; e.g. outside Dusseldorf there is a light industrial estate and a local educated, flexible workforce for direct selling.

The health insurance company said that with regard to labour input, there has been a move toward lower managerial staffing since the mid-1980s. The company has found that an increased concentration of scale and buying power in its operations had been quite influential in changing unit costs over the late 1980s. Increased contracting out has also had some influence.

A.9.8. Role of the single market

The Association of British Insurers noted that the free movement of products and services and also people and skills have been highly significant factors in permitting a 'single business' structure in the EU in commercial lines. The free movement of capital has also been significant in both personal and commercial lines. Harmonized technical standards have been only a moderate factor in personal lines and a rather low factor in commercial lines. Public procurement liberalization has not been a great factor in either area.

The non-life insurer found there to be little impact of the SM programme on either marketing, or product or service development. However, EU insurance directives, it believes, will drive changes in training and recruitment in future as the company anticipates multi-tasking.

One of the composite insurers said that the SM programme has had no impact whatsoever on the possibility of gaining greater scale economies. The other composite insurer said that the SM programme had minimal impact on 'best practice' but that underwriting and claims handling is now done in local markets on a branch basis (rather than subsidiary companies) due largely to the second Directive. The SM has facilitated (but not driven) decentralization that allows for movement of people. In addition, greater opportunities were opening up in Germany as the insurance directives would lead to greater price differentiation in the non-life area, which would have the effect of breaking the German insurance industry's former *de facto* cartel.

The health insurance company said it believes that common technical standards will drive changes in product/service development in future. EU insurance directives will impact the three areas of marketing, product/service development, and training/recruitment only with regard to national implementation in Spain. It believes a side-effect of these directives will be the squeezing of smaller Spanish competitors.

The company representative said that the SM has not brought economies of scale to the health insurance sector, and nor have reductions in non-tariff barriers to trade been influential in changing unit costs over the period 1986–91. Health insurance tends to complement state health finance, which is vastly different in each EU country. There is therefore little transferability of product design or service experience. Ideas are freely exchanged at European trade association level, but no significant cross-border businesses have yet been built on them. The 'single passport' opportunities introduced by the Third Directive are less applicable to health insurance, because health policies and claims are market-sensitive to local language, and the necessary cost containment pressures on local institutions can only really be sourced from local establishments.

The company has had an opportunity to establish business in another EU country, but that country's failure to implement the 'freedom of product design' permitted in the Third Directive has frustrated their attempt. Furthermore, it believes its market share is now under threat from continental bancassurers who might be able to loss-lead in the health sector via their UK acquisitions.

In summary, most of the respondent insurers did not believe that their companies had achieved significant economies of scale, either due to dynamic factors or to input cost factors. Where any economies were achieved they did not attribute them to the European Commission's insurance directives (though in some cases they did facilitate change). It is likely that insurance will continue to be written locally by agents or subsidiaries of insurers in the other country, because a local presence is necessary in order to inspire confidence in claims-paying ability. Furthermore, access to an efficient distribution network is vital; in practice this means the branches of banks and/or building societies. Hence, insurers will continue to form joint ventures or mergers with banks and building societies in order to grow. Bancassurance would have happened without the formation of a single European market, and this convergence of the money management business is the crucial development. The respondent companies share the view that the single market by itself is unlikely to produce dramatic effects on the growth of their companies, nor on their ability to reap greater dynamic or external economies of scale.

Figure A.9.1. Sector shares of the UK insurance market

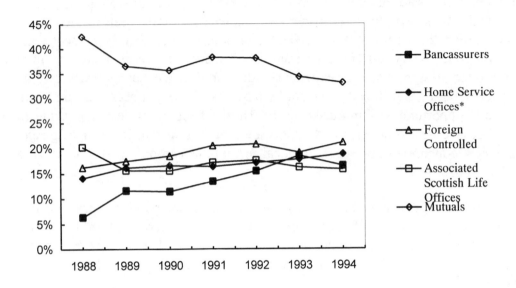

* Premiums are collected by an insurance company agent at the policyholder's home
Source : Association of British Insurers.

Figure A.9.2. Overseas general business net written premiums by territory

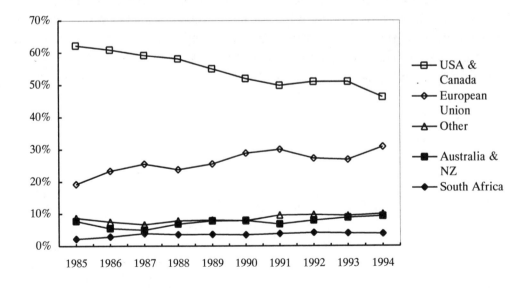

Source : Association of British Insurers.

A.10. Retailing

A.10.1. Market trends

Demand trends

The period has seen substantial change in the structure of the retail sector in many EU countries. The industry still accounts for the overwhelming majority of the number of enterprises in the EU, and in every individual country market, as well as for the largest single employment contribution of any sector. In all countries where reliable statistics exist, the numbers employed in retailing increased throughout the 1980s and into the early 1990s, even in those national markets where firms in the sector had invested most heavily in automation.

Retail sales growth has been less steady than employment. Retail turnover has shown at least one year-on-year downturn in real volume in each of the national markets except the Netherlands and France since 1985. In 1993 the weighted average volume retail sales index for the EU as a whole declined. Despite growth in the period, and strong investment in the sector, retailing has not been a low risk area for participating firms.

Almost by definition, store retailing is a local activity, whose outlets exist to serve customers in a specific area. The impact of single market measures on shop operations is, therefore, limited by local constraints. In this analysis we aim to examine the changes which have taken place for retailers in the EU in product specification and purchasing, in distribution, and in the operation of retail premises themselves. In each area we shall see that differences in market environment due to geography, to consumer tastes and behaviour, to ownership structure and firms' strategy play a major part in determining the realization of available scale economies.

Technology impact

At the level of the individual retail outlet there has been a major and continuing shift to larger units, both in grocery and other convenience shops, and in some areas of comparison shopping, with supermarkets, hypermarkets and cash & carry units replacing small traditional units. In part this shift has been driven by technology change with the automation of till operation, including scanning systems, increasing both the maximum selling capacity of shop units and ability to replenish them through an integrated warehousing and distribution system. The scope to take advantage of unit scale advantages depends on a large number of locally determined factors, including planning regulations, population density and the willingness of shoppers to travel. These vary enormously from country to country.

In distribution and warehousing the scope to realize economies of scale is influenced by available technology, and by the quality of transport networks. In both areas there have been changes which have tended to increase the scale of individual operations. The costs associated with warehouse operation, and with the information technology linking stores, warehouses and the purchasing operation, represent fixed costs and sunk costs respectively which benefit from being spread over a greater volume. A significant driver of business performance in this sector over the period has been the ability of businesses, through the use of technology, to increase the rate of stock turnover, both through stores and through warehouses. By better availability and analysis of consumer data, firms are able to predict purchasing patterns more accurately, reducing the need to carry stock and the degree of wastage; this type of advance often also increases the capacity of warehousing systems.

In the firms we have spoken to, a typical warehouse supports around 50 to 70 stores, normally within a geographically limited region. However, as transport links have improved it has been possible for firms to support stores which are further removed from their home region – including, within our respondent group, distances of over 800 km. For firms which operate the warehouse/superstore model, however, it is usually uneconomic for more than a small number of stores to be supported in remote sites; there are therefore barriers to entry for a retailer building up a critical mass of stores in a new country/region to support a new warehouse. The hypermarket and cash & carry models, on the other hand, where producers deliver direct to store, are in principle more readily transferable.

Purchasing arrangements have changed over the period for many of the large retailers. Improved transport links, and harmonization of product regulations, have provided more scope to purchase across national borders. There has also been a technological shift towards closer links between retailers and their larger manufacturing suppliers. Integration of store and warehouse IT systems with manufacturers' order processing, designed to improve utilization of stocks and of capacity, has tended to limit the number of suppliers to those prepared to make additional fixed cost investment.

In parallel with this cost effect, there has also been an increasing tendency for retailers to examine more critically the profitability of each metre of shelf space, and to reduce numbers of brands on offer. The ultimate example of this process is a store such as Aldi, which carries a limited number of manufacturers' brands alongside its own in order to maximize the productivity of its space. This trend – prompted both by technology and by competitive pressures – may reduce the costs of products for trading, but at the expense of consumer choice.

Our respondents in this case study include directors from two firms involved in the grocery trade, one a retailer and the other responsible for distributor relations for a pan-European supplier, and from the comparison goods sector which operate in more than one EU country. Two of the firms have extended the scope of their international activities in the last ten years, but in a relatively limited way, and are still overwhelmingly based in a single country.

Structural differences – and changes

The birth of global retailing, which has been heralded in some reports, is still very much a minority interest. In considering it, one must not confuse ownership with co-operation or the sharing of experience. One of the earliest examples of a multinational retailer, BAT, owned comparison goods stores of different formats in at least three different countries, and did not encourage them to co-operate or learn from each other. Each was treated as a free-standing investment, to which the corporate organization added very little value, and all were eventually divested as independent entities. In Associate Marketing Services (AMS) by contrast, the collaborative purchasing and learning venture between Ahold, Casino and Safeway, a mutual shareholding was considered a useful declaration of intent when setting up in 1989. However, by 1995 the benefits of intercompany learning were seen as sufficiently strong for the firms to dissolve the shareholding links without putting the collaboration at risk.

Transnational ownership of major grocery and comparison goods retailers has so far been limited. Acquisitions in Eastern Europe have been more common than purchases of retail networks – or the creation of new networks – across intra-EU boundaries. There have been some high profile exceptions (e.g. Marks & Spencer, Laura Ashley) but these have tended to focus on specific product areas and customer groups.

Opinion among our respondents is divided as to whether the current bid by UK-based Tesco for Docks de France will 'break the log jam' and begin a process of transnational concentration, but they are agreed as to why so many previous attempts to build international retail businesses have had limited success. Retailers have found it difficult to replicate in non-domestic markets their ability to predict the changing pattern of customer needs, and to manage their offering to meet customer expectations. These two factors are critical to competitive success.

However, there has been concentration in the pattern of retail supply in almost all EU countries over the last 15 years, both as a result of acquisitions and via the construction by a relatively small number of firms of large retail units, either large superstores (shops over 2,500 m^2 supplied via warehouses) or hypermarkets (large stores big enough for supply direct from manufacturers). The impact has been determined by differences in national planning and licensing regulations governing the building of new stores. The range of supply patterns by country is illustrated in Table A.10.1, showing concentration (top three firms) in grocery, and the proportion of trade by type and size of outlet.

Table A.10.1. Concentration and pattern of grocery supply, 1993

Country	Grocery share of top three firms	% via hypermkts & large supermkts	% via small supermkts *	% via other outlets
Sweden	95%	38	34	27
Finland	80%	36	32	32
Denmark	77%	37	31	32
Belgium	58%	56	29	14
Austria	56%	26	34	40
Netherlands	47%	31	55	15
Germany	46%	40	33	27
Ireland	43%	53	16	31
UK	43%	70	12	18
Portugal	41%	43	11	46
France	38%	76	15	8
Spain	20%	35	13	52
Greece	17%	na.	na.	na.
Italy	11%	26	22	52

* 'Small' supermarkets are under 1,000 m^2.
Source: Nielsen.

This pattern illustrates the very different structure between four main groups of countries. Scandinavia shows a very concentrated ownership structure, but a relatively strong smaller shop sector, reflecting both the dispersion of population and a strong social commitment to equality of access and national average pricing. Norway, outside the EU, fits the same pattern. Austria shares some of these characteristics, but the ownership pattern is not yet so concentrated.

Germany and Belgium have a somewhat higher proportion of trade through large outlets, and a lower firm concentration ratio. The number three retailer in each country is Aldi – so far the only example of a strong share company in more than one national market. The Netherlands has an intermediate firm share structure, but its proportion of smaller stores is affected by short journey shopping, much of it by cycle.

The UK and France have the highest proportion of sales via large stores – although in France the proportion of hypermarkets is larger. This reflects a less restricted planning system during the 1970s and 1980s, which is now becoming more regulated with fewer opportunities for new large out-of-town stores.

Portugal, Spain and Italy (and Greece) have a much higher proportion of small stores than the other markets, reflecting a more fragmented retailing and distribution pattern, and different consumer behaviour. In Spain and Italy firm concentration is also low, although acquisitions by French retailers and developments by local firms have made a significant impact.

The distribution of grocery retail firm activity across EU, and adjacent, markets is shown in Table A.10.2. Some of the firms are co-operatives, consortia or franchise operations, with ownership structures which affect their ability to compete in particular ways. For example, in many of the franchise operations, including Spar, separately owned shops retain the right to choose stock items for stores independently, which limits their ability to take advantage of technology for automatic replenishment. This type of arrangement extends into some relatively large retail brands including some in both Germany and France, and it limits the ability of retail networks to take advantage of both operational scale economies, and marketing economies. In the other large and developed market in the UK, on the other hand, most of the main retail brands are owned by quoted companies, which are run as single entities.

The retailer activity pattern shown in Table A.10.2 emphasizes the different position in the more fragmented markets of Portugal and Spain. None of the retailers shown is among the top three firms in any of these countries; for example, despite the presence of major French firms in Spain, their market position there is not yet strong. These markets are led by local retailers which operate almost exclusively within the country, and have some way to go to develop the benefits of scale. Also in Ireland, which is a relatively concentrated market with a large proportion of grocery sales through large stores, local firms lead with little competition from outside.

The rate of penetration in opening up transnational retail outlets has started to pick up in the grocery area since 1992, particularly by French stores. In addition to the entry into Spain by Carrefour and Intermarché, the French group Promodès has entered Greece, and now has six stores in Italy. The complex system of permits required to open supermarkets in Italy is clearly a strong barrier for non-domestic firms, but it appears somewhat easier for hypermarkets and cash & carry operators to enter, as evidenced by the 19 stores that Metro has succeeded in establishing. However, in a market such as Italy, hypermarkets supply the many small retailers and therefore perform a rather different economic role from that in their home market in

Germany. Since 1993, Metro has also opened in Denmark, further evidence of the mobility of this format. During the late 1980s Marks & Spencer expanded its operations in France. During the early 1990s it opened outlets in the Netherlands and Spain, and in 1996 it opened its first store in Germany.

Table A.10.2. Retailer activity by national grocery market (1993)

Firm	S	FIN	DK	B	A	NL	D	I	UK	P	F	E	GR	I
Metro					*		*							
Edeka			*				*							
Rewe							*							
Aldi			*	*	*	*	*	*	*		*			
Spar	*	*	*	*	*	*	*	*	*	*	*	*	*	*
Carrefour								*			*	*		
Intermarché				*							*	*		
Promodès							*	*			*	*	*	
Leclerc											*	*		
Sainsbury									*					
Tenelmn					*	*	*	*						
Tesco									*		*			
Auchan							*				*	*		
Casino							*				*			
ICA	*													
Argyle									*					
Migros					*						*			
Asda									*					
Co-op Ital.							*							
Ahold						*				*				
Co-op Swe	*													
System U											*			
Co-op CH											*			
Docks de F.											*	*		
Cora				*							*			
Somerfld.									*					
GIB				*										
Kesko		*												

National markets in order of local concentration (share of top three as in Table A.10.1).
Retailers in order of share of Europe turnover (from Metro 3.2% to Kesco 0.5%).
Source: Nielsen.

Economic analysis of purchasing and distribution structure is complicated by the different roles of store types in different countries. UK stores are reasonably homogeneous in their approach to integrated distribution and supermarket operation, although there has been some penetration by hypermarkets and discount warehouses. The UK approach to organization is also used by Ahold, Casino and Promodès. But in France, Germany, and other markets, firms such as Intermarché, Leclerc and Edeka – as part-franchise operations – are effectively wholesalers rather than integrated retailers. The French No. 3, Carrefour, is in the process of centralizing logistics to the UK model in order to reduce costs and increase stock turnover.

A.10.2. Overview of respondents' operations

Location and scope

All our respondents had their operations overwhelmingly based in a single EU country. Each operates over 400 stores, from around six or seven warehouses. One had increased its number of stores by over 30% in the period, with some increase in average size. Another has reduced its number of stores by over 40% in the last six years, with a significant increase in average store area. Each firm has operations outside its domestic market, but only a few stores. In each case their initial ventures outside the domestic base were supplied from the 'home' logistics system, and shop locations were confined to similar markets with shared language and tied – or almost tied – currencies.

Each of our respondents had spent a considerable amount of effort attempting to understand the significant differences in margins between retail operations in different European national markets, not just between categories but within them. In deciding whether or not to invest in market entry they had analysed:

(a)   whether there were factors affecting costs and margins for all operators in a market;
(b)   whether there were specific problems in 'managing at a distance' in the market;
(c)   whether the offering was appropriate to the market.

None yet had a warehouse infrastructure outside the domestic market, although one was in the process of assembling a store network to support one. Its plans for logistics post-2000 were based on increasing the average size of warehouse, and making greater provision for cross-border supply. Two problems needed to be overcome before the company could confidently commit to this. Firstly, the control systems for dealing with fluctuating currency relationships have to be perfected (or a single currency established). Secondly, the ability to understand and predict consumer needs and buying patterns accurately needs to be built into the stocking and replenishment systems to be used – which even firms such Marks & Spencer found difficult in its initial stores outside its home market, 20 years ago. This problem is not yet solved! An example was quoted of Tesco finding it difficult to service its Calais store from a Kent warehouse, although it had no problem supplying Northern Ireland from Scotland.

Purchasing is international for all the firms contacted, but controlled from a single centre. One respondent had pursued a strategy of dual responsibility for purchasing, in the UK and France, but is now concentrating this activity back in the home country. Respondents with a leading share in three or four product categories of one or two EU national markets are able to negotiate effectively at a global level. For another respondent in grocery, who is a member of Associate Marketing Services (AMS), procurement is partly co-ordinated with other members of the group, which includes Casino, Argyle, Ahold, ICA, Mercandona (Spain), Kesko, Danske Supermarked, Allkauf and Edeka. Migros of Switzerland was a member but has now left. The operation of the group is managed after consultation with the EU's competition directorate to avoid the exercise of excessive market power, and many of its initiatives are bilateral (agreements between two members to share costs of development or distribution), rather than Europe-wide purchasing deals. The respondent company retains control of its own purchasing function, based in its home market.

New market entries

Only one of our respondents has made an entry into another EU national market at anything like the critical mass of shop units required to support a fully integrated distribution system. There are examples of other entries described previously, but many of these are into Eastern Europe (Ahold, Tengelmann, Aldi, IKEA) or South America (Carrefour) as well as in the EU. The drive for growth is what has led retailers to look outside the EU, once the major opportunities for development in the Spanish, Portuguese, Greek and Italian markets have been addressed. The need for growth has proved a more powerful driver in directing entry investment than the impact of the single market. One of the reasons cited for this in our interviews was the tightening of planning controls on availability of sites for new stores in the major EU markets.

Mergers, acquisitions and strategic alliances

Two of our respondents had been through the acquisition process at the beginning of the period, but in neither case had it served to increase transnational scale. Both had been divested by a larger group, essentially as national units, and had subsequently focused the majority of their efforts on organic growth.

AMS clearly fulfils the role of a well-functioning strategic alliance for our member respondent. Those responsible for business development within the firm see it less as a tool to negotiate lower prices, than as a platform for innovation. For example, it has been used recently to develop and test a new scanning system to offer better service to customers, and it operates shared procurement in areas of the world where individual stores would find it hard to operate – thus increasing choice. It has also developed new approaches for refrigeration and display, sharing the advantages between participants.

Perhaps most interestingly AMS has been used to develop common specifications for store brand products, together with key suppliers. For example, by agreeing a joint specification for disposable diapers with supplier Kimberly Clark, the group has been able to create with the manufacturer both development and production scale economies, shared between producer, retailer and consumer. This combination of strategic alliance in both horizontal and vertical directions may extend to sourcing outside the EU, so is not necessarily linked to the single market.

One of our respondents emphasized how important it was to work with partners or franchisees in many of the Mediterranean markets, but this has more to do with local market access rather than scale *per se*.

A.10.3.   Factors driving dynamic economies of scale

Differences between national customer needs are quoted by all our respondents as a major barrier to integrated transnational operation of retail networks. In the words of one, 'Retailing competence has not yet proved to be exportable between countries', while another said 'Our format, which is very successful in two countries, fails when operated by others elsewhere, not just in the EU but also in the US'. The importance of developing systems to understand, predict and provide for local consumer behaviour is paramount. Customer tastes, travel patterns, shopping frequencies, response to advertising and promotion, seasonal behaviour and price sensitivity are all to some extent national characteristics. Firms' ability to transfer their understanding of these factors from one market to another is limited – much more so than appears to be the case in the marketing of individual products.

The scope for common marketing approaches is limited both by lifestyle differences, and by variations in national food safety regulations. One of the AMS members said 'We would like to be able to transfer our marketing approach for cheese from France to the UK, but it wouldn't be legal'.

There is no 'lead' market for retailing innovation in the EU, but different countries' retailers have focused on different strengths. Within the AMS group, for example, Germany is recognized as having developed store operational approaches which maximize space productivity, in response to planning constraints. The UK is seen as the leader in IT-based logistics as a result of intense competition between the major players in a 'Porter'-type cluster.

Free movement of products is limited in some areas by food health regulations as noted above, but the improvement in trans-European transport links has lowered distribution costs, and increased the incentives for firms to co-operate in areas such as seeking return loads for partners. Free movement of capital is cited as significant by one of our respondents, but only indirectly. 'It was probably important in facilitating the shareholding exchange which helped to create AMS. This was a symbolic anchor, a statement of intent and mutual confidence, to underpin the relationship when it started. Now we value the relationship enough not to need the capital tie.'

Knowledge transfer within firms is illustrated by our respondent which has entered a market adjacent to its home base. Proving that its models of consumer behaviour could be modified and transferred required significant internal study; dealing with currency differences was a major learning experience in itself, from which the company hopes to benefit when it enters another market. But the most important transfer the firm considers it has to make is the ability to manage stores at a distance. Many retail firms are tightly controlled, and across Europe many successful firms are owner-managed and privately owned. Even where this is not the case, our respondent operating in two markets has put significant effort into management systems for devolved operation – which has so far been successful.

Knowledge transfer between firms, in a framework like AMS, seems to those involved to offer benefits of scale without many of the risks outlined earlier. Each of the participants nominates a co-ordinator who identifies issues which their own store is concerned to explore, and the firms seek areas in which they can exchange experience, learning from one another's strong points. In part this depends on the companies involved not having 'head to head' competitive issues. The three main players in AMS have had fundamentally different strategies over the last few years. Ahold, having saturated its main EU markets, is targeting North America and other new growth areas; Casino has been through a domestic acquisition programme and is now targeting Eastern Europe; while Argyle is developing both share and quality in its main domestic market. Within these different objectives, it is possible for firms to share technology, procurement, logistics and new product ideas without conflict of interest. Scanning systems, return load arrangements, logistical systems and development of store label product specifications have all been shared over the five years, and the process has delivered benefits on quality and costs.

A.10.4. Influence of external economies of scale

The ability to secure competitive sources of supply is a crucial determinant of retail business success. This is why large sections of the industry are consolidated into buying groups, such as Cometca in France, which comprises the top four retailers. In some of these groups it is difficult for a supplier to obtain shelf space in any of the member stores without 'buying in' to become a supplier to the group – viewed by some suppliers as an anticompetitive practice. But these groups do provide networks for information exchange, and stronger bargaining power to the retail members. The disadvantage which is seen in some groups, including co-ops, is over-emphasis on price as a buying criterion as opposed to quality and innovation. In buying groups which are shared within a country this does not necessarily benefit either the retailer, whose scope for differentiation is reduced, or the final consumer, whose choice may be limited.

Some international buying groups have proved less successful than others. For example, Deuro, established by Metro (Germany), Macro (Netherlands), Asda (UK), and Carrefour (France), has been wound down. These are four partners containing quite different formats, which may have made external economies hard to realize.

Within AMS the scope for this type of conflict is somewhat reduced because retailers tend to reach bilateral arrangements for specific products, and for the most part the group only has one or two members in each national market. External economies are achieved in this system through the use of local procurement expertise; for example, Mercandano procures Spanish olives for other members using its local knowledge, and Argyle procures whisky and smoked salmon. In cases where bilateral procurement arrangements involve products with similar transport needs, they can also help achieve external economies through better utilization of vehicles and distribution capacity.

Whichever type of arrangement retailers choose – or if they choose to operate independently – the ability to purchase across Europe subject only to local health and safety regulations has increased both choice and price competition. The existence of 'arbitrage' by retailers and wholesalers, shipping products into higher priced markets and eroding local premiums, has affected the way in which producers market and price their products both within the EU and outside it.

At least one respondent made it clear that its adherence to an alliance was originally seen as a response to 'Europeanization' by manufacturers. The introduction of European sales organizations by some brand owners was seen as a potential threat by strictly national retail buyers. In the event, apart from levelling down prices in some peripheral markets, the impact has been less dramatic. Producers have introduced European branded products, with labelling to meet all national requirements, which simplifies the logistics for wholesalers or retailers who move products across borders. But the structure of commercial arrangements has remained largely national, reflecting the different consumer needs and different procurement models for most markets.

A.10.5. Impact of the single market

Interestingly, the retailer among our respondents which had made the most significant move into an adjacent market gave the single market least credit for its ability to carry out this move. If a single currency had been in place it would have counted for more. However, the existence of common product standards, and the free movement of products and capital was an important condition for this firm.

Another respondent commented that expansion into other EU markets initially led to diseconomies, through the complexity of managing different retail environments and serving different consumer tastes. Even where the retail formula did prove exportable, success was less to do with economies of scale over the longer term and more with targeting growing consumer markets in growing national economies. Cost advantages of different locations (e.g. in property as well as purchasing) were not significant.

Our AMS member credited the ability to take shareholding stakes in partners without added risk as having given an important impetus to the development of knowledge sharing and development collaboration. Enhancing the ability of stores to innovate, perhaps when they are not among the top few EU firms, appears to be a significant benefit from the collaboration which requires this degree of interdependence. Retail innovation, both in products and in systems, is a high fixed cost/high capital process, and so frameworks which permit cost sharing should help boost the number of effective competitors. It is difficult to point to effective transfer of innovation from partnerships across the EU boundary, although there have been many attempts and it will be interesting to see how the eastern European ventures work.

But real benefits in procurement, in product innovation and in developing store systems have been identified by respondents as being at least partly aided by the existence or the expectation of the single market. Without the collaboration which it has permitted, products, R&D, and operating technology would have cost more or carried higher risks. Increasingly, as competitive advantage in retailing depends more on personnel and service development and an operator's relative learning rate, the ability to transfer knowledge between markets becomes more important; and one respondent saw their membership of the European Council as highly relevant in this respect.

APPENDIX B

Outline technological assessments by industry sector

This section draws on recent experience from PIMS consultants and company contacts of technology changes related to scale and scale economies over the period 1980–95. In addition, where sufficient observations are available, it provides a brief profile of business characteristics from PIMS observations within each sector.

It is not complete across the sectors identified by Buiges et al [1990] as 'sensitive' to the single market, since there are some in which we do not have either recent international experience, or sufficient sector-identified data to provide a robust sector profile. Where one is available without the other, we have provided it.

We comment on the cost impact of changes in technology under four headings:

(a)   technology inherent in the product (e.g. switch to mobile communications);
(b)   technology in process of manufacture (shift to capital intensive mass production);
(c)   technology development costs;
(d)   marketing and distribution systems.

The sector profiles focus on quantitative measures for which the sector observations show a systematic tendency across the sector sample. Usually a characteristic is mentioned only if it lies in the top or bottom quartile of the range of values found for all sectors.

B.1.   High technology/public procurement NACE groups

330   Office machines/computer hardware

(1)   Technology, products and scale

Downsizing in products delivered to customers from mainframes to minicomputers, then to PCs has been carried through since 1980 for many applications. The impact of technology change at each stage was to bring down both costs of production and barriers to entry. However, measured in terms of functionality and performance, the maximum size of computer installation continues to grow. Technology change has transformed monolithic computers into systems which can be built up from discrete, relatively cheap, but powerful elements.

A major technology change in peripheral equipment has been the shift from mechanical to optical/electronic systems. For example, the substitution of jet/laser printers for dot matrix has pushed some suppliers out of the European market, and brought in others from adjacent markets such as copiers – effectively enlarging the market and increasing the scale leverage of optical technology research.

Although software systems are not part of this NACE category, the computer market is increasingly affected by them, because they are sold as complementary products in the same package. Economies of scale here – in the consumer segment and in standardized business applications – can be inexhaustible. However, in tailored software systems for business, where an increasing portion of value added is taken by 'value added resellers', it is clear that diseconomies of scope exist alongside economies of scale. Specialists in many particular niches of the business systems market, for example, exist alongside large scale generalists such as Andersen.

(2)   Technology, processes and scale

The shift to minicomputers, then PCs in the late 1970s and 1980s permitted new manufacturers to enter the market at significantly lower scale than market leaders. This suggests either that at first economies of scale were not large, or that market leaders' costs or prices were unreasonably high. As entry to markets increased the number of suppliers, standardized products and techniques to speed manufacture came to dominate processes:

(a)   in chip manufacture (optical processes and techniques for placing atoms in crystals);

(b)   in PCB stuffing (optical process replacing printing, and press/glue replacing solder);

(c)   assembly (more robotics and automated testing).

As the number of suppliers in the global market has increased, many of the businesses involved in supply have become more specialized and less vertically integrated. Instead of IBM producing processors, computer assemblies and software, the global industry is now dominated by Intel developing chips, clone/Unix manufacturers designing and assembling machines, and Microsoft providing software.

Economies of scale driving down manufacturing costs of hardware are very different from behaviour of costs in one-off big system software. System complexity can make the production of large solutions for corporate systems costly. An increasing part of this activity, which used to be given away free to sell computers is now being undertaken by independent consultants, because hardware prices are being bid down faster than software in competitive markets.

(3)   Technology development

Development economies for major parts of the office machinery market are obvious. In the processors sector Intel has established a commanding position, and has maintained the importance of innovation (and hence its scale advantage) by linking the expanded capability of its new products to the increasing complexity of software systems. Development costs, if anything, are getting larger, and so the importance of spreading them over increased output of standardized product increases.

Standardization and innovation have similarly affected optical systems (printers and copiers) and software (Microsoft for business PCs and the consumer market).

(4)   Marketing costs

Marketing approach for big business users has changed less than the products through much of the 1960s and 1970s, but is a significant cost. For consumer marketing the introduction of direct selling/making to order has made a difference, offering new routes to market for smaller suppliers.

[*Source*: Consultants working with global and European-focused IT companies.]

Sector profile for NACE 330 – 22 businesses

Businesses in this sector experienced relatively rapid real market growth of 6% per annum. Their market sectors were fairly highly concentrated and had high product differentiation. Marketing expenses were very high at 15% of revenue.

Production was primarily in small batches. Value added was high, typically 75% of revenue. These businesses had low dependence on a few suppliers for their purchases.

The investment to value added ratio is low at 67%, and fixed capital intensity (measured as gross book value of plant and equipment/value added) is particularly low. Major technological change was experienced by 58% of these businesses in the last eight years. R&D expenses are fairly high at 3.5% of sales, and the development time for new products long – typically about four years.

344   Telecommunications equipment

(1)   Technology, products and scale

Products in this industry have undergone major changes, and their adoption has been accelerated in many countries by deregulation of user industries. Development of more powerful switches and network systems have increased functionality and reduced cost of equipment. The introduction of IT into telecommunications systems has increased the carrying capacity of conventional lines, led to the explosion of demand for high capacity optical lines, and broadened the range of applications for telecommunications equipment. In the corporate market, IT is also increasingly being used to develop customized systems for companies, using standard hardware components and made-to-order software.

As in office equipment/computers, costs for individual products have fallen sharply, but increasing functionality and complexity of systems have kept system costs high. Development of mobile communications has changed market structure, opening up competition between system operators but also making economies of scale more important to them.

(2)   Technology, processes and scale

Economies of scale in production of equipment have become more significant, with similar effects to those in office equipment/computers, because the major components of equipment and elements of cost are similar:

(a)   system design and development;
(b)   microprocessors and other electronic components;
(c)   PCB manufacture and assembly;
(d)   box and system assembly.

As in office equipment/computers there has been a steady trend towards outsourcing parts of the value chain. Component manufacture and PCB production are subject to external scale economies for many producers except the very biggest.

(3)   Development costs

R&D continues to rise as telecommunications and IT converge – intelligent communications equipment is a fast-growing sector of the market, and the IT required to underpin mobile communications is also substantial.

(4)   Marketing costs

These are becoming more important in the telecoms industry now, because regulated monopolies have been turned into competitive markets. In many countries this is because mobile communications entrants are challenging state monopolies, or because rules of access to former monopoly networks have been changed. Marketing scale economies for those parts of the equipment industry selling to end-users are therefore growing in importance, as the complexity of routes to market increases.

[*Sources*: Consultants working with UK telecoms company, and global 'intelligent telecoms' suppliers.]

Sector profile for NACE 344 – 17 businesses

These market sectors had highly differentiated products and services with a very high rate of new product introductions. Marketing/revenue was high at 14%.

Value added for the businesses was relatively high at 73% of revenue. Production was primarily in small batches with low customization of products. Fixed capital intensity was low. Major technological change occurred for 53% of these businesses. R&D expenses were high at 4.8% of sales.

These businesses had many suppliers.

372   Medico–surgical equipment

(1)   Technology, products and scale

Most of the interesting areas of medical equipment where technology is changing – IT and electronically based diagnostic and measuring equipment – appear to be included in NACE 344. Many products are highly specialized, and often customized – which limits scale economies in product use or production.

Medical equipment has seen steady substitution of disposable for reusable items, so volume production has become more important in the industry. Many equipment markets (e.g. syringes) have been global for ten years because of this effect.

Main technology trends have come about as a result of improved materials, the search for better control of treatment, and – in the US and some other markets – simplification and cost reduction in diagnostic and treatment systems which means that their use can be decentralized from hospitals to doctors' offices. This means smaller, more standardized items of equipment, which are more susceptible to scale economies in production.

[*Source*: Consultants working with firms based in France and UK.]

Sector profile for NACE 372 – 19 businesses

Real market growth was high at 6.2% p.a. Market concentration was very high, with the top four companies having 90% of the market. Market differentiation was also very high, as were marketing expenses at 13% of revenue.

Vertical integration was high with value added at 71% of revenue. Fairly high R&D/revenue costs were incurred and product development times were fairly long. Over 30% of these businesses had the benefit of product or process patents. Customization of products was low.

B.2.   Public procurement/regulation

257   Pharmaceuticals

(1)   Technology, products and scale

Some of our industry contributors believe that the ability of drug companies to deliver more 'blockbuster' drugs is declining. Product innovation is becoming more incremental and also more related to delivery systems, and to 'packages' of therapeutic treatment rather than the traditional 'silver bullet' approach. However, the basic development model of the industry is still the same shape as it was ten years ago. Economic pressures come from the fact that the rise of generic products has shortened the effective lifespan of branded ethical products, during which they can command a high premium over possible substitutes, to terminate very soon after the life of the patent.

(2)   Technology, processes and scale

Production costs have to date been an almost insignificant part of pharmaceutical cost structure – typically under 20% of revenue. However, traditional chemical production processes for many active ingredients are long and complex, with interdependent multistage processes. Ineffective use of capital assets is often a problem with these processes. Scale economies, where they exist, are due to shared know-how in process design and management within companies, rather than production scale economies.

The development of biological routes to active ingredients offers significant potential gains – lowering barriers to entry and reducing effects of scale economies – but has so far not delivered in a big way.

In generic drugs and some OTC products, however, production costs normally account for significantly more of the overall product value, and so are more susceptible to competitive pressures. Technology changes in these areas parallel what is happening in other mass production industries for packed products for human consumption. Improvements in process control, packaging methods and process speeds through automated controls have had a large impact.

(3)   Development costs

These dominate the economics of ethical drugs. Here development of technology for designing molecules may have helped reduce initial costs, but these are dwarfed by costs of trials, which are driven by regulation. Economies of scale here – in the development of applicable and approved intellectual property – are huge, and are driving mergers of pharmaceutical companies globally.

(4)   Marketing costs

Marketing costs in the pharmaceutical sector need to be considered separately for different classes of drugs. For ethical drugs, marketing effort is directed towards prescribing doctors, distributors and public authorities, and its total cost is often significantly more than either production costs or even development costs. For OTC drugs marketing is directed to distributors, opinion formers and end-users – and its costs are also high – again underlining the importance of in-market scale. For generic drugs, marketing costs are usually much lower, and directed mainly to public purchasers or to large distributors. Growth in the proportion of the market taken by OTC and generic drugs is expected to continue.

[*Source*: Consultants working with UK and a number of German pharmaceutical companies.]

315   Boilers and metal containers

This is a very diverse sector, in which we see no overriding technology shifts in products. Boilers for electricity generation may be an exception, as design changes to make major energy savings have altered minimum efficient scale in user industries (see electrical machinery below).

The sector contains both industrial products (often made to order), and commercial/domestic products which are usually mass produced. Deregulation of energy suppliers has given rise to greater demand for innovative, energy-saving products and has opened up new routes to market; technology changes have been sector specific for different groups of end users, and demand led.

General trends which apply are:

(a)   better process control in finished products, which may reduce the severity of conditions under which equipment is required to operate – decreasing its capital cost to users – and increase the potential efficiency of smaller units;

(b)   increasing automation of design and fabrication process, through IT. This sector shows the same sort of effects as other engineering and assembly industries.

[*Source*: Consultants working with UK energy utilities, and European/American boiler component suppliers.]

Sector profile for NACE 315 – 14 businesses

The businesses in this sector suffered a decline in real market size of 7% p.a. Market differentiation was low, and new product innovation virtually zero. Marketing expenses were low at 6% of sales.

Value added was low at 43% of revenue. Production is mainly in small batches with a high degree of customization, but about 30% was produced on assembly lines. Businesses experienced little technological change.

362   Railway equipment

(1)   Technology, products and scale

No major changes in technology which are driving scale are apparent. Across the industry it is rather a case of technology adapting to smaller scale applications – light rail, trams for urban transport systems – and at the same time to larger, faster trains to compete in Europe on long distance travel. Product changes are mainly caused by the increasing sophistication of rail systems, which make modular construction approach for trains a better approach. This has been evident in most areas of the market.

The modular approach has led to more specialization, and hence a greater role for subcontractors. This should show up in reducing value added/sales ratio for individual companies in the industry. Fundamental product technology development, such as linear motors, has shown up only in specialist applications.

(2)   Technology, processes and scale

Production processes have become more IT intensive, as in most areas of engineering. Processes are therefore more capital intensive, with lower variable costs and higher breakeven points.

[*Source*: Former project director Franco-British electrical company, and consultants working with German electrical manufacturer.]

425   Brewing and malting

(1)   Technology and products

The trend in demand from distributors in this sector has been towards products which are easier to handle, with longer shelf-life and less loss during the process to final consumption. Improvements in process control and in packaging have therefore been the most important factors in changing the type of products sold. Scale economies achieved in packaging have mirrored those in other canned and bottled products, with significant increases in packaging speeds, and therefore in minimum scale, achieved during the 1980s.

(2)   Technology, processes and scale

Response to changes in scale of brewing technology in this industry have historically been slow, but steady. For example, Whitbread's City brewery was the largest in the UK when it opened around 1740, and was still above UK average scale when it closed in 1976. The major changes in process technology and control which led to a revolution in scale and significant gains in productivity largely occurred between 1970 and 1985; however, industry investment determining how far they were put into effect in different countries was partly dependent on changes in national product regulations (e.g. Germany) and on monopoly power in distribution (e.g. the UK).

(3)   Marketing costs

Growth in national and international brand marketing has been substantial, raising the threshold scale for major brands. In most countries this is related to a shift in distribution patterns towards supermarkets. However, the impact of marketing costs may be unrelated to production, because some brands get licensed to local brewers in individual countries.

In the UK changes in regulatory frameworks have driven changes in marketing scale by breaking the tie between breweries and pubs. The German market has been changed by relaxation of laws on products. In both cases the result has been for bigger producers to gain in 'mass' brands, and smaller breweries to focus on specialist products. The main losers have been medium-scale firms with undifferentiated products.

[*Source*: PIMS consultants with UK and German brewing companies.]

428   Soft drinks and spa waters

(1)   Products and processes

We are not aware of major technology changes in the product itself; the sector has been highly automated since the 1970s. There have, however, been shifts in packaging which represents a significant part of the value chain. Substitution of glass by cans, PVC and most recently PET has been accompanied by a major speeding up of production/bottling. There are significant economies of scale in bottling, but in most cases they are most important at national market level, because of the relatively high costs of transporting products. Local franchising is often used to overcome this problem in soft drinks; in spa waters this may not be possible due to regulation.

(2)   Marketing costs

Marketing economies have driven concentration and internationalization of this market rather than production – which tends to be national/local rather than continental. A substantial part of enterprise cost is usually in sales, marketing and advertising for 'image' products.

[*Sources*: Consultants working with European PET business, and with German packaging conglomerate.]

341   Electrical wires and cables

Technology and products

The major technology impact on this sector is substitution by optical fibre in the communications sector, and downstream substitution of mobile for fixed communications, which is undermining demand for traditional products but greatly expanding the total market. Optical fibre growth has been driven by global companies.

Sector profile for NACE 341 – 28 businesses

The real market size for these businesses has declined by 4% p.a. Market concentration was low, the top four companies having 58% market share. Product and service differentiation was low, as was marketing at 4% of sales.

Vertical integration is very low with value added only 36% of revenue. Capital intensity was very high (capital employed/value added = 123%). Businesses used a mixture of production processes. R&D expenses/sales were low and product development times short. Businesses typically depended upon three suppliers for 45% of their purchases.

342   Electrical equipment

(1)   Technology and products

Scaling up of power generation units, which happened steadily for 30 years up to 1975, has significantly slowed. The biggest generation sets are unchanged at around 1,200–2,000 MW, because of limits to boiler/turbine capacity. The introduction of combined cycle technology over the last 15 years, which offers greater efficiency at lower scale and capital intensity, has significantly reduced the minimum size of new generating units, particularly where gas is available as a feedstock.

Distribution/conversion technology has been largely stable since the early 1980s.

(2)   Technology and processes

There has been no real change in manufacturing processes, except the steady substitution of IT for people. Robotic control on machinery for making components of generators and motors has increased but basic technology is broadly the same. The trend towards modular production systems has been steady, as in other engineering sectors, permitting increased use of outsourcing by main contractors.

[*Source*: Former projects director, Franco–British electrical company.]

Sector profile for NACE 342 – 65 businesses

Market growth rate, concentration and differentiation were below median levels but the level of new product activity was high.

Value added/revenue was high at 66%. Although production was primarily on assembly lines, a relatively high proportion of products and services were customized. The incidence of major technological change was low, as was the development time for new products. R&D expenses were fairly high at 3.5% of revenue.

421   Cocoa, chocolate and sugar confectionery

(1)   Technology and products

Changes in products have been made to exploit available technology (e.g. ice cream/chocolate composite products) and economies of scale through global products with uniform ingredients and process control. Advances in packaging materials have had an effect in improving shelf-life and marketing presentation. Nestlé's redesign, and internationalization, of selected Rowntree products after takeover in the late 1980s provides clear examples of how in-company know-how provides scale advantages through production and packaging.

(2)   Technology and processes

Basic process technologies are largely unchanged, except for progress evident in other sectors of the food processing industry on measurement and control, process speed increases, substitution of automatic control for people, and focusing of people input in support functions – which increase scale economies available. Action by large confectionery companies to take advantage of these economies predates, and is independent of, the EU single market.

(3)   Development costs

Since innovation is now an important competitive weapon in chocolate confectionery, economies of scale on development costs are increasing in importance. This has driven one US manufacturer to reposition European brands to align with US formats and positioning.

(4)   Marketing costs

Economies of scale on marketing and procurement/logistics are seen as the most significant sources of cost savings by major producers. The growth of international branding, within Europe and beyond, has expanded to take advantage of this.

[*Source*: Consultants working with chocolate producers.]

B.3.   Sectors with moderate non-tariff barriers

B.3.1. Consumer products

345   Electronic consumer goods

(1)   Products, technology and scale

Since 1980, the main characteristic of this sector has been a continuing stream of innovative products, to meet new needs and to extend the performance and functionality of products meeting existing needs. Product advantage has been established by leading firms by 'setting the standard' (as in VCRs); by achieving reputation for reliable innovation and good design; or by rapid exploitation of scale economies.

(2)   Technology and processes

Effects of technology on process scale have been similar to those in office equipment and telecommunications – because the technology itself, and the core competencies required for success in each area, are themselves converging. The increasingly modular approach to production, with outsourcing of components where a producer does not possess cost or technology advantage, has changed the character of competition. It has led to substantial investment in Far East production of modules, by companies competing in markets which are effectively global. Scale economies achieved in individual production steps do not show up in terms of business size because of this modularization of production.

(3)   Development costs

Most leading producers depend for maintenance of their competitive position and innovation edge on some key product module. Development costs are therefore high, and scale economies very significant. In some of the most development intensive product module areas there is effectively room for only four or five global suppliers.

(4)   Marketing costs

Costs of getting the product into markets in this sector are also relatively high, even for global players. This has served to reinforce the concentration effects of high R&D.

[*Source*: Consultants working with European electronics businesses.]

Sector profile for NACE 345 – 28 businesses

Average real market growth was 7% per annum. Market concentration was fairly low at 68% share for the top four businesses. New product activity was high.

Production was largely on assembly line processes. 40% of businesses had process patents. Value added/revenue was high at 74%. On average, businesses depended on only three suppliers for 40 % of their purchases. Capital employed was low relative to value added at 62%.

Over 50% of businesses experienced major technological change. R&D expenses were relatively high at 3.4% of sales, but product development times were fairly short at less than two years.

Sector summary for domestic-type electrical appliances (NACE 346 – 25 businesses)

Market growth rate, concentration, differentiation and new product activity for businesses in this sector were fairly close to the median levels for all sectors in these profiles. Marketing expenses were fairly high at 12% of sales.

Production processes were entirely by assembly line with little product customization. The fixed asset intensity (GBV of plant and equipment/value added) was low at 32%. There was little technological change. Development time for new products was short at a little over a year, and few businesses held either product or process patents. Dependence on a few suppliers for purchases was low.

351 Motor vehicles

(1) Technology, products and scale

Changes in products have included increasing use of electronic control systems, and increased emphasis on quality – possible through more precise process control. Ford have led the US and Europe's 'quality movement' in response to Japanese competition, which has radically changed the relationship between major producers and their suppliers. Movement to modular product design has also influenced assembler/supplier relationships. Modular design is in part a reaction to the increasing technical complexity of the car as a whole – no supplier can master all the technology.

(2) Technology and processes; development costs

The just-in-time approach and the use of dedicated suppliers reflect a new approach to process integration in the vehicle industry. It may have increased barriers to entry in some components, but flexible modular approach has moved minimum scale down in a number of areas.

The way in which economies of scale in car development and production are being affected by more flexible approaches to manufacture is illustrated by a current Volvo/Mitsubishi project in the Netherlands. Two companies have built common plant, with a single production line and common 'platform' for two different cars. This approach shares all the costs of platform development, and the basic robotics on line. The line operates flexibly, taking Volvo components from one side and Mitsubishi components from the other to produce cars with different engines and designs.

Normal costs of a line and model development for Volvo would be SEK 12 billion; under this joint approach it is reduced to SEK 8 billion. Mercedes also has lines which can produce more than one model.

[*Source*: Consultants working with German and Scandinavian vehicle companies.]

438   Carpets, lino, floor covering

(1)   *Technology and products*

The European floor covering industry has been significantly affected by Scandinavian innovation, using printed laminate. Printed foil is stuck onto chip-based backing with plastic sealant, substituting for lino, vinyl, wood and ceramics over the last few years.

(2)   *Technology and processes*

Production economics of the new process depend on the printing process, where economies of scale are large. The leading firm has only one printing centre in Europe and one in the US. But lamination is local, because of the logistical cost of backing and finished products.

[*Source*: Consultants working with Scandinavian and German floor covering firms.]

B.3.2. Capital goods

322   Machine tools for metal

(1)   *Technology, products and processes*

The economics of machine tool manufacture in Europe changed significantly during the late 1980s and early 1990s. Particularly in Germany many small, profitable, machine tool firms crashed in the 1989/90 recession because they had over-invested in 'flexible systems' of manufacture. Most such systems installed in the early 1980s were not flexible, but were very capital intensive. This combination of over-investment and inflexibility – and underutilization – killed smaller competitors and concentrated the market.

More successful machine tool businesses have made the switch from mechanical to electronic/optical control technology for their products, and for their own manufacturing processes where appropriate. Flexible manufacturing systems are now in place, which are closer to the original intention.

[*Source*: PIMS consultants with German machine tool companies.]

Sector summary of plant for mines (NACE 325 – 28 businesses)

Real market growth for these businesses was high at 7.5% p.a. Market differentiation and new product activity were low.

Production was almost entirely in small batches, and about 50% of products were customized. Capital intensity was low (capital employed/value added = 39%). Few businesses had process or product patents. Development time for new products was high at about four years, but R&D expenses were low at 1.6% of sales. The three largest suppliers provided only 15% of purchases.

347   Lamps/lighting equipment

(1)   Technology and products

Steady substitution of more energy efficient products for traditional tungsten filament light has been going on for years – first by fluorescent tubes, then by more compact alternatives. Product technology has evolved rather than radically changed over the 1980s, stretching design parameters for better product performance.

(2)   Technology and processes

Process technology has benefited from better process control/speed of working, but no radical changes in technology. Scale economies appear to be significant in this industry, because it is so concentrated. Although there is a sizeable market for 'own label' products in supermarkets etc., there are no purely own label producers, which suggests that the substantial scale possessed by branded product manufacturers is required to compete.   As an example, GE (No. 3 in Europe, but No. 1 in the US) make all their tungsten bulbs for Europe in one factory (in Hungary) and all fluorescents in another (in Leicester in the UK).

[*Sources*: Consultants who have worked with US and European lighting manufacturers.]

364   Aerospace equipment – manufacture and repair

(1)   Products and processes

Technology change in this sector has been mainly incremental. Improved materials, production control systems, and flexible manufacture have changed the products and processes used, but have not really changed the basic economics. A modular approach to manufacture has become more common.

(2)   Development costs

An important element of the economies of scale available is on development costs, which only main contractors can bear fully. Subcontractors for specific items/subsystems in planes may bear part of a technical risk, but proportionately less.

Increasing complexity of systems/subsystems has increased the tendency for subcontracting, and has thus reduced the average size of enterprises at a time when scope for scale economies is actually increasing. If this is true, it may show up in reducing value added/revenue for companies in the sector.

[*Source*: Consultants working with European manufacture and repair company.]

B.3.3. Industrial products

247   Glassware

This sector contains at least three subsectors with different economic structures.

(a) Containers (bottles). The market has been shrinking in many areas due to substitution by PVC and PET. Products have changed incrementally – light-weighting, composites with polymer sleeving, etc. – but not in a way to affect basic scale economies.

The bottle-making process has been scaled up over recent years (more 'gobs and sections' per machine) to the point where logistics and order book define the limit of plant size – because glass bottles are not cheap to transport. Much larger plants exist in France, where the order book is dominated by standard wine bottles in certain regions; big plants in the UK focus on standard milk bottles. Such plants are inflexible, and leave a significant gap in the market to permit entry by smaller rapid response suppliers, who are able to fill gaps and produce short runs.

(b) Flat glass technology has been broadly stable since the float process revolution of the 1960s, with some scaling up, but also some scaling down. The size of plants is partly limited by logistics, but process control improvements over recent years have made it possible to introduce float technology economically in smaller units where this would previously have been uneconomic (e.g. Pilkington in Finland). Pilkington no longer build plants which employ more than 500 people because of diseconomies in labour relations and productivity.

A recent, and growing, product development is coated glass, which has better heat properties. In initial stages this has been more difficult to transport than float glass, which may temporarily limit scope for further scale economies.

(c) Glass fibre products are produced mainly for a range of uses in building, and product development over recent years has tended to focus on products which provide 'easy to use' modules at the building assembly stage. Costs of complexity tend to offset economies, as scale usually requires a difficult mix of products in one plant. Plant size is mainly limited by order book. Successful high output plants tend to be limited in range to simple building products.

Glass fibre is in competition with basalt melting and spinning, based on plants which require less capital and produce higher output, but which have been the source of much innovation over the last decade.

(d) Tableware is dominated by one huge French producer, plus a few other national majors. There are significant economies in standard machine-made products. For more upmarket, labour-intensive products some companies selling under EU brands are moving production east to Poland and the Czech Republic, where low labour costs offset any possible scale factors.

[*Source*: Consultants and managers working with companies in bottle, glass, glass fibre and tableware businesses.]

Sector profile for NACE 247 – 15 businesses

Market concentration was very high with the top four businesses achieving 91% of sales. New product activity was low, as were marketing expenses at 4% of sales.

Production was primarily by continuous processes and customization of products was high. Capital intensity (capital employed/value added) was low at 69% but fixed asset intensity (GBV of plant/value added) was high. Total R&D was low at 1.6% of sales, but the incidence of process patents was fairly high.

251   Basic industrial chemicals

(1)   Technology and products

Products in this sector are mainly, but not exclusively, commodities, and unchangeable. However, there have been shifts for certain products – e.g. PET – towards the emergence of concentrated demand for large users in consumer markets, which have given opportunities for differentiation. However, this appears to be exceptional.

(2)   Technology and processes

'Economies of scale in basic chemicals are virtually over in manufacturing, except in certain specific products; the main economies now are in business support functions and logistics,' (quote from a chemicals planning manager with a European industry leader). Most of the major technology changes in basic chemicals production took place in the 1960s and 1970s, when some plants still in operation today were built. For example, the UK's biggest ethylene cracker (1978) was rated at 500,000 t, but now produces significantly more and is comparable in cost to a new German 750,000 t cracker. An important factor which has stopped bigger plants being built, placing a brake on the exploitation of theoretical engineering scale economies, is the logistics cost of assembling an order book for huge plants like this.

Some technology changes have been in the direction of smaller economic scale – e.g. the shift from mercury to membrane cells in electrolysis of brine to make chlorine and caustic soda. This has opened up the market to potential smaller scale competitors – but so far the infrastructure costs (handling etc.) show economies of scale to offset production technology effects.

The main areas where changes have taken place are in new growth products. Here normal technology changes to improve measurement and process control have made:

(a)   bigger plants possible without losing control of reaction;
(b)   reactions possible to run at less extreme conditions (lower temperature/pressure).

For example, PET plants have scaled up from 30kt to 120kt, and PTA plants up from 300 kt to 500 kt. These changes have come about with capital savings, both from increased scale and from better process control.

Catalyst advances have opened up new routes to specific products, drastically cutting the capital intensity of the production chain in certain areas. Examples are Dupont's new route in nylon during the 1980s; the switch to gas phase polymerization of polypropylene which cuts out liquid handling etc. – and scales up from 50 kt to 120 kt; and Union Carbide's linear low density PE process – which cuts capital and has similar effects on operating costs.

[*Source*: Managers and consultants working with European and North American chemical companies.]

Sector profile for NACE 251 – 79 businesses

Markets grew in real terms by 6% p.a. and were relatively concentrated. Product and service differentiation were low but new product activity was fairly high.

Both capital intensity and fixed asset intensity were high, particularly the latter at GBV/VA = 149%. There was a high incidence of patents, particularly for processes, and 43% of businesses experienced major technological change. On average, businesses relied on only three suppliers for over 50% of their purchases.

Sector summary: Other chemical products for industry (NACE 256 – 56 businesses)

This industry sector has very few characteristics that distinguish it from the others. This is probably because the NACE category definition is very wide, and businesses lack the homogeneity of activities found in other sectors.

A few distinguishing characteristics do stand out. These are high levels for product and process patents, low product customization, and high reliance on a few suppliers.

481   Rubber

Products and processes

This sector is dominated by the large tyre companies, whose products have changed over the last 15 years in that the switch – in developed country markets – to radial tyres has been virtually completed, and the proportion of product from synthetic rubber has steadily increased. However, there has been little change apart from this in the basic technology of products or processes. Some significant improvements in process control have driven increases in plant sizes. The industry is now effectively global, dominated by half a dozen major producers, of which half are big European manufacturers.

[*Source*: Consultant working with supplier to rubber companies.]

APPENDIX C

Community legislation, etc.

C.1. Directives

70/156/EEC: Council Directive of 6 February 1970 on the approximation of the laws of the Member States relating to the type approval of motor vehicles and their trailers (OJ L 42, 23.2.1970, p. 1), as amended by Decision 73/101/EEC (OJ L 2, 1.1.1973, 1) and Directives 78/315/EEC (OJ L 81, 28.3.1978, p. 1), 87/358/EEC (OJ L 192, 11.7.1987, p. 51), 92/53/EEC (OJ L 225, 10.8.1992, p. 1), 93/81/EEC (OJ L 264, 23.10.1993, p. 49), 95/54/EC (OJ L 266, 8.11.1995, p. 1) and 96/27/EC (OJ L 169, 8.7.1996, p. 1).

73/239/EEC: First Council Directive of 24 July 1973 on the co-ordination of laws, regulations and administrative provisions relating to the taking up and pursuit of the business of direct insurance other than life assurance (OJ L 228, 16.8.1973, p. 3), as amended by Directives 76/580/EEC (OJ L 189, 13.7.1976, p. 13), 84/641/EEC (OJ L 339, 27.12.1984, p. 21), 87/343/EEC (OJ L 185, 4.7.1987, p. 72), 87/344/EEC (OJ L 185, 4.7.1987, p. 77), 88/357/EEC (OJ L 172, 4.7.1988, p. 1), 90/618/EEC (OJ L 330, 29.11.1990, p. 44), 92/49/EEC (OJ L 228, 11.8.1992, p. 1) and 95/26/EC (OJ L 168, 18.7.1995, p. 7).

73/241/EEC: Council Directive of 24 July 1973 on the approximation of the laws of the Member States relating to cocoa and chocolate products intended for human consumption (OJ L 228, 16.8.1973, p. 23), as amended by Directives 74/411/EEC (OJ L 221, 12.8.1974, p. 17), 74/644/EEC (OJ L 349, 28.12.1974, p. 63), 75/155/EEC (OJ L 64, 11.3.1975, p. 21), 76/628/EEC (OJ L 223, 16.8.1976, p. 1), 78/609/EEC (OJ L 197, 22.7.1978, p. 10), 78/842/EEC (OJ L 291, 17.10.1978, p. 15), 80/608/EEC (OJ L 170, 3.7.1980, p. 33), 85/7/EEC (OJ L 2, 3.1.1985, p. 22) and 89/344/EEC (OJ L 142, 25.5.1989, p. 19).

79/267/EEC: First Council Directive of 5 March 1979 on the co-ordination of the laws, regulations and administrative provisions relating to the taking up and pursuit of the business of direct life assurance (OJ L 322, 17.12.1977, p. 30), as amended by Directives 90/619/EEC (OJ L 330, 29.11.1990, p. 50), 92/96/EEC (OJ L 360, 9.12.1992, p. 1) and 95/26/EC (OJ L 168, 18.7.1995, p. 7).

88/357/EEC: Second Council Directive of 22 June 1988 on the co-ordination of laws, regulations and administrative provisions relating to the taking up and pursuit of the business of direct insurance other than life assurance and laying down provisions to facilitate the effective exercise of freedom to provide services and amending Directive 73/239/EEC (OJ L 172, 4.7.1988, p. 1), as amended by Directives 90/618/EEC (OJ L 330, 29.11.1990, p. 44) and 92/49/EEC (OJ L 228, 11.8.1992, p. 1).

90/619/EEC: Council Directive of 8 November 1990 on the co-ordination of laws, regulations and administrative provisions relating to direct life assurance, laying down provisions to facilitate the effective exercise of freedom to provide services and amending Directive 79/267/EEC (OJ L 330, 29.11.1990, p. 50), as amended by Directive 92/96/EEC (OJ L 360, 9.12.1992, p. 1).

92/49/EEC: Council Directive of 18 June 1992 on the co-ordination of laws, regulations and administrative provisions relating to direct insurance other than life assurance and amending Directives 73/239/EEC and 88/357/EEC (Third Non-life Insurance Directive) (OJ L 228, 11.8.1992, p. 1), as amended by Directive 95/26/EC (OJ L 168, 18.7.1995, p. 7).

92/96/EEC: Council Directive of 10 November 1992 on the co-ordination of laws, regulations and administrative provisions relating to direct life assurance and amending Directives 79/267/EEC and 90/619/EEC (Third Life Assurance Directive) (OJ L 360, 9.12.1992, p. 1), as amended by Directive 95/26/EC (OJ L 168, 18.7.1995, p. 7).

C.2. Other

76/492/EEC: Council recommendation of 4 May 1976 on the rational use of energy by promoting the thermal insulation of buildings (OJ L 140, 28.5.1976, p. 11).

76/493/EEC: Council recommendation of 4 May 1976 on the rational use of energy in the heating systems of existing buildings (OJ L 140, 28.5.1976, p. 12).

79/167/ECSC, EEC, Euratom: Council recommendation of 5 February 1979 on the reduction of energy requirements for buildings in the Community (OJ L 37, 13.2.1979, p. 25).

85/326/EEC: Council Resolution of 15 March 1985 on the rational use of energy in the building sector (OJ C 78, 26.3.1985, p. 1).

Bibliography

Acs, Z.J. and Audretsch, D.B. [1991a], 'Innovation and technological change: an overview', in Acs, Z.J. and Audretsch, D.B. (eds), *Innovation and technological change*, London, Harvester Wheatsheaf.

Acs, Z.J. and Audretsch, D.B. [1991b], 'Firm size and innovative activity', in Acs, Z.J. and Audretsch, D.B. (eds) [1991], *Innovation and technological change*, London, Harvester Wheatsheaf.

Arthur, W.B. [1989], 'Competing technologies, increasing returns, and lock in by historical events', *Economic Journal*, Vol. 99, 1, March.

Audretsch, D.B. [1993], 'Industrial policy and international competitiveness', in Nicolaides, P. (ed.), *Industrial policy in the European Community: a necessary response to economic integration?*, The Hague, Martinus Nijhoff Publishers.

Baldwin, R. [1992], 'The measurable dynamic gains from trade', *Journal of Political Economy*, 100, Feb., pp. 162-74.

Baldwin, R. [1994], *Towards an integrated Europe*, London, Centre for Economic Policy Research.

Birindelli, L. [1995], 'Il numeri del setore', Quaderni No. 3, Osservatorio sul sistema moda, February.

Brusco, S. [1995], paper presented at the seminar, 'Sistema moda Italia', Sissma-Cna-Confartigianato, Rome.

Buigues, P., Ilzkowitz, F. and Lebrun, J-F. [1990], 'The impact of the internal market by industrial sector: the challenge for the Member States' in *European Economy*, special edition, Luxembourg, Office for Official Publications of the EC.

Buzzell, R.D. and B.T. Gale [1987], *The PIMS principles*, New York, Free Press.

Caballero, R.J. and Lyons, R.K. [1990], 'Internal versus external economies of scale in European industry', *European Economic Review*, 1990, Vol. 34, 4, pp. 805-30.

Caves, R.E. [1989], 'International differences in industrial organization', in Schmalensee, R. and Willig, R.D. (eds), *Handbook of industrial organization*, Vol II, Amsterdam, North-Holland.

Caves, R.E. et al [1992], *Industrial efficiency in six nations*, Cambridge, Mass., MIT Press.

Cecchini, P. (ed.) [1988], *1992: The European challenge*, Aldershot, Wildwood House.

Centrale dei Bilanci [1995], *Economia e finaza delle imprese Italiane*, Bacaria Editrice, Rome.

Chandler, A.D., Jr. with the assistance of Hikono, T. [1990], *Scale and scope: the dynamics of industrial capitalism*, Cambridge, Mass, Belkman Press.

Chaudhry et al [1994], 'The pharmaceutical industry and European integration', *European Management Journal*, Vol. XII, No. 4, December.

Clayton, T. and Carroll, C. [1994], *Building business for Europe, evidence on intangible factors behind growth, competitiveness and jobs*. Report submitted to the European Commission (DG III), December.

Coffey and Bailey [1991], 'Producer services and flexible production: an exploratory analysis', *Growth & Change*, Vol. 22.

Cohen, D. [1990], Comments on Caballero, R.J. and Lyons, R.K. [1990], 'Internal versus external economies of scale in European industry', *European Economic Review*, 1990, Vol. 34, 4, pp. 827-8.

Cohen, W.M. and Levin, R.C. [1989], 'Empirical studies of innovation and market structure,' in Schmalensee, R. and Willig, R.D. (eds) *Handbook of industrial organization*, Vol. II, Amsterdam, New-Holland.

Cominotti, R. and Mariotti S. [1994], Italia Multinazionale 1994, Milan, Etas Libri.

Comité Européen des Assurances (CEA), *European insurance in figures*.

Cool, K., Neven, D.J. and Walter, I. (eds) [1992], *European industrial restructuring in the 1990s*, London, Macmillan.

Dasgupta, P. and Stiglitz, J. [1988], 'Learning-by-doing, market structure and industrial and trade policies', *Oxford Economics Papers*, June, Vol. 40, 2, pp. 246-68.

Davies, S. and Lyons, B. (eds) [1996], *Industrial organization in the European Union: Structure, strategy and the competition mechanism*, Oxford University Press.

Davis, E. [1993], 'Industrial policy in an integrated European economy', in Nicolaides, P. (ed.), *Industrial policy in the European Community: a necessary response to economic integration?*, The Hague, Martinus Nijhoff Publishers.

Davis, E. et al [1989], '1992: Myths and realities', London Business School, Centre for Business Strategy Report Series.

De Jong, H.W. (ed.) [1993], *The structure of European industry*, third revised edition, The Hague, Kluwer Academic Publishers.

Dunning, J.H. [1993], *Multinational enterprises and the global economy*, Reading, Mass. and Wokingham, Addison Wesley.

Emerson et al [1988a], *The economics of 1992: the European Commission's assessment of the economic effects of completing the internal market*, Oxford University Press.

Emerson et al [1988b], *Research on the 'cost of non-Europe': Basic findings*, 16 volumes, European Commission, Luxembourg, Office for Official Publications of the EC.

Ethier, W.J. [1988], *Modern international economics*, second edition, New York, London, W.W. Norton & Company.

European Commission [1988], 'The economics of 1992', *European Economy*, No 35, Luxembourg, Office for Official Publications of the EC.

European Commission [1990], 'The impact of the internal market by industrial sector: the challenge for the Member States', *European Economy/Social Europe*, special edition, Luxmbourg, Office for Official Publications of the EC.

European Commission [1996], *Panorama of EU industry 1995/96*, Luxembourg, Office for Official Publications of the EC.

European Commission [1997], *The Single Market Review*, Vol. I:6, Impact on manufacturing: Motor vehicles, Luxembourg, Office for Official Publications of the EC and London, Kogan Page.

Farrands, C. and Totterdill, P. [1993], 'A rationale for an appropriate level of regulation in the European Community', in Sugden, R. (ed.) *Industrial economic regulation*, London & New York, Routledge.

Farrell, M.J. [1957], 'The measurement of productive efficiency', *Journal of the Royal Statistical Society*, Series A, 120, part 3, pp. 253-81.

Federtessile [1995], 'Dinamica della distribuzione in Europa 1988–1993', Milan.

Feldman, M.P. [1993], 'An examination of the geography of innovation', *Industrial and Corporate Change*, Vol. 2, 3, Oxford University Press, pp. 451-470.

Flam, H. [1992], 'Products markets and 1992: full integration, large gains?', *Journal of Economic Perspectives*, Vol. 4, pp. 7-30.

Freeman, C., Sharp, M. and Walker, W. [1991], *Technology and the future of Europe*, London, Pinter.

Ginzburg, A. and Simonazzi, A. [1995], 'Patterns of production and distribution in Europe: the case of the textile and clothing sector', Eiba Conference, Perugia.

Hobday, M.G. [1989], 'Corporate strategies in the international semiconductor industry', in Dodgson, M. (ed.), *Technological strategy and the firm: management and public policy*, London, Longman.

Holmes, P.R. [1989], 'Economies of scale, expectations and Europe 1992', *The World Economy*, Vol. 12, London, Basil Blackwell, pp. 525-538.

Holmes, P.R. [1992], 'The political economy of the European integration process', in Dyker, D.A. (ed), *The European economy*, London and New York, Longman.

Hooper, P. and Larin, K.A. [1989], 'International comparisons of labor costs in manufacturing', *Review of Income and Wealth*, Series 35, 4, December.

Ice [1995], Rapporto sul commercio esterio, Rome.

Jewkes, J., Sawers, D. and Stillerman, R. [1958], *The sources of invention*, London, Macmillan.

Johnson, P. [1993], *European industries*, Aldershot, Elgar.

Krugman, P.R. [1979], 'Increasing returns, monopolistic competition and international trade'. *Journal of International Economics*, Vol. 9, pp. 469-480.

Krugman, P.R. [1991a], 'Increasing returns and economic geography', *Journal of Political Economy*, Vol. 99, 3, June.

Krugman, P.R. [1991b], *Geography and trade*, Leuven University Press, Leuven, Belgium, and Cambridge, Mass., London, MIT Press.

Krugman, P.R. and Venables, A. [1990], 'Integration and the competitiveness of peripheral industry', in *Unity with diversity in the European Community*, Bliss, C. and Braga, J. (eds), Cambridge University Press.

Lansbury, M. and Mayes, D.G. [1996a], 'Productivity growth in the 1980s', in Mayes, D.G. (ed.), *Sources of productivity growth*, Cambridge University Press.

Lansbury, M. and Mayes, D.G. [1996b], 'Shifts in the production frontier and the distribution of efficiency', in Mayes, D.G. (ed), *Sources of productivity growth*, Cambridge University Press.

Leibenstein, H. [1966], 'Allocative efficiency vs X-efficiency', *American Economic Review*, 56, pp. 392–415.

Mayes, D.G. et al [1991], *The European challenge: industry's response to the 1992 programme*, London, Harvester Wheatsheaf.

Mayes, D.G. and Hart, P. [1994], *The single market programme as a stimulus to change: comparisons between Britain and Germany*, Cambridge University Press.

Mayes, D.G. (ed.) [1996], *Sources of productivity growth*, Cambridge University Press.

Mayes, D.G., Harris, C. and Lansbury, M. [1994], *Inefficiency in industry*, London, Harvester Wheatsheaf.

Nerb, G. [1988], 'The completion of the internal market: a survey of European industry's perception of the likely effects', in *Research on the 'costs of non-Europe': Basic findings*, Vol. 3, European Commission, Luxembourg, Office for Official Publications of the EC.

Netherlands Economic Institute in cooperation with Ernst and Young [1993], 'New location factors for mobile investment in Europe', Final Report, European Commission, Directorate-General for Regional Policies.

Neven, D. [1990], 'Gains and losses from 1992', *Economic Policy*, April.

Osservatorio Acquisizioni ed Alleanze [1995], Acquisizioni, accordi e joint venture nell'industria tessile-abbigliamento 1985–94, Modena.

Oulton, N. [1996], 'Increasing returns and externalities in UK manufacturing: myth or reality?', *The Journal of Industrial Economics*, Vol. XLIV, 1, March.

Owen, N. [1983], *Economies of scale, competitiveness and trade patterns within the European Community*, Oxford, Clarendon Press.

Pavitt, K.L.R. [1992], 'Some foundations for a theory of the large innovating firm', in Dosi, G., Giannetti, R. and Toninelli, P.A. (eds), *Technology and enterprise in a historical perspective*, Oxford, Oxford University Press.

Pavitt, K.L.R. and Patel, P. [1991], 'Technological strategies of the world's largest companies', *Science and Public Policy*, Vol. 18, 6, December.

Pelkmans, J. [1984], *Market integration in the European Community*, The Hague, Boston, Lancaster, Martinus Nijhoff Publishers.

Porter, M. [1980], *Competitive strategy*, New York, Free Press.

Pratten, C. [1971], *Economies of scale in manufacturing industry*, Cambridge University Press.

Pratten, C. [1988], 'A survey of the economies of scale' in *Studies on the Economics of Integration*, in *Research on the 'costs of non-Europe': Basic findings*, Vol. 2, European Commission, Luxembourg, Office for Official Publications of the EC.

Scherer, F. [1991], 'Firm size, university-based research and the returns to R&D', in Acs, Z.J. and Audretsch, D.B. (eds) [1991], *Innovation and technological change*, London, Harvester Wheatsheaf.

Scherer, F. and Ross, D. [1990], *Industrial market structure and economic performance*, third edition, Boston, Houghton Mifflin.

Schmalensee, R. [1992], 'Sunk costs and market structure: a review article', *Journal of Industrial Economics*, XL, 2, pp. 125-34.

Scott, A. [1986], 'Industrial organization and location: division of labour, the firm and spatial process', *Economic Geography*, Vol. 62.

Sda-Bocconi [1995], Il fabbisogni professionali dell imprese tessili, Milan.

Sharp, M. [1992], 'Changing industrial structures in Western Europe', in Dyker, D.A. (ed.), *The European economy*, London and New York, Longman.

Shepherd, W.G. [1990], *The economics of industrial organization*, third edition, Englewood Cliffs, New Jersey, Prentice Hall.

Smith, A. [1992], 'Measuring the effects of "1992"', in Dyker, D.A. (ed), *The European economy*, London and New York, Longman.

Steele, P. [1995], 'Textile and garment sourcing and the Single European Market', *Textile Outlook International*, January.

Sutherland, P. et al [1993], 'The internal market after 1992: meeting the challenge', report to the European Commission by the High Level Group on the Operation of the Internal Market.

Sutton, J. [1991], *Sunk costs and market structure: price competition, advertising, and the evolution of concentration*, Cambridge, Mass., London, MIT Press.

Texco International-Roland Berger [1991], 'Lo scenario della distribuzione di abbigliamento in Europe negli anni 1990', Milan, Edizioni Studion Sabatini.

Torii, A. [1996], 'X-inefficiency in measured technical inefficiency', in Mayes, D.G. (ed.), *Sources of productivity growth*, Cambridge University Press.

Venables, A. and Smith, A. [1988], 'The cost of non-Europe: an assessment based on formal model of imperfect competition and economies of scale', in *Research on the 'costs of non-Europe': Basic findings*, Vol. 2, European Commission, Luxembourg, Office for Official Publications of the EC.

Yip, G.S. [1992], 'A performance comparison of continental and national businesses in Europe', *International Marketing Review*, Vol. 8, No. 2, 1991, pp. 31–39. Quoted in *Total Global Strategy*, G.S. Yip, Englewood Cliffs, New Jersey, Prentice Hall.